PRAISE FOR PARENTING IN A CHANGING CLIMATE

"Bechard traverses the experience of parenti\
breakdown with insight, compassion, an\
honesty. This beautifully written book invite\
terms with the grief and travails that accom\
life into an increasingly damaged world. It's a book that our time
badly needs; and if you are a parent whose eyes are open, it's a
book that YOU need."

—**Professor Rupert Read, author of *Parents for
a Future: How Loving Our Children Can
Prevent Climate Collapse***

"At a time when many people are questioning whether or
not to have kids at all because of the severity of the climate
crisis, *Parenting in a Changing Climate* does something profound. It
calls for parents' moral clarity, emotional intelligence and resilience,
showing that these are indeed possible to practice when facing the
crisis, and supports the climate-concerned who haven't turned
away from having kids despite the existential threat humanity now
faces. Increasing numbers of people will be needing this book as
ecological losses and a warming world bear down on their family
relationships, and through it, they'll find strength."

—**Dr. Britt Wray, author of *Gen Dread*, Human and
Planetary Health Fellow at Stanford University
and the London School of Hygiene and
Tropical Medicine**

"If our real job as humans is to engage more *emotionally* with the
climate crisis then Elizabeth's book is an invaluable tool in that
process. She presents facts and fears with warmth and humor in a
way that opens the road to all travelers. She very successfully blends
the journey into and through parenthood with our parallel path

into climate change and how we can live with the changes wrought by both. Elizabeth seemingly effortlessly combines well-researched data with personal experience and her years of working with families. This book articulated what I felt as a parent working on the climate crisis, but hadn't ever put into words. You will find a newfound sense of your ability to make a difference and your relevance to the crisis. Beautiful, tender and truly eloquent, Elizabeth's writing is at once gentle, funny, bluntly honest and heart-rending. She deftly handles two very emotive subjects in this, unbelievably, her first book. I very much hope that she writes more."

—Charly Cox, coach and Founder
of Climate Change Coaches

"Bearing witness to a set of interlocking issues, including eco-anxiety and climate grief, Elizabeth Bechard has penned an extraordinarily sensitive, evocative, and beautifully moving portrait of parenthood in this time of severe climate disruption. Her book is heartbreaking, yet ultimately healing and validating to read. It is also one of the most immediately useful books I have read in years, including an invitation to simply feel what we are feeling, and to build our resilience, as first steps in moving towards meaningful and open conversations, and from there to engage in effective collective action. Any parent, or anyone considering having children, will find their concerns and thoughts reflected in these pages, along with tools and practices to move us in a positive direction.

The crux is that we would all do whatever it takes to protect our children, all children, and that is the call here. As she writes, 'What would it take for us to act as if our collective house is on fire, acting with the same fierce protective instinct that guides us in caring for our families every day?' Answering that call, she also helps us envision what our future could look like... 'Somehow, one day a time, we've become the parents our children needed us to be: parents who showed up when it mattered the most. Parents who helped to bring a future worth living for to life.'"

—Peter Tavernise, coach and Executive Director
of the Cisco Foundation

"*Parenting in a Changing Climate: Tools for cultivating resilience, taking action, and practicing hope in the face of climate change* is a highly personal and at the same time completely relatable account of a mother of young children waking up to the stark realities of our climate emergency. Bechard uses her background in public health and coaching to weave into her story practical actions and important questions for each of us to ponder including the most complicated question of all: 'What did you do once you knew?' The book helps us find direct and straightforward ways to answer this question and many others and to build up our resiliency to face head on what lies ahead."

—**Harriet Shugarman, award-winning author of *How to Talk to Our Kids About Climate Change: Turning Angst into Action***

"I love this book. It is told with honesty, integrity and vulnerability, is compassionate for self and the planet and it is embracing, insightful and has humor. Yes, it is a serious subject, but Elizabeth draws you in with wonderful stories (look forward to meeting Heimlich and some bugs!) highlighting the reality and challenges of parenthood, alongside of course the seriousness of what we are facing. Elizabeth has dealt with infertility personally and professionally, and the question 'Are you sure you want the babies want to come?' still stays with me. It is such a powerful thought, when we reflect on climate change and the ecological crisis, and what this means for future generations. The book also makes clear the interconnectedness of the issues facing us—climate, economic and racial justice, as examples. Alongside this reality, we are offered a range of 'tools' in the Appendices which I know will be useful to me both in my personal life and in my work."

—**Eve Turner, Co-founder, Climate Coaching Alliance, www.climatecoachingalliance.org, coach, supervisor, author and mum, friend, relative and partner**

TOOLS FOR CULTIVATING RESILIENCE,
TAKING ACTION, AND PRACTICING HOPE
IN THE FACE OF CLIMATE CHANGE

PARENTING IN A CHANGING CLIMATE

ELIZABETH BECHARD

This is a work of nonfiction. Nonetheless, some names, identifying details, and personal characteristics of the individuals involved have been changed. The author of this book does not dispense medical advice or prescribe the use of any technique as a form of treatment for physical, emotional, or medical problems without the advice of a physician, either directly or indirectly. The intent of the author is only to offer information of a general nature to help you in your quest for well-being. In the event you use any of the information in the book for yourself, which is your constitutional right, the author and publisher assume no responsibility for your actions.

This book includes excerpts from: UPSIDE: The New Science of Post-Traumatic Growth by Jim Rendon. Copyright © 2015 by Jim Rendon. Reprinted with the permission of Touchstone, a division of Simon & Schuster, Inc. All rights reserved; and THE FUTURE WE CHOOSE: SURVIVING THE CLIMATE CRISIS by Christiana Figueres. Copyright © 2020 by Christina Figueres & Tom Rivett-Carnac. Used by permission of Alfred A. Knopf, an imprint of the Knopf Doubleday Publishing Group, a division of Penguin Random House LLC. All rights reserved. The author thanks all others for the correspondence extending permission to quote the material cited in this book.

This book is printed on partially recycled paper with ink that does not contain animal byproducts. Cover design by Simon Avery.

Library of Congress Cataloging-in-Publication Data
Bechard, Elizabeth / Parenting in a Changing Climate: Tools for cultivating resilience, taking action, and practicing hope in the face of climate change
p. cm. / Paperback ISBN: 978-1-947708-57-0 · Ebook ISBN: 978-1-947708-51-8
Library of Congress Control Number: 2021918315 · 1st Edition, September 2021

CITRINE PUBLISHING
Brasstown, North Carolina, USA
(828) 585-7030 · www.CitrinePublishing.com

*For Minnie, Milo, and Haven
and for all of the Minnies, Milos, and Havens*

CONTENTS

APPENDICES 191

INTRODUCTION

IN AUGUST 2020, THE fire season texts started rolling in. Friends on the West Coast of the United States sent photos of the apocalyptic red skies in Oakland and San Francisco, with messages describing packing toddler-sized clothing into go bags, planning evacuation routes, running air purifiers, and trying to keep their young children occupied indoors. One was pregnant; another named being so anxious she couldn't sleep. More than one reported wondering whether their children's coughing was due to COVID-19 or wildfire smoke. This was nearly six full months into the COVID-19 pandemic, and less than twelve months after unprecedented wildfires had ripped through Australia, sending families on the other side of the world running for cover as well.

As a lifelong resident of central North Carolina, I've never experienced the threat of a wildfire, but heat waves and hurricanes roll in on a yearly basis. During the same summer that unprecedented wildfires terrorized West Coast parents, North Carolina experienced the sixth hottest July in 125 years, and the edges of several tropical storms and hurricanes soaked the state with an unusually high level of precipitation. Blistering heat and long stretches of rain kept my family indoors for much of that summer as well, a challenge for two high-energy four-year-olds (and their

1

parents). We were trapped in place not just by the pandemic, but also by the weather. I thought often of a text from one of my Bay Area friends, describing the sense of panic at feeling unsafe in her own home amidst the wildfires. She posed a question that was simultaneously rhetorical and literal: *where can we go to be safe?*

Parents around the world are increasingly concerned about climate change, which has been directly linked to a dramatic rise in frightening extreme weather events. Three years ago, *I* became increasingly worried about climate change. Though I've long considered myself someone who cares about the environment, in truth, climate change was barely on my radar as a parent amidst the chaos of life with twin toddlers. My body, brain, and heart were still recovering from a difficult pregnancy and C-section birth. But in 2017, I started to notice the escalating presence of climate change stories in the mainstream media, and the following year, a series of events that transpired within a matter of months forced climate change into the center of my reality: the death of my grandmother, who had lived for most of her ninety-seven years in the port city of Wilmington, North Carolina; Hurricane Florence's brutal landfall on the North Carolina coast; and a landmark report from the Intergovernmental Panel on Climate Change triggered a flood of anxiety and grief that I couldn't shake, and couldn't look away from.

Panicked, dread-filled visions of future apocalypse looped on repeat in my mind, not unlike the photos my California friends would send me a few years later. Amidst my own heightened climate distress, I started to hear my coaching clients—all women navigating various versions of infertility and pregnancy loss—worry about climate change, too.

Waking up to climate change as the parent of young children had a particular slant of cruelty to it: knowing that I needed to *do* something about climate change during a season of life where I already felt stretched beyond my capacity on a daily basis felt like an impossibly heavy burden to carry. What could I possibly do? If I did know what to do, when would I find the time to do it? And then, would it even make a difference? Would it ever be enough?

As I'm writing this, it's a typical Wednesday afternoon in early March, and all four of the following sentences have come out of my mouth in the last hour:

"Milo, DON'T pee on your sister!"

"Why did you pour the popcorn onto the neighbor's garden?"

"No, I can't help you find those missing LEGO legs right now; Mommy's working."

"I'm not sure onions and bananas will taste good in a smoothie together, sweetie. Maybe swap the onions out for some peanut butter?"

My twins will turn five years old in less than a week. We are still in the thick of what mindfulness teacher Jon Kabat-Zinn calls "full catastrophe living" every day, and some days, the catastrophes are painfully literal. Or at least, they *seem* that way. Hell hath no fury like a small boy who has lost his favorite Spider-Man LEGO figurine, or a sister who has been peed on.

Alongside the chaos of parenting, today has also been a typical day of climate action. I've called my senators to ask them to prioritize climate change, as I do on a weekly basis. Their numbers are programmed as contacts on my phone, which makes calling a relatively easy task to take care of in the fragmented time that is so often parents' reality. With my noise-cancelling headphones on, the kids' cartoons are a muffled cacophony in the background as I squeeze in twenty minutes of volunteer work for a local climate action group. I've posted about climate change on my social media feeds, as I try to do often. Earlier in my workday, while my parents were watching the kids for a few hours, I spoke to a health coaching client who's trying to reduce her meat consumption for health and environmental reasons. During lunch, I caught a lecture on the health risks of climate change for pregnancy.

Tomorrow, I might not manage to make time for any of this. Some days—many days—the exhausting combination of work, graduate school, and parenting wins, and it's all I can do to make sure that my kids are fed, that I've brushed my teeth, and that I've said hello to my husband at least once during the day. Yet more often than not, I'm able to find some way to take action on climate change several times a week. It has taken me a few years to find my way from paralyzing climate anxiety to consistent climate engagement, and it's a journey that's ongoing. I still experience surges of climate distress on a regular basis, and my family's carbon footprint is far from perfect. But my life as a climate-engaged parent is also far better than it was three years ago. I feel more hopeful for the future, more resilient, and more confident that my actions, as part of an emerging wave of active, climate-concerned citizens across the globe, can and will make a difference. The tools that have helped me the most are the same tools I've worked with for a decade as a coach with specific training in supporting bereaved parents, and as a research coordinator in an integrative medicine clinic, organizing and implementing numerous studies on human resilience, wellness, and behavior change. I believe they can help you, too.

Parenting in a Changing Climate is divided into three sections: *Pain, Possibility,* and *Practice.* The first section, *Pain,* deals with the emotional landscape of climate change awareness and parenthood. In Chapter 1, I share my own personal story of waking up to climate change, while in Chapter 2, I discuss the broader dilemmas of waking up to climate change as a parent of young children. Chapter 3 examines how parenthood changes our perception of risk and offers a primer on how climate change will affect our children's health. In Chapter 4, I talk about the "earth emotions" we'll increasingly experience as the climate rapidly shifts, from climate grief to *solastalgia.*

The second section, *Possibility,* aims to help readers think about climate change from a different perspective and begin to cultivate a positive, resilient vision for the future. In Chapter 5, I explore how intentionally shifting our perspective on difficult circumstances can help us to cultivate resilience, sharing my personal and professional experience with expressive writing. Chapter 6 considers the power of engaging in positive visions for the future as an antidote to the "disaster framing" approach so often used by the media.

The third section, *Practice,* is an invitation to consider how climate engagement might fit practically into your life. In Chapter 7, I discuss my own experience with challenging conversations about social and environmental change, bringing in the perspective of climate communications experts and addressing the importance of conversations about racism in the work of climate justice. Chapter 8 describes what current research tells us about the most impactful climate solutions we can engage in within the context of our everyday lives, and in Chapter 9, I explore what it can look like to embrace activism in parenthood. Chapter 10 invites readers to consider how accepting the reality of loss and heartbreak may be exactly what allows us to love the future into being. Finally, a set of appendices at the end of the book offers practical guidance and ideas for taking action: if you're already wondering what you can actually *do* about climate change, these resources will help you to make a plan.

Each chapter is written as a blend of personal story and journalistic nonfiction, as one of the things that helped me the most in learning how to engage in climate action was reading and hearing other parents' stories about their lives. My own journey of navigating infertility, pregnancy loss, and reproductive anxiety is used as a frame throughout the book, as I found that these experiences offered unexpected practice in navigating a complicated dance between anxiety, grief, and hope. While your journey to parenthood may look very different than mine, I hope you'll be able to see parts of yourself and your family reflected in the details of my life. At the end of each chapter, you'll find a set of questions that are designed to help you reflect on your own climate story, and ideally, engage others in discussions about climate change, too.

It's important to acknowledge that I'm writing this book as a white, cisgender, socioeconomically privileged North American. My journey of waking up to climate change has been explicitly informed by the privileges I've held all my life, including the fact that it took as long as it did for climate change and environmental injustice to fully land as realities that required my attention and action. I was born in Durham, North Carolina in 1983, on stolen land that was originally the territory of several Indigenous nations, including the Eno and Occaneechi Native American tribes. Durham is just sixty miles from the site of a 1982 protest in Warren County, North Carolina that is often credited as the initial spark of the modern Western environmental justice movement. After the state of North Carolina designated a small, predominantly Black community as the site of a hazardous waste landfill, the community rose up in massive protest against this blatant act of environmental racism. Were I Black, Indigenous, Asian, or Latinx, or had I lived in another part of the world (or another part of my own home state), environmental injustice might well have been a priority for me years earlier. Though I've lived through my fair share of Atlantic coast hurricanes, I have never feared that I might not have the resources to evacuate if needed, or that my home might not make it through a storm. Though I've experienced plenty of North Carolina heat waves, I have always lived in neighborhoods sheltered from the harshest heat by trees. I have never not had access to air-conditioned spaces. I have never not had the privilege of access to safety.

My experience of climate anxiety is also explicitly informed by my whiteness: before waking up to climate change, I had never experienced a sense of dread about what the future might hold for me or my children. Many vulnerable and marginalized communities, on the other hand, have experienced the existential threats of genocide, slavery, forced migration, and systemic oppression for generations. For them, climate change is one of many existential threats, a multiplier of harms that are already far too familiar, and already killing them. What is new about climate change, author

Sarah Jaquette Ray notes in an essay in *Scientific American* aptly titled "The Unbearable Whiteness of Climate Anxiety," is that people who had previously been sheltered from systemic oppression—people like me—are finally waking up to the possibility of our own "unlivable future."

And as we are waking up, we are often taking up more than our fair share of space in the climate movement. I'm aware of the complexity of writing a book about climate change as a white person, and adding another white voice to a movement that is already disproportionately white. I'm aware of the complexity of writing a book that features two white children on the cover, children who look so much like my own, when the children who will be most impacted by climate change will be children of color. Research indicates that while Indigenous communities and communities of color are far more likely to be impacted by air pollution and other environmental threats, they are vastly underrepresented in the leadership of environmental organizations. While oppressed and marginalized communities in the United States and around the world have fought for environmental justice for generations, their contributions are often erased by the media. According to The Solutions Project, an organization that supports grassroots climate solutions, the vast majority of funding for environmental causes—up to 95%—goes to organizations led by white people (and 70 to 80% goes to organizations led by white men). I'm writing this book to speak directly to readers who, like me, have privileges and resources that can be leveraged in allyship with parents who have been systematically denied access to the same privileges and resources, parents whose families will likely be far more impacted by climate change than ours. It's my intention to reflect on my social identities and privileges throughout the book, and to highlight the necessity of approaching climate change from the lens of environmental justice. There will undoubtedly be places where I get this wrong, and I welcome feedback from readers that might help me get it right next time.

I also want to acknowledge that the book touches on subjects that may be especially tender for some readers: infertility, pregnancy loss, and reproductive choice. I've written about my own experience of these subjects, but want to be clear that—especially in the reproductive choice department—I fully honor experiences that are different than mine. If you have chosen to have fewer children than you'd like because of climate change, I stand with you. If climate change hasn't factored into your decisions around having children at all, I stand with you. And if you are still in the process of deciding whether or not to become a parent, or how many children to have, I stand with you. I honor the courage and soul-searching that goes into these decisions. I am of the firm belief that every child who is here belongs and deserves a safe, livable planet.

Ultimately, *Parenting in a Changing Climate* is a book for any parent who has found themselves lying awake at night worrying about climate change, or constricting with fear for their children's future at the latest climate headline in *The Guardian* or *The New York Times*. It's for any parent who knows that climate change is a problem that needs their attention, but can't yet fathom how to make room for *one more thing* in the mayhem of their everyday family lives. It's a book about my own experience of navigating climate anxiety and grief as a white mother of young children in the southeastern United States, and how I've found ways to cultivate resilience and take concrete action in the midst of a profoundly demanding season of parenthood. What I know for sure from my professional and personal experience is that people *can* change their lives to bring them into alignment with their values, sometimes overcoming overwhelming barriers. In all likelihood, you've picked up this book because your values around the environment may seem at odds with the reality of your life as a parent. I know how painful this is. And I know that positive, transformative change is possible.

Writing this book was an emotional journey for me, and reading it may feel like an emotional journey at times, too. But in the context of climate change, bringing our lives as parents into alignment with our values around the environment may be among the most important journeys we'll ever undertake. I'm excited to walk alongside you in the coming pages. Parenting is hard; parenting in a changing climate is harder. But we can do this together, and I believe we can and *will* rise to the challenge of engaging fully in climate action while raising the children we love so much. They're counting on us, and we can't let them down.

Part I
PAIN

WAKING UP TO CLIMATE CHANGE

"Inside the word 'emergency' is 'emerge'; from an emergency new things come forth. The old certainties are crumbling fast, but danger and possibility are sisters."

—Rebecca Solnit, *Hope in the Dark:*
Untold Histories, Wild Possibilities

WHEN A SWALLOWTAIL CATERPILLAR is threatened, it will inflate a fleshy organ called an *osmeterium* from the back of its head. Meant to deter potential predators, the organ protrudes as two jelly-like, neon orange horns, emitting a pungent, fruity odor. At close range, the display is alarming: it's not hard to imagine how it could frighten away a swallowtail's typical predators, like spiders, small birds, or mice.

If, however, the potential predator is a four-year-old boy who loves bugs, the osmeterium does not adequately accomplish its mission. A four-year-old boy may try to provoke the osmeterium in order to touch it, and then lick his hands after successfully making contact. If you are that four-year-old boy's mother, you will remind him a hundred times in a summer to sing the "happy birthday" song at least twice each time he washes his hands—only because you insist on it—after licking his fingers after touching small, crawling things.

Being the type of person who strongly prefers my encounters with nature to occur within close range of running water and electricity, I never imagined being so personally grateful for small, crawling things. But they were without a doubt the surprise heroes of the COVID-19 pandemic at our house, offering an anchor of wonder during a season that often felt chaotic and anchorless. Like countless other families, my husband and I were attempting to juggle two careers without the level of childcare that would typically make such a feat possible. It was going badly. And as in countless other families, my job was deemed the "flexible" one. For me, working remotely meant navigating dozens of interruptions an hour and a daily fear of accidentally forgetting to push the mute button on Zoom during a meeting.

I coped by texting my other mom friends about the simmering, just-under-the-surface rage that had become the norm of my pandemic experience; they all understood. I also coped in other ways, trying to channel my rage into constructive activities: I baked yeast bread for the first time in years, because punching dough was more socially acceptable than punching anything else. Anxious about politics and worried about all that was at stake in the upcoming U.S. election, I poured myself into efforts to get out the vote. I did yoga (usually with a few extra pairs of small feet on my mat), went for runs (leaving to a chorus of *MOMMY! DON'T GO!!!* wails almost every time), stayed hydrated, listened to angry feminist music. Everything helped.

But honestly, the bugs helped the most.

Milo is the sort of child who can become intensely devoted to a single subject for months on end, and during the first nine months of the pandemic, the focus of his laser-like attention was tiny creatures. (It was also, for a time, The Flash: he wore a shirt bearing the Flash's lightning bolt logo for 137 days straight at the beginning of the lockdown, not that I was counting.) Nearly every morning before my remote approximation of a workday started, I'd take the kids out on the trails for a nature walk. While his twin sister Minnie would delight over wildflowers and various plants, Milo searched for creatures.

And he found them. In April, he collected dozens and dozens of snail shells (which we'd later find "decorating" all of the surfaces in our house at a four-year-old's eye level, such as doorknobs). In May and June, he caught tadpoles and tiny frogs. In July, a generation of seventeen-year cicadas emerged, several of which made their way onto my kitchen counters. In August, a nearly-dead dragonfly was flung in my face during a Zoom meeting. September offered a praying mantis, a katydid, numerous spiders, and an ample cohort of caterpillars.

The caterpillars were my favorite.

Several months earlier, I'd had a conversation with Sara Peach, a journalist with the Yale Climate Connections blog, about what it meant to consider becoming a parent in an age of climate change. Alongside my day job as a research coordinator, I'd had a small private practice as a fertility coach for a few years, and loved my work supporting people who were navigating infertility and pregnancy loss. Becoming a mother in 2016 after our own journey through infertility and loss had, in the most pedestrian of clichés, transformed me. It felt like an extraordinary privilege to be able to support others in trying to bring children into the world, too.

In 2018, I had taken on more clients as I began to emerge from the fog that had been the first two years of parenthood, excited to be stepping back into my professional identity as a coach after a postpartum hiatus. Just as becoming a mother had transformed me, so had becoming a coach years earlier. For me, coaching was the thing I couldn't believe I got paid to do: have conversations with people about their most deeply held desires and values.

Helping people navigate conflicting values and desires is central to the work of a coach, and it was a common theme in many of my conversations with fertility clients. There's a values conflict present when you had your heart set on conceiving naturally, but your doctor has told you that your egg quality is rapidly declining and you're running out of time. There's a values conflict present when you want to move forward with IVF, but aren't sure you want to risk having to take another $15,000 from your savings account for a treatment round that has a 70% chance of failure. There's a values conflict present when you desperately want a baby, but aren't sure you can bear having your heart broken by yet another miscarriage.

By the time I spoke with Sara Peach, another values conflict had emerged as a theme that my training hadn't prepared me for. Once, in the span of just a few weeks, I'd heard three separate clients name some version of the same fear: "What if the babies don't want to come?" They were all navigating particularly painful fertility journeys that had each been punctuated by repeated disappointments, each moment of disappointment a fresh opportunity to second-guess the whole idea of having kids. All of my clients were highly attuned to issues of social and environmental justice, reading the same frightening headlines that I was about the Trump administration's repeated assaults on marginalized communities and increasingly dire climate change reports.

What I heard underneath the surface of their words were deep, existential fears. *What if the world is too dark, too scary, too hopeless a place for children to want to be here? What if I don't know how to face this kind of world as a parent? What if I don't get to experience parenthood at all?*

There's a values conflict present when you desperately want to become a parent or to have another child, but climate scientists tell us that the earth's capacity to sustain human life for future generations is rapidly declining, and we're running out of time.

What if the babies don't want to come?

Climate change had been on my radar during the months that my husband and I were trying to conceive, but in 2015, it hadn't been a dealbreaker for us. We'd had a few conversations about how big we wanted our family to be. In the Global North, one child was clearly the most eco-friendly approach to parenthood, if you looked at it purely from a carbon footprint perspective. But few people look at something as intimate and personally consequential as the decision to become a parent purely from a carbon footprint perspective. I didn't; I wanted a baby. Our values around the environment didn't dissuade us from agreeing to a course of fertility treatments that offered us a 30% chance of conceiving twins and a 2% chance of conceiving triplets. When our first ultrasound revealed that we were among that 2%, I wasn't thinking about the impact that three new heartbeats would have on the environment. When the fifth ultrasound revealed that one of the heartbeats was gone, my environmental values didn't keep me from secretly wondering if we might later try for a third baby, carbon footprint be damned.

In October 2018, the Intergovernmental Panel on Climate Change (IPCC) released what later came to be known as the "1.5°C Report." I read the headline first online in *The Guardian*, just above a photo of a California firefighter battling apocalyptic flames: "We have twelve years to limit climate change catastrophe, warns UN." Almost reflexively, I did the math in my head. I'd be forty-seven in twelve years. My children, who had just started preschool, would be fourteen. The *Guardian* article summarized the key points of the IPCC report alongside a brightly colored table illustrating the potentially catastrophic impact of various degrees of warming on coastal flooding, crop yields, extreme weather events, and coral reef die-off. If the world didn't pull out all the stops to try to keep warming at or below 1.5°C, the report had made clear, we risked passing irreversible climate tipping points that could cripple younger generations' ability to defend their own right to live on a safe planet.

It was far from the first terrifying climate headline I'd read, but the framing of the article had the effect of planting a ticking time bomb in my psyche. Twelve years is less than the length of a childhood.

Specifically, twelve years was less than the length of *my* kids' childhood.

Out of all the options on the menu of climate horrors, sea level rise and increasing hurricane intensity hit closest to home. A lifelong North Carolina resident, I'd experienced hurricanes many times, and each year, the threat of "the big one" felt noticeably more present than it had when I was a child. In the fall of 2018, as I ruminated about the IPCC report, I was still grieving the death of my beloved grandmother and the loss of her Wilmington, North Carolina home. Wilmington had been my second home throughout childhood, and it had been a joy to be able to take the twins to visit my grandmother at the coast during their first year of life. As soon as I had known I was pregnant, I had also known that I wanted my kids to come to love Wilmington as much as I did, even if my grandmother wouldn't always be there as the family's taproot at the coast.

Her funeral was in August. We buried her in a cemetery full of majestic magnolia trees and live oaks draped with Spanish moss, alongside several generations of family members on my mother's side before her. After the ceremony, my husband and I took the twins to the beach to take in the medicine of saltwater and sand. Minnie wanted to dash headlong into the water and delighted in the froth and the waves; Milo clung to me like a frightened tree frog. There is a picture of my father and me at Wrightsville Beach in 1985 in the same position: my father trying to encourage two-year-old me to dip my toes into the ocean, and me hanging on for dear life.

In September 2018, Hurricane Florence battered the North Carolina coast with a direct hit, and images of Wrightsville Beach and the flooded streets of Wilmington were splayed across the national media less than a month after my grandmother's funeral. Wilmington's historic district, where my grandmother spent her childhood, sustained catastrophic damage as the banks of the Cape Fear River overflowed. Over 200 trees in the cemetery we'd just buried her in were severely damaged, with local news outlets sharing photos of downed live oaks collapsed over gravesites that looked far too familiar.

In nearly a century of life, my grandmother had never once evacuated her home for a hurricane. But I was grateful she hadn't lived to see this one.

As I eased back into my fertility coaching practice, my growing awareness of climate change paralleled a growing interest in the intersection between the environment and reproductive health. I'd noticed that conversations about environmental pollutants were almost entirely absent in my clients' conversations with their doctors, in spite of a wealth of evidence that pregnancy loss and a wide range of fertility challenges are strongly associated with exposure to certain environmental toxicants. I started accumulating a collection of books on environmental health. On a trip to visit my husband's family in Vermont several months after Hurricane Florence, a well-worn book caught my eye in our favorite independent bookstore: *Raising Elijah: Protecting Our Children in an Age of Environmental Crisis*, by Sandra Steingraber. I hadn't heard of Sandra Steingraber before then, but within the first few pages of her book, she became an instant heroine. Writing as both a mother and an ecologist, Steingraber's message was intimate and urgent: the people we love most, our children, are directly threatened by environmental hazards. As parents, we are responsible for protecting them.

I am my son's mother, and I am also capable of becoming intensely devoted to a single subject for months on end. *Raising Elijah* catalyzed my casual interest in environmental health into a nascent career shift, though I wasn't yet sure of the direction this pivot would take. I spent a year learning more and more about environmental health and climate change, devouring every book and article I could find on the subject. Looking for ways to build a bridge from my current professional skillset to the new direction

I felt drawn to, I signed up for distance-learning trainings on climate change coaching, climate change yoga, and a graduate-level certificate program on climate change and health.

It was inspiring to be in community with others in these trainings. But for me, learning was also a well-practiced escape route from pain and anxiety. If I could armor myself with enough knowledge about a subject, I could almost avoid having to know the truth about it. During the first few months of this self-imposed immersion, I'd find my heart racing with anxiety while reading books or watching slideshows that etched out bleak, sometimes terrifying visions of a climate-changed future. Often, what I was learning on the science front left me feeling more paralyzed and grief-stricken than motivated.

The truth was that my own climate distress had reached a fever pitch that I rarely spoke about out loud. I'd learned quickly that bringing up the topic of climate change in social conversations sucked the air out of a room, and others rarely brought up the topic with me. There was a growing dissonance between going through the motions of my everyday routines and my increasing awareness that underneath the facade of normalcy, things were definitely *not* normal. There were cracks in the safe, stable future I'd assumed my children and I would have, thanks to a lifetime of privilege. Some alternate, entirely unknown future was intruding in moments when I least expected it. It was a future I didn't even have language for.

Months after the bruising shock of Hurricane Florence, spring came too soon. The year the twins had been born, the pear tree in our front yard was in full bloom during the week in early March that we traveled back and forth from our house to the NICU. An exuberant swath of white blossoms had been a comfort in our bedroom window while I was trying to master pumping breast milk from bed, baby-less, in the evenings. It seemed that the tree had exploded in bloom just for the event of the twins' birth. Three years later, the same tree had shed nearly all of its blossoms by the twins' birthday, the timing amiss. All of the trees bloomed early that year, and while I knew that the onset of a North Carolina spring had some natural variability, there were news articles pointing to a larger trend of erratic weather and "global weirding" that scientists suspected was related to climate change. What's the word for the specific flavor of grief when a favorite tree blooms at the wrong time?

I found myself heartbroken by trees on the other side of the world, too: in early 2019, a series of wildfires ripped through the Amazon rainforest in Brazil, gathering enough momentum to gain international attention by that summer. A longtime ethical vegetarian, I knew intentional fires were often set in the rainforest to clear land for agricultural use to satiate the world's appetite for beef. I also knew the fires were releasing extraordinary amounts of carbon into the atmosphere, while destroying acres of one of the planet's most critical carbon sinks. The surge of headlines about the fires was accompanied by a surge of donation requests from aid organizations. Minnie saw me crying as I pulled out my debit card one afternoon, devastated by images of irreplaceable acres of rainforest going up in flames. I explained to her what I was upset about, using as simple terms as possible. She seemed satisfied, and went off quietly to play. Later, I saw she'd constructed a "rainforest" out of LEGOs and was flying a toy helicopter over an invisible fire, spraying buckets of imaginary water over it to put the fire out. How do you describe being simultaneously proud of your three-year-old child's creativity and horrified by the innovation and resilience her future will require?

There were other moments, too: once, I broke down weeping after a PowerPoint presentation had shown climate projections for the U.S for the next several decades. Even the most conservative estimates projected that by 2050, the climate in North Carolina would feel far more like the climate of northern Mexico than the North Carolina of my youth. I did not want to live in the climate of northern Mexico—I wanted crisp autumns, distinct springs. I cried each time news broke that another critical environmental protection had been rolled back by the government. I teared up watching my daughter play "family" with her dolls, and not just because it was sweet. By the time she would be old enough to think about having a family of her own, I wasn't sure the world would feel like a safe place for children anymore.

Publicly, I kept talking about my fertility coaching practice as if it was a path I was certain I wanted to pursue. I truly loved my clients, and it was a joy to receive the photos of their ultrasounds and babies after witnessing their journeys through pregnancy loss and rounds of failed fertility treatments. The work of walking alongside someone in their journey to build a family felt sacred. But privately, I also felt increasingly conflicted. Though the role of a coach is clearly to focus on the client's agenda, rather than the coach's, I felt like I was hiding something from my clients when I didn't warn them that they were trying to enter parenthood during a decade so delicate that the future would quite literally depend on our every move.

Are you *sure* you want the babies to come?

Motherhood was not going as planned, and it wasn't just because we'd had multiples and a fertility journey with more than a few plot twists. I didn't regret having children. I loved my kids more than I had ever loved anything, but I'd been underwater for the first two years of parenthood, the time a blur of trying to juggle work with endless diapers, feeding schedules, and very little sleep. As soon as I was able to start coming up for air, the world itself seemed to be drowning. I'd been looking forward to the experience of seeing the world through my children's eyes, excited to watch them fall in love with nature as they learned to walk, explore, and play. But as the twins transformed from toddlers into intrepid, exploring preschoolers, I felt my heart begin to break under the weight of two exacting questions:

How could I bear to teach my children to fall in love with a world that would inevitably break their hearts?

And how could I bear to look them in the eyes in twenty years—even ten years—if I didn't do more to preserve a livable planet when there was still time?

During the first summer of the COVID-19 pandemic, we made a valiant attempt at growing carrots in a row of narrow containers on our back deck (and by "we," I mean my husband Bart, who was less afraid of accidentally killing plants than I was). By late August, the carrots had grown abundant greens that became a magnet for swallowtail caterpillars. Bright green, slow-moving, and delightfully chunky, the caterpillars razed through our carrot tops with astonishing speed. Milo poked at them to provoke the osmeteria. (*They like me!* he cried. *Maybe,* I countered. *Please wash your hands.*) Both kids begged me to let them bring one inside as a pet. Seeing as a caterpillar seemed less likely to escape into the house than the other "pets" that had also been suggested, I agreed.

Delicately, I broke off a carrot frond that held the chunkiest one. It flared bright orange horns at me.

It's hard not to grow fond of a caterpillar if you spend time with it, especially one that so closely resembles Heimlich, the jolly, German-accented caterpillar in *A Bug's Life*. I became attached. For the first two days, we fed it fresh carrot greens and watched it traverse a landscape of moss, rocks, and sticks in a modified fish tank-turned-terrarium in our kitchen. On the third day, it crawled up to the top of the tank and stayed. Either it had decided to die upside down on the ceiling, or it was about to transform into a chrysalis; for a caterpillar novice, it was hard to tell.

We missed the first transformation entirely; it happened overnight. Most days, I wake up before the rest of the household to steal as much of the day's precious silence as possible, and was the first to notice what had transpired. After hanging motionless on the lid of the tank for over twenty-four hours, Heimlich had been replaced by a small, humble sac. In mottled shades of brown, it looked like a piece of wood the size of a child's thumb. I drank my coffee on the floor, at eye level with the tank. I'd gotten used to checking on Heimlich every time I went into the kitchen and felt a small stab of grief that he was gone. It was another tiny loss in a season of losses.

Also, I couldn't believe we'd missed the event: a small, shriveled mass of black and green on the ground of the tank was evidence that Heimlich had completely shed his skin. *How had he done that?* I was determined that we wouldn't miss the next transformation.

For nearly two weeks, I peered into the tank dozens of times a day, looking for any signs of change or movement; at this point, I was far more interested in the whole thing than the kids were. Each day, nothing. The chrysalis remained an immobile brown sac. I began to wonder if we might have accidentally killed it, several of the summer's earlier creatures (quite a few earthworms; quite a few snails) having met with unfortunate early demises. Our household track record for keeping bugs alive was admittedly bad. I was losing faith.

At 5:30 in the morning on September 11th, I checked the tank before making coffee, as I had been for days. This time, the chrysalis looked different. Still motionless, but distinctly darker, the wood-like markings having been replaced by neatly arranged rows of tiny yellow dots. I settled onto the couch in the living room with my mug and a book. If I hadn't gotten up to microwave my coffee twenty minutes later, thanks to an eccentric preference for nearly scalding beverages, I would have missed the second transformation entirely, too.

Coffee in the microwave, a tiny flash of motion in the tank caught my eye, just as the morning's small window of quiet came to an abrupt end with Milo's feet pattering down the stairs. Unlike his sister, who likes to sleep late and often enters wakefulness with a loud protest of beast-like groans, Milo wakes fully articulate and ready to go. I motioned for him to join me at the tank and held an index finger to my lips to head off his typical morning monologue about superheroes or bugs. In all of ninety seconds, Heimlich emerged after a riveting tug-of-war between butterfly and chrysalis, no longer looking like a Heimlich at all.

You can gather all the knowledge in the world about a thing and still not know the truth of it.

During the previous two weeks, I'd searched for "black swallowtail chrysalis" at least a dozen times, looking for clues that might indicate when our butterfly would emerge. (Googling "How long does black swallowtail chrysalis take" was my version of asking the universe, "Have we killed it? Is there still hope in the world?")

The larval stage of a black swallowtail lasts three to four weeks; as caterpillars, they shed their skin up to five times. They are herbivores, preferring vegetation from the parsley family: fennel, dill, Queen Anne's lace, carrots. The pupal stage generally takes ten to twenty days, unless it's late in the season. In that case, the chrysalis may "overwinter," a process in which the chrysalis hibernates until completing its development the following spring. Black swallowtail butterflies closely resemble their poisonous cousins, pipevine swallowtails, whose wings are tinged with a wash of blue. Their primary predators are birds, spiders, insects, and four-year-old boys.

Met immediately upon waking by an exciting event, Minnie skipped her typical groaning routine. The twins broke off a stem of purple flowers from the butterfly bush in our front yard and put it in the tank as breakfast for our reborn friend. All four of us marveled as a brand-new set of velvety, orange- and yellow-spotted black wings began to stretch for the first time.

There were other Heimlichs that month, each a mirror of the inward battle between grief and love that had been raging in me for nearly four years. I loved my children desperately. The world I had brought them into shattered my heart on a daily basis. I grieved the deep national wounds the Trump administration had both revealed and deepened, and felt terrified that he might win the election again in just a few short weeks, knowing what that might mean for vulnerable populations, for the environment, and for American democracy. I grieved the state of the natural world. It had broken me to realize that climate change would be the defining backdrop of my experience as a parent, even as I understood how privileged I was to have ever assumed that the world would be a safe, stable place for my white, North American children. It had broken me to wonder, every time one of them expressed delight at some marvel of nature, if they'd later come to resent me for letting them grow attached to a version of the world that might disappear before their eyes.

Climate change, at the speed it's currently happening, isn't natural.

It took the tiny, brave wings and the fumbling first flight of a butterfly to remind me that transformation is.

There's a gut-wrenching moment in the first few months of every new parent's life when we realize the truth of the old saying: babies don't keep. The seven-pound lump we brought home from the hospital is suddenly crawling, babbling, and eating mashed carrots. *How did that happen so fast?* But there's also an aspect of parenting that teaches us to be brave in the face of inevitable change: our hearts might be broken that we'll never hold the seven-pound version of our child again, but this doesn't keep us from loving the forty-pound and the sixty-pound versions of her. It's excruciating to know that someday, Milo won't wake up with me at 5:30 in the morning requesting a banana and an episode of "Monster Bug Wars" on YouTube as I drink my coffee and try to read. I desperately miss my morning quiet; I will miss four-year-old Milo more. But I'm not afraid to meet his teenage self, either.

As parents, we know something about how to love what is disappearing. We know how to love what is disappearing with our whole hearts, even as they break.

Climate science is clear: the world as we grew to love it in our own childhoods is irreversibly changing. The winters, springs, summers, and autumns our children and grandchildren experience won't feel like the ones we remember. We know that hurricanes and wildfires are becoming more intense, that the planet is getting hotter, that precious biodiversity is being lost, and that all of this directly threatens our health, our children's health, and the well-being of future generations.

But we can't yet know what kind of people, and what kind of parents, we will become as the world's form radically changes.

In the wake of Heimlich's release—a glorious, if tentative first flight—I thought of activist Valarie Kaur's words, spoken nearly four years earlier in the grief-filled wake of the 2016 U.S. election: "The future is dark. But what if—what if this darkness is not the darkness of the tomb but the darkness of the womb? What if our America is not dead but a country that is waiting to be born?"

As parents, we know how to love what is waiting to be born.

Climate change will shape the experience of parenthood for all of us moving forward; anxiety and grief will inevitably be our companions as we watch the world we knew change form. But climate change also offers us the opportunity to become something new, both individually and collectively: if we are willing to accept our responsibility to take climate action on behalf of our children, even as our hands shake and our hearts are breaking, something new *will* be born. The outer appearance of a transition—a country embroiled in political divisions and strife; a tiny, tomb-like chrysalis—is no indication of what might emerge on the other side.

Chapter 1 Reflection

Key practice: Explore your own evolving relationship with the natural world and our changing climate. Whenever possible, cultivate wonder (I recommend caterpillars).

Questions for reflection and discussion with others:

- What is your own "waking up to climate change" story? What moments stand out to you as being significant? What emotions have you noticed?

- What changes in the natural world have you noticed that might be related to climate change?

- How have your social identities (gender, race, geography, etc.) influenced your experience of climate change?

- How has parenthood affected your experience of climate change?

- When was the last time you experienced a sense of wonder in the natural world? In what ways have your children influenced your relationship to the environment?

THE DILEMMAS OF PARENTING IN A CHANGING CLIMATE

"Ultimately, the environmental crisis is a parenting crisis. It undermines my ability to carry out two fundamental duties: to protect my children from harm and to plan for their future."

—SANDRA STEINGRABER, *Raising Elijah: Protecting Our Children in an Age of Environmental Crisis*

IN CASE YOU'RE WONDERING what it's like to choose a sperm donor with your husband, it's like this: there are two glasses of wine, and two laptop computers positioned on opposite ends of a dining room table that you never imagined would be ground zero for sperm hunting. You've pre-agreed on the selection criteria you'll both be using for your separate sperm bank searches, which are surprisingly streamlined, considering what you're endeavoring to do: make a human. The donor must have a clean bill of health. And he must be able to write a compelling essay that doesn't come off as too stiff, too politically extremist, or too immature (this eliminates a fair number of candidates in the first round of picks, such as the one whose profile features multiple Will Ferrell quotes). You want to *like* the human whose genetic material may be fused with yours for generations to come. As you scroll through pages and pages of baby photos of the sperm bank's most eligible candidates, you'll find yourself wondering whether you should want to date these men or mother them. (You'll also find yourself wondering if you should share this thought with your husband.) It's both awkward and thrilling, and it feels like a scene from a movie of someone else's life.

At least, that's what it was like for me.

After months and months of rumination about whether to use a sperm donor at all, my first-choice donor was a man of Puerto Rican descent whose essay described a love for music and a dedication to animal and human rights. His writing was beautiful, and as far as I could gather from a few short paragraphs, our values seemed compatible. There's no right or wrong way to choose a sperm donor, but for me, this was the most important thing: I wanted to be able to tell my future child that their genetic donor was a good person. I wanted our choice of donor to reflect our values, even though I'd felt deeply conflicted about whether to use a donor in the first place. We'd chosen to go with an open donor, which meant that when our child or children reached legal adulthood, they would have the option of choosing to reach out to the donor to make contact. Before my children were even conceived, I had daymares of them turning eighteen and finding out that their genetic father was a sociopath. There was no way to *completely* prevent this possibility, but choosing a donor based on shared values instead of physical attributes seemed like as strong of a filtering mechanism as we'd be able to implement. The part of me that wondered if I should want to date these men felt comfortable with the Puerto Rican donor: in entirely different circumstances, this might have been someone I would naturally mate with, unlike the donor the sperm bank had bestowed with the moniker "HotHunter24."

We went with Bart's first choice instead.

Given the situation, it only felt fair to let him choose the donor that would serve as proxy for his absent sperm. After an hour or so of leads that mostly led to rejections at the essay stage, Bart glanced up from his computer with a look on his face that told me he'd found someone promising. I read through the donor profile:

Vegetarian. Environmental studies graduate student. Likes science. Does yoga. His essay about himself meandered philosophically through various topics in a way that reminded me of… my husband. Born over two decades apart, the donor and my husband seemed like kindred spirits, and even shared the same Myers-Briggs type. I felt no special connection when I looked at the donor's baby photos, as I had with the Puerto Rican donor, but I also felt no inner resistance. I could picture weaving a narrative about this donor that my future children would be proud of. This one could work.

Every part of our journey to become parents felt weighted by consequential decisions that forced us to consider our values more closely than ever before, and each decision was fraught with the knowledge that our future child or children would live with the outcome of each choice at least as much as we would. We chose a donor based on what we imagined our child's needs might be, more so than our own. We opted for fertility treatments that might give us the chance of twins so they'd have a better chance of having a sibling, in case we didn't have it in us to try again for another child. When the possibility of twins turned into the reality of triplets in that first ultrasound, we deliberated whether or not to reduce to a twin pregnancy, told by the doctors that triplets would be extremely risky for both me and all of the babies. It was a decision we were both devastated and grateful to have taken away from us by nature.

Almost nothing in our road to parenthood went as planned. Naively, I suppose I had assumed that once the babies actually arrived, the chaos might at least be predictable: sleepless nights, endless diapers, colic, and strange rashes. There were plenty of sleepless nights and diapers and rashes, but for all of my anxious planning, I hadn't anticipated the unsettling impact climate change would have on my experience of parenthood.

As parents, we wonder about our children's futures from the moment they're on the way (and in many cases, long before). Those of us who have always longed to be parents have names in mind before our children are even conceived. We imagine the trips we'll take them on, beloved places we'll share, experiences we'll teach them to love. And as any veteran parent can attest, our experience of parenting is often vastly different than we expected it would be. Nothing shatters our assumptions about the world or ourselves like the arrival of a tiny, screaming bundle of flesh and bones that we're assigned to love for the rest of our lives. (After the birth of her second son, a friend once confided to me: *The first one was pretty quiet. I didn't expect this one to be so* loud!)

But though we can take many of the plot twists of parenthood in stride, the late Gen-Xers and millennials who came of age in the 1990s and early 2000s didn't grow up dreaming of parenting in a world so starkly shadowed by climate change. It might have been on our radars, but throughout most of our generation's childhood, climate change was framed in the media as a distant threat whose impact wouldn't be felt by humans for generations more to come. If we learned about it at all in school, we learned that polar bears were endangered and didn't fully grasp what it meant that the glaciers were melting. We didn't grasp what it would mean for *us*. As we grew up and fell in love with potential partners, for most of us, climate change didn't figure into our calculations about whether or not we should aspire to have children. If climate change registered at all, it didn't land as a factor that would significantly impact our experience of parenting.

Until, for some of us, it did.

One evening, after listening to a lecture on the hurricane-related health impacts of climate change as my husband navigated the twins' bedtime routine, I realized I would have to think about the future entirely differently than my own parents had when I was young. That I would have to consider how to prepare my children practically and emotionally for frequent, intense natural disasters as a way of life. I realized they might need skills that I didn't yet have in order to thrive (and even survive) in the world that was coming, like how to grow food at home if—when—climate change caused major disruption to agricultural systems. I ordered three books on home gardening that night.

I heard my own awareness of the starkly unsettling truth about climate change echoed within the intimate space of conversations with my fertility coaching clients, and increasingly, in conversations with friends who were parents or considering becoming parents. In the fall of 2019, I posted a link to a survey about climate change and parenting on my Instagram account, curious to find out how those in my small band of followers felt about the topic. The responses came fast; they were poignant and sometimes heartbreaking. Clear themes emerged. Climate anxiety was definitely present, and it was definitely affecting respondents' experience of parenting.

"I worry every day about the future my children will inherit," one respondent said. "I wonder whether they'll even want to have children at all, with the world on course to be dramatically different in the next twenty years. I wonder if I'll ever get to be a grandparent."

Another remarked: "I'm very concerned about climate change, but when I read about something frightening—like a big wildfire or some other natural disaster—I just numb out because it's too much to process. I care, but I often feel too overwhelmed to actually *act.*" Several respondents expressed that parenting itself made acting difficult: "I feel super-caught in knowing this requires action, and feeling so overwhelmed by the day-to-day requirements of parenting small children. I hate that I'm not 'doing more,' but I'm also aware of how maxed out I am."

A few noted that climate change was a painful factor in their family-building decisions, a significant source of reproductive anxiety: "We constantly question if we'd like to try to have a second child," one wrote. "I also find a nagging in my head—worry, maybe—about how our child will handle her future." Another, several years into a challenging fertility journey, responded: "Every time I see another terrible climate headline in the news, I question whether moving forward with IVF is the right decision. I'm still questioning whether it's the right path for me to become a parent at all."

And one mother wrote: "Sometimes, I regret having children because of how uncertain their future is, even though I love them intensely. It's heartbreaking no matter which way I think about it. I hate knowing their lives will be burdened by a damaged planet. And I hate that it feels like there isn't much I can do about it."

My small sample was admittedly biased. It was a cross-section of attitudes among politically progressive, predominantly white, socioeconomically well-off, mostly cisgender women in the United States and the United Kingdom. It was a snapshot of the impact of climate change on parenting in parents who hadn't directly experienced environmental injustice, like so many communities of color have experienced for decades. It was a snapshot of the impact of climate change on parents who had, so far, largely been spared from the harshest impacts of the natural disasters, temperature extremes, and food insecurity that many families in the Global South have already begun to experience. I could only begin to guess at what it must be like to parent young children in a country where climate change had already contributed to worsening water shortages, devastating air pollution, emerging waves of climate migration, or where sea level rise was already an imminent threat—that was another world of experience entirely.

But in reading through the responses to my informal Instagram survey, I could relate to every comment. I, too, had wondered whether I might ever become a grandparent, as I heard more and more people questioning the decision to have children. I, too, felt utterly overwhelmed by what parenting two small humans required of me on a daily basis and how hard this made it to live into my own environmental values. One respondent had written: "I have found that I have made a lot more compromises in terms of my environmental impact as a parent than I ever thought I would. I've used disposable diapers. I've driven my kids around to get more sleep. I've purchased cheap plastic party favors and bought cheap processed food. This is due to exhaustion and general lack of support. Time and time again, I've chosen convenience in order to preserve some level of sanity in motherhood. My twenty-two-year-old self would be appalled."

My twenty-two-year-old self, too, would have been appalled at the environmental indiscretions that my thirty-something self had committed since becoming a parent: disposable diapers were just the start.

For many of us, becoming a parent presents a strange, unsettling paradox: when our children arrive, the stakes are suddenly raised. We grasp what it means to be connected to future generations in a visceral new way. We'll fight for our children in ways that we might not fight for ourselves. We'll fight for *other* people's children in ways that we might not for ourselves. And just as this new awareness dawns on us, we're also more sleep-deprived and exhausted than we've ever been in our lives. Our relationship with time is fragmented and rearranged in unfamiliar configurations. The same children who need us to work towards a world that is just, safe, and livable also need us to tend to a seemingly endless stream of diapers. If we're breastfeeding or chestfeeding, their bodies literally depend on our bodies for food, twenty-four/seven, for months on end.

At times, the physically grueling work of early parenthood can feel nearly impossible to reconcile with living fully into the very values we considered so carefully before our children were born. Choosing a sperm donor is hard. Reducing the amount of cheap plastic crap in a household with small children is harder.

Many of my clients trying for second children spoke wistfully of earlier days of social activism and change-making, and how they'd engaged their values before becoming parents. They spoke of years spent volunteering in the Peace Corps, of working to preserve the Brazilian rainforest in college, of going to protests and working long hours for nonprofit organizations. Several of them knew of mothers who had managed to continue engaging in intense social change work after having babies—mothers who strapped their babies onto their backs and kept marching for justice, or mothers who ran for office while breastfeeding—but spoke of these parents with a sense of resigned awe.

"Those mamas are superheroes," a friend said, "but I'm still barely managing to get a shower in every day."

Parents of small children, especially mothers, are constantly bombarded with messages that we're not doing enough. Advertisers show us images of mothers gracefully juggling babies with careers, looking chic in the clothes we can buy to look just like them. At the checkout line at the grocery store, magazine covers remind us nearly every week how quickly the celebrity of the moment lost her baby weight. Social media reminds us that our friends and favorite influencers are breastfeeding with ease, keeping their freezers stocked with ice cube trays of organic baby food, and taking their little ones to weekly mommy and me yoga classes. If we're not managing to do all of these things (or any of them), there must be something wrong with us. And while many of us know that these curated images don't necessarily represent real life, and while we might have a magnet on our fridge reminding us that "comparison is the thief of joy," it's profoundly difficult to counter the effects of living in a culture that constantly tells mothers that they need to do and be *more*. Embracing a sense of "enoughness" as a parent requires heroic levels of resilience and inner confidence.

Therein lies a second paradox for parents: we become aware that we really might not be doing enough to make the world a safe place for our children in the very same season of life that we're desperately trying to claim a sense of enoughness. We're trying to figure out how to hold a complicated truth. We *are* enough, but we also need to do more.

My own first year of motherhood brought these paradoxes home in dramatic fashion. The first several months of the twins' lives coincided with campaign season for the 2016 U.S. election. They'd been born on International Women's Day, delivered via C-section by an entirely female surgical team, and as I watched them learn to smile, babble, and crawl, I'd felt buoyed by the prospect of the election of the first female president in U.S. history. Like many other white women, the mirage of social progress on the gender front lessened my own sense of urgency to act on my values in an overtly political way as the Obama years drew to a close. Also, I was tired: two years of navigating infertility and a pregnancy defined by months of violent nausea and vomiting had left me feeling physically and emotionally depleted as I entered parenthood. In the fall of 2016, I was as bone-tired as every new mother is, still trying to figure out how to integrate my new identity with full-time work, marriage, friendships, and some semblance of self-care. I was far from apolitical, putting in a few phone banking shifts and donating as much to progressive candidates as my bank account would allow, but as November came closer, I largely assumed that others would do the work of making sure the United States elected a highly-qualified woman to the country's highest office, rather than a reality show buffoon.

"Tomorrow, when you wake up, there's going to be the first girl president!" I had whispered to Minnie before she went to bed on Tuesday, November 8th. I didn't stay up to watch the results. When my stomach turned with the next morning's shock, I was glad she wasn't old enough to have understood anything I'd said. I still felt a crushing sense that I'd let her down.

In the months that followed, the horrors of the Trump administration's racist, xenophobic, environmentally and socially destructive policies unfolded in parallel to my own growing awareness of the gravity of climate change. I felt a sense of urgency to act. At the same time, I felt so overwhelmed by what motherhood required of me on a daily basis that any intimation that I should be doing *more* was paralyzing.

How could it be right that I was mothering two babies, working full-time, desperately trying to maintain my marriage, friendships, and some semblance of personal well-being, and still not doing enough?

And yet, how could I face my children if I just stood by as the planet their future depended on was being destroyed, assuming that someone else would do the work of protecting it? How could I expect them to learn to stand up for their values in moments of moral consequence if I wasn't willing to do the same thing myself?

If we care about living in a world that's safe, equitable, just, and healthy for all, the paradoxes of early parenthood are essentially values conflicts, not unlike the values conflicts many of us face when we're in the process of trying to conceive. We value preserving the environment for the sake of our children, but we also value convenience and ease when we're exhausted from long days of parenting, and that convenience is often delivered at the expense of the environment. *Conflict.* We value the ideal of being responsible parents and making the world a safe place for our children, but we also value claiming a sense of enoughness in our identities as parents. *Conflict.* When it comes to climate change, many of us find ways to avoid looking at values conflicts altogether, because seeing the reality of the disconnect between our values and our actions can be so painful. We know that our Western lifestyles are inextricably part of what's causing climate change, biodiversity loss, and rampant deforestation. It can seem nearly impossible to imagine what it might look like to extricate ourselves from the only lifestyle we've ever known. Without a vision that allows us to honor both the environment and the practical realities of our lives, it may often feel easier to check out altogether.

"Honestly, sometimes I just want to look away and pretend it's not happening," a friend confessed once. "I know that nearly everything I do pumps more carbon into the atmosphere—driving, using my computer, cooking, turning on the lights. But what am I supposed to do—move to the middle of nowhere and live off the grid? Nothing I could ever do to lessen my impact on the environment seems like it would be enough to make a difference, and sometimes, it's easier to just not try."

Checking out is an understandable, even *normal* response in the face of circumstances that seem hopeless to change. I've heard my friend's candid comments echoed in a hundred other conversations, many of which have taken place in my own head. Yet there's an inevitable cost to looking away from our values conflicts, rather than towards them. The cost might come in the form of a nagging feeling of guilt every time we book a cross-country flight, or a sense of low-level anxiety that inflames each time we see another frightening climate headline—emotions we quickly assuage with our distraction of choice, be it shopping, ice cream, or Netflix. It's painful to carry the awareness that we're complicit in systems that don't align with our ideals, especially when it feels impossible to extricate ourselves.

But the steepest price we pay for numbing out in the face of the environmental crisis might be the experience of love. To the extent that we shield ourselves from feeling pain about environmental loss and its accompanying cascade of other losses, we also shield ourselves from feeling the full extent of how much we love what is or could be lost. Anyone who has navigated a devastating season of grief knows this excruciating truth all too well. Underneath any measure of grief, fear, anxiety, or sadness is the truth that something we love and care deeply about is at stake. It's an extraordinary loss to lose access to our own capacity for love.

A few months after being told that my husband's azoospermia was the reason we hadn't conceived yet, I went for a run with my friend Jessie. I needed a sounding board as I thought through our menu of options: adoption, embryo adoption, using a sperm donor, or choosing not to become a parent at all. I'd looked deeply into each of these potential paths and felt angry at all of them. None of them felt simple, and none of them perfectly aligned with all of my values. I hated being in a situation where there was no clear, morally "right" choice.

"I just can't see us using a sperm donor," I told her, breathing heavily as we ran on a trail we'd traveled together dozens of times. "It doesn't seem fair to have a baby that's only genetically related to one of us. Sperm donors are probably all college students who are just looking for extra cash, and that feels icky. And how can we go through all of the expense and risk of fertility treatments when there are so many children who already need homes?"

"There's no such thing as perfect in parenting, you know," Jessie said. She had known me since my first semester in college, and had watched me wrestle with a tendency towards self-righteous ethical perfectionism at close range for years. It was as loving a way as someone could have said to me the obvious: *you can't do this perfectly, so you're going to have to make an imperfect choice and find a way to live with it.*

I grieved all of the options we left behind. I grieved all the children who needed homes and all of the tiny "snowflake babies" we wouldn't adopt. I grieved the fact that there was no way our children would ever be genetically related to Bart, and that I would never get to experience what it's like to look at your child and see a physical reflection of the person you love staring back at you. I grieved the loss of a simple, straightforward version of motherhood—the loss of a fantasy I hadn't even realized I wanted until it was already gone.

And somehow, the grief allowed us to move forward. With expert reassurance from a skilled therapist at our fertility clinic, we talked through ways to honor our values in making the choice that was simplest on a practical level: using a sperm donor. There was a strange sense of freedom in embracing the messiness and complexity of the situation, and in walking through uncharted territory with an open heart.

Parenting in a changing climate requires exactly this: that we embrace the messiness and complexity of the situation we're in, and that we walk through uncharted territory with open hearts. Those of us raising young children in the coming decade will be doing so in a climate that is both literally and figuratively different than the parenting climate of any previous generation. The years that we'll be watching our children learn to walk, talk, read, and ride bicycles are the same years that climate scientists tell us we have an urgent mandate to stop carbon emissions and preserve what biodiversity is left on the planet. If we *don't* look honestly at the climate crisis and allow ourselves to feel our full range of emotions about it, we also won't have full access to our capacity to be part of creative, imperfect solutions, or to cultivate authentic resilience. We can't afford to lose that—and neither can our children.

Chapter 2 Reflection

Key practice: Acknowledge ambivalence and conflicting values—they have much to teach us about what we love.

Questions for reflection and discussion with others:

- What values conflicts have you navigated since becoming a parent? What conflicts have you noticed between your values around the environment and your lifestyle?

- When confronted with a values conflict, how do you tend to respond?

- This chapter describes the experience of wrestling with messages of "not-enoughness" that parents (especially mothers) are bombarded with from the moment our children arrive in the world, and the paradox that just as we become aware of the stakes of the future in a new way, we're also more exhausted than we've ever been. How do you relate to the statement: "We *are* enough, but we also need to do more"?

- How have your social identities impacted your engagement in issues of social and environmental justice?

- What "imperfect" choices have you had to grieve in parenting so far?

RISK PERCEPTION AND OUR CHILDREN'S HEALTH

"We deserve a safe future. And we demand a safe future. Is that really too much to ask?"

—GRETA THUNBERG
GLOBAL CLIMATE STRIKE, *New York, September 2019*

IT TOOK APPROXIMATELY A week after bringing the twins home from the hospital to throw the first of many parenting maxims out the window. The ubiquitous new parent advice to "sleep when the baby sleeps" is utterly useless, we discovered quickly, when there are *two* babies. Two babies, it turns out, rarely have synchronized sleep schedules. When one falls into a nap, the other will decide that this is the perfect time to claim a parent's uninterrupted attention. One will have the nocturnal bent of a night owl; the other will wake for the day at ungodly early hours of the morning. There was some blessing, in those early months, in not knowing how long this sleep deprivation experiment would last. Neither Bart nor I got a solid night's sleep for well over a year after the twins were born.

One evening when the twins were about six months old, I found myself—miraculously!—with two simultaneously sleeping babies. I wasn't sure how it had happened, or how to make it happen again the next evening, but I was determined to relax and enjoy at least a few minutes of peace and quiet before crashing into sleep myself, knowing the peace and quiet probably wouldn't last long. Another new facet of parenting: the way the feeling of *determination* accompanied the desire to relax.

Sitting in bed, determinedly relaxing, I wondered what to do with myself: Watch trashy television? Read an edifying book? Call a friend? Stare vacantly at the wall? I was staring vacantly at the wall when Bart came in to check on me.

Earlier that day, he'd made me a batch of lactation cookies. I was breastfeeding the twins, but not producing nearly enough milk to feed both of them without supplementing with formula. The internet offered a wealth of advice for increasing milk production naturally, and I was trying it all. I ate more oats, took fenugreek pills that made my armpits smell like maple syrup, drank organic lactation tea, tried to get more rest. My personal favorite was "cluster pumping," which sounded like an obscene CrossFit exercise and involved pumping breast milk at frequent intervals to mimic babies' cluster feeding. Lactating was a lot of work, and it called for cookies.

"I think I'm ok, sweetie," I said, mentally noting how thoughtful it was for Bart to check in.

He left, determined to relax himself. I realized I was thirsty. My attempt to relax was failing anyway, so I went downstairs to fix myself a cup of Mother's Milk tea. As I reached up to the shelf where we kept the tea boxes, I felt something warm pressing against my belly. The oven was on. Hours earlier, Bart must have forgotten to turn the oven off after making the cookies.

Whatever gene running through my dad's side of the family that's responsible for being safety conscious to the point of obsessive-compulsive neurosis had just turned on in me, activated in full force by the trigger of an oven left on in a house with sleeping babies. Bart grew up in a small town in Vermont where his parents still left the door unlocked during the day, and neighbors often wandered in and out without knocking. In the house I grew up in, the door had never once been left unlocked. Not once. Every time we'd leave for a road trip when I was a child, my dad would check the house at least three times to make sure that appliances were unplugged, that doors and windows were locked, and most importantly, that the oven was turned off.

My mom had always disparaged this tendency, but suddenly, I understood it completely. I confronted Bart with his transgression. There were words exchanged between us, and the words that came out of my mouth were not, "Thanks again for the cookies, love!"

Any attempts at relaxing went out the window after that. It was hard to be angry at Bart, because he'd clearly only been trying to help (and the cookies, it must be said, had been delicious). But inwardly, I panicked. What if this happened again? Would I have to check to make sure the oven was turned off every night for the rest of our marriage? What if I forgot to check the oven and a fire started? What if a fire started and all four of our smoke alarms failed? What if we were trapped upstairs with the babies with no way out?

Fiery, smoke-filled terror fantasies played out in my head. I tried to go to sleep, but couldn't turn my mind off. Finally, after an hour of anxious rumination, I pulled my iPhone under the covers and searched for "fire safety" on the Amazon app. The first result that came up was a two-story fire escape ladder with anti-slip rungs. Sold, in ten seconds flat. Sleep cost $39.99 plus two-day shipping that night.

Becoming a parent—and sometimes, an accompanying cocktail of postpartum hormones—changes our perception of risk. It's why we can drive a clunker that barely passes inspection for years, but the minute we learn we're expecting a child, we're examining vehicle safety ratings and reviewing Consumer Reports' list of the year's safest car seats. It's why we can live for thirty-something years in two-story homes without ever having owned a fire escape ladder, and then be unable to fall asleep without one once we've imagined the threat a fire could pose to our little ones. It's why we go to great lengths to insert small plastic prongs into every outlet in our homes, dull sharp coffee table corners with padding, and buy organic baby food whenever possible, even though it's far more expensive than non-organic.

Intuitively, we know that children are inherently more vulnerable than adults in a vast variety of ways. I'll never forget how tiny the twins' bodies looked when we brought them home from the hospital after a week in the NICU, still weeks before their original due date. At four and five pounds, they still seemed far too fragile to exist outside of my body or a hospital incubator. It was difficult to be attuned to anything other than an overwhelming instinct to protect them.

When we're tasked with keeping these precious little bodies safe, the world can feel like a more dangerous place, and we adjust our behaviors accordingly. Social psychology research suggests that parents whose parental role is "salient"—or more central to their identity—perceive greater risk, make more risk-averse choices, and trust strangers less than non-parents or parents whose role is less salient. "A risk-vigilant mindset," say researchers Richard Eibach and Steven Mock, "may be an important psychological adaptation to the parental role." Children need parents who can protect them, and we're wired to adapt to this need.

The concept of salience factors prominently into why the risk of climate change feels qualitatively different than the risk of an oven left on inadvertently, or an unprotected electrical outlet. Humans, especially those who are parents of young children, have evolved to respond efficiently to risks that feel immediate and personal. Psychologist Daniel Gilbert uses the acronym PAIN to summarize the four key triggers that cue us to respond to a threat: we respond when risks feel Personal (they impact something of personal importance); Abrupt (we are most attuned to sudden changes, and far less attuned to slow-moving threats); Immoral (we respond to threats that seem repulsive, immoral, or indecent); and to risks that threaten us Now. Threats that trigger our PAIN points have salience, demanding our attention and action.

Unlike a hot oven, ironically, climate change has tended not to push our collective PAIN buttons. Throughout much of the last few decades, climate change has been framed in media messages as a distant, far-off threat—something that might affect other people in other places in the future, but not us, and not now. Images of vulnerable polar bears might pull on the heartstrings of animal lovers, but few of us have a meaningful personal connection to polar bears that might motivate us to act decisively on their behalf. Climate change has often been presented in the media with what's known as "disaster framing." This is what's happening when you read a news article or book that's focused heavily on describing how terrible the impacts of climate change are or will be. The information presented in a disaster-framed piece may be entirely factual, and the author's hope is usually that the reader will be frightened into action by words and statistics that paint a vivid picture of how bad things are going to get.

But according to researcher Per Espen Stoknes, disaster framing isn't effective at motivating us to take action. Instead of provoking a clear, engaged response to the problem of climate change, it tends to provoke cognitive dissonance and denial. The more terrifying climate headlines we read, the more we instinctively create a sense of inner distance from the problem. We use an impressive array of psychological defense mechanisms to create this distance, not the least of which is a remarkable capacity to check out in the face of emotionally difficult circumstances.

"After thirty years of scary climate change communications," Stoknes says in his 2017 TED talk, "more than 80% of media articles still use disaster framings, but people habituate to and then desensitize to doom overuse. So many of us are now suffering a kind of apocalypse fatigue, getting numb from too much collapse porn."

There is only so much collapse porn we can take before our brains start tuning out the gnawing, just-under-the-surface anxiety that many of us feel about climate change. The more inner distance we create from climate change, the less PAIN we feel. Historically, most of us in the Global North haven't experienced climate change as a salient threat.

But this may be rapidly changing.

For years, the Yale Center for Climate Change Communication has collected data on climate beliefs and risk perceptions. In 2014, the year my husband and I started trying to become parents, Yale's data suggested that only 34% of Americans felt that climate change would personally impact them to a great or moderate degree. By 2020, a year when wildfires raged through Australia and California with unprecedented intensity, 43% of Americans felt personally threatened by climate change. More and more of us have directly experienced the impact of natural disasters the mainstream media openly associates with climate change, and more and more of us can name personally beloved places that are at risk of further harm. When climate change starts to feel personal, our perception of risk begins to shift.

Climate communications researchers at Yale and George Mason University have also collected years of data on Americans' perceptions of the health risks of climate change. In a 2015 report, researchers demonstrated that perception of climate-related health risks varies greatly by level of climate belief. Over 1200 survey respondents were divided into "Six Americas" according to six distinct patterns of belief about global warming. At one end of the belief spectrum were those whose belief statements categorized them as *alarmed, concerned,* or *cautious* about global warming; on the other end were those who were *disengaged, doubtful,* or outright *dismissive.* A moderate majority (60%) of the alarmed segment could name at least one health risk associated with global warming, but they were the only group in which a majority did so. The vast majority of respondents overall could not accurately name *any* health problems associated with global warming.

Climate change is associated with a vast array of adverse health impacts, and children are among the most vulnerable to almost all of them. For parents, nothing feels more personal than a threat to our children.

During the week my children spent in the NICU after their birth, Minnie received several doses of surfactant as a treatment for respiratory distress syndrome. Surfactant is a liquid produced by the lungs that helps keep the airways open, and it's what makes it possible for babies to inhale air after delivery after months of "breathing" aquatically. Bart recorded a voice memo on his iPhone of the twins' entire C-section delivery. Amidst a cacophony of hospital voices and rhythmic beeping sounds, Milo's first cry rang out clear and strong, while Minnie's sounded more like the scratchy mewl of a sick kitten. Babies start to produce surfactant in utero at around twenty-six weeks, but if they're born prematurely before thirty-seven weeks of gestation, they may not have made enough surfactant to breathe well on their own. Most babies with respiratory distress syndrome are premature; C-section delivery adds another layer of risk, as the process of going through labor helps ready babies' lungs to breathe air.

There are other risk factors for infant respiratory distress, including maternal exposure to air pollution, and this is where climate change comes in: climate change makes air pollution worse. Scientists predict that climate change will increase ground-level ozone, a key component of smog, thanks to a complex synergy of chemical reactions that are altered as temperatures rise. Climate change is linked to more frequent and intense wildfires, which can significantly reduce air quality and affect lung health in a variety of ways. Warmer temperatures can also increase the amount of seasonal pollen in the air, adding to an alarming cocktail of particulate matter and gaseous pollution.

When pregnant people are exposed to air pollution, their babies face higher risk of impaired lung development in utero, increased risk of preterm birth, low birth weight, and stillbirth, and higher likelihood of childhood asthma and respiratory distress. In research that examined studies of more than 32 million U.S. births, authors found that climate change-related higher temperatures and exposure to ozone and particulate matter were clearly associated with higher risk of low birth weights and stillbirths. Black mothers and babies are at highest risk for all of these outcomes in the United States, thanks to racial disparities in exposure to environmental risks and access to health care and to the trauma-tizing impact of racism itself. One of the studies reviewed found that each temperature increase of 1°C during the week before delivery corresponded with a 6% greater likelihood of stillbirth between the warm-weather months of May and September. The risk of having a stillbirth is twice as great for Black mothers as for whites. Once, while giving a talk on grief rituals after pregnancy and infant loss at a fertility clinic, I met a woman who'd had two stillbirths in a row. It is still impossible for me to imagine a world in which this level of grief is magnified.

The burden of air pollution is not evenly distributed among children after they are born, either: Black children, again, are most vulnerable. They are twice as likely to be hospitalized for asthma, and four times more likely to die from it than white children. In February 2013, nine-year-old Ella Kissi-Debrah died in south London from asthma attacks that were later ruled by a coroner to be related to uncontrolled air pollution levels. Kissi-Debrah lived just twenty-five meters from a congested London road, having spent her entire nine years of life in close proximity to toxic air; her death was the first death in the U.K. to be specifically attributed to air pollution. Poor communities of color are more likely to live in areas with polluted air than affluent white communities. Across the globe, the World Health Organization estimates that more than 90% of the world's children breathe toxic air, and climate change will dramatically exacerbate the levels of air pollution that already exist. It is still impossible for me to imagine a world in which the grief of bereaved parents, whose children die from breathing dirty air, is magnified.

Much to the annoyance of the hospital staff member whose job it was to finalize the details of the birth certificate, we couldn't firmly commit to a middle name for Minnie for the first three days of her life. Resting prone in a tiny incubator, her five-pound body was plastered with electrodes hooked to a tangled web of cords, her skin yellowed with jaundice, and the half of her face that we could see swollen with edema. We hadn't seen her full face yet. We couldn't be sure if her middle name should be Wren or Sage until we'd been able to look her directly in the eyes.

I did not get to hold her in my arms until she was five days old. *Sage.* Taken through the shield of the Ziploc bag that the NICU required us to place our phones in during visits for infection control, all of the pictures we have of the twins' first week of life are blurry.

The same environmental factors contributing to distressing increases in air pollution are contributing to an equally distressing shift in natural disasters. Thanks to climate change, natural disasters like wildfires and hurricanes are becoming more intense, and in some cases, more frequent. In August 2020, as an unprecedented season of wildfires raged through California, I started receiving text messages from my West Coast friends. They sent pictures of an apocalypse that had arrived at their front doors: hazy red skies, cars covered in skins of ash, suns blotted out by dark, enveloping clouds of smoke.

One message came from my friend Alix, who lives in Oakland with her husband Nate and one-year-old son Oren:

> *"The scariest feeling is feeling unsafe in our home. It's a drafty house so we can't really escape the smoke (we do have filters running) and we can't go outside because of the smoke, so I'm left with this panic: Where can we go? Where can we go to be safe? I'm scared for Oren as much as for myself. I feel it in my body. And we have a home. I think of all the migrants and the homeless. It's really really scary and sad. I'm having pretty detrimental anxiety—it ramped up as COVID started, then the political/racial/immigrant sadness, and now with the fires I'm having so much trouble managing it. I have pretty terrible insomnia because of it. All my practices for relaxing and trust are not working. I feel disconnected from any sense of work or purpose in the world. But I am running on very, very little sleep, so I know that*

impacts my emotions a lot. Going to go drink a lot of water! I remember in 2018 when it was terrible I thought—if this happens again, we're moving. It's terrifying. Not even the fire danger, but the smoke. Today, we're barely going outside, running all our air purifiers that we bought in 2018. And we have a home, and purifiers. And then with coronavirus, we can't see friends, can't invite community over, or even my brother and his kids. It's like: fear, sadness, loneliness... and then crammed in a city. And each summer now has major fires. It's the new normal but I question staying here almost every day. Nate is open to moving, but I also want to remember the good things that are here."

In addition to its hazardous impact on prenatal development, wildfire smoke is particularly dangerous for children's still-growing lungs. Children spend more time outside than adults, increasing their risk of exposure to smoke, and research has shown that a higher proportion of inhaled smoke goes directly into their lungs than in adults, where more particulate matter may be captured in the nose. Pediatric exposure to wildfire smoke can cause chest pain, coughing, wheezing, dizziness, and a burning sensation in the nose and throat, and the adverse effects of smoke on developing lungs may last into adulthood. For children with asthma or other underlying respiratory issues, risks can be far more serious and may include emergency room visits, hospitalization, or even death.

The physical risks of wildfires are unnerving enough, but of course, the impact is not just physical. It can be traumatic to experience the threat of evacuation, to be stuck indoors for days on end because of smoke, or terrifyingly, to experience the loss of a home or another beloved place due to fire. In May 2016, a wildfire ripped through Fort McMurray in Alberta, Canada, forcing the largest wildfire evacuation in Alberta's history. Over 88,000 people had to leave their homes, and 10% of homes in the evacuation area were destroyed. Eighteen months after the fire, researchers surveyed over 3,000 grade 7-12 students—70% of the total student population—to assess possible long-term mental health impacts. Forty-six percent of all students met criteria for one or more probable diagnoses of PTSD, depression, anxiety, or substance abuse, with students who had experienced greater impact from the fire exhibiting higher scores on all mental health measures. This study did not explore the impact of the fire on the mental health of the students' parents, but it's easy to imagine that many of them were traumatized, too.

Where can we go to be safe?

When I was eight years old, I watched the collapse of a giant southern live oak tree from a back window of my grandmother's house in Wilmington. A nor'easter tore through in January of 1992, the second winter storm in a fourteen-month series of nor'easters to produce strong winds, high tide, and flooding across the East Coast of the United States. With my five-year-old brother at my side, I watched with a dizzying sense of excitement as the tree veered more and more precipitously to the left, its enormous root system starting to emerge through the soil. My grandmother's house was positioned at the edge of a golf course, and thankfully, the golf course was between us and the tree; the tree posed no direct threat to us. The next day, when the storm had passed, we examined the fallen goliath. While the root system of an oak tree is fairly shallow, extending just two or three feet below the surface of the ground, it's incredibly wide, spreading as much as ninety feet from the trunk. An entire universe had been uprooted, exposing an enormous mouth of soil.

Others in the path of the same storm were not as lucky. Flooding closed highways in the Outer Banks, high winds downed power lines, and wind gusts across the East Coast approached the strength of a category one hurricane. Flooding in Dewey Beach, Delaware contaminated the town's water supply. As far north as Maine, injuries and deaths were reported from storm-related accidents.

The Rio Earth Summit also happened in 1992, and representatives from 172 countries gathered in Rio, Brazil to discuss the damage that human activity was causing in the natural world. Interest in the event was considered unprecedented, representing a distinct shift in global attitudes about environmental issues. One of many outcomes of the event was the establishment of the United Nations Framework Convention on Climate Change, which continues to be one of the major organizational bodies tasked with supporting the global response to climate change.

In 1992, climate change was on the radar of scientists and world leaders, but not yet taught in North Carolina's third-grade science classes. I did not learn in school that year that the string of nor'easter storms might have been related to human activity's toll on the environment, nor did the popular media link climate change to Hurricane Andrew, which also wrought immense damage on the southeastern United States in 1992. That August, Hurricane Andrew was one of only four hurricanes to make landfall in the country as a category five storm. Research on the psychological impact of Hurricane Andrew on elementary school children in Miami, which took a direct hit, painted a clear picture of emotional distress. Eighty-seven percent of children who had experienced high impact from the storm—such as having a window or door broken open, a roof caved in or blown off, or an injured pet—reported symptoms of post-traumatic stress in the months after the hurricane.

Be it a storm or a wildfire, the intensity of exposure to a natural disaster is directly correlated to the level of adverse mental health impacts experienced afterwards. As a child in central North Carolina, buffered by almost 200 miles of land from the highest intensity of coastal storms, hurricanes and nor'easters were more often exciting than frightening. We'd pile pillows into a downstairs hallway during tornado warnings, light candles when the power went out, delight in our freedom on days when school was cancelled. Sheltered from the storms by geography, privilege, and parents who didn't want to frighten me, I did not understand that there were children who had lost homes, pets, and loved ones to the same storms that I experienced as an adventure.

But as a parent, as the storms worsen, each hurricane brings the same nightmare: I dream that a giant tree will collapse on our house. I dream that my children will fall into the gaping earth-wound left by its roots.

Learning about the health impacts of climate change on children is like learning about a rapidly metastasizing cancer. The effects are staggering, complex, far reaching, and likely to only get worse. The same increasing temperatures that are worsening air pollution and contributing to more violent storms are also a direct threat in and of themselves: children are more vulnerable to heat-related illnesses than non-elderly adults, because their small bodies are less efficient at cooling and because they spend more time outside. A warmer world will be a world in which droughts are more likely, in which food and water insecurity mean more and more children will be malnourished and forced to migrate from their homes to faraway countries that may not welcome them. Changing climate patterns will put children at greater risk for contracting vector-borne diseases that thrive in the aftermath of intense bursts of precipitation, such as malaria and dengue fever. Scientists already know that climate change is dramatically expanding the habitable zones for ticks that carry the bacteria responsible for Lyme disease, which, if left untreated, can attack a child's heart, nerves, and joints.

If either of my children had cancer, I would do everything in my power to save them. I would spare no cost to try to protect their chance at a healthy future.

Public health experts estimate the burden of specific diseases using a variety of measures. Mortality rates, for instance, summarize the number of people who have died in a particular population of a particular cause. Predictive mortality rates use complex statistical algorithms to guess at the toll a disease might take on a population. Disability-adjusted life years, or DALYs, describe years of life prematurely lost to ill health, disability, or early death. DALYs come closer than mortality rates to estimating what's actually lost in an encounter with life-threatening disease. When calculating DALYs, the loss of a year of childhood is generally weighed as more costly than the loss of a year of senior adulthood. The loss of a child's entire potential future is counted as a greater toll than the loss of the last few potential years of an elder's lifetime.

Researchers anticipate that climate change will have a dramatic impact on all of these measures, and that globally, children will bear the vast majority—close to 90%—of the burden of disease. The World Health Organization estimates that in 2030, there will be 77,000 to 131,000 additional deaths in children under age five from climate-related malnutrition; others put this estimate higher. Health economists use quality-adjusted life years, or QALYs, to assess the value of health outcomes with an acknowledgement that *quality* of life matters as much as length of life. But QALYs are an imperfect measure, often inadequately capturing what matters most to people in assessing what makes a life worth living. To my knowledge, there is no scientific measure that can account for the loss of childhood summer days spent leisurely outside without fear of dying of heat stroke or having a fatal asthma attack. I don't know how to measure the cost of parenting in a world where each wildfire is accompanied by the fear that you might have to evacuate your children with an hour's notice. I don't know how to measure the loss of a pregnancy free from the fear that a heat wave might cause a miscarriage, or that simply breathing polluted air might cause a stillbirth. I don't know how to measure the loss of a childhood free from the threat of unrelenting natural disasters.

Intergenerational equity, or the concept of justice between generations, attempts proactively to account for these intangible, hard-to-quantify future losses. In the context of climate change, intergenerational equity reminds us that we will have to answer to our children and our grandchildren for the consequences of our actions, and that future generations have a fundamental right to a future that is safe, healthy, and just. Intergenerational equity demands that we acknowledge our moral responsibility not just to intellectually understand, but to *respond* to the risks that may threaten future generations. It asks us to act on behalf of our children's future as much as we act on their behalf in the present.

All of the parents I know are vigilant about fire safety. We'll strategically place fire extinguishers in key rooms, make sure our smoke alarms and carbon monoxide detectors have working batteries, ensure that matches are out of reach of little hands, and give our spouses icy stares when they inadvertently leave the oven on. In the domain of our homes, fire safety habits are just a small portion of the actions we take every day to ensure that our families are as safe and healthy as possible. There are risks we know how to respond to proactively and consistently; as parents, we practice risk management all the time.

In a January 2019 speech at the World Economic Forum in Davos, climate activist Greta Thunberg urged an audience of high-level politicians, executives, and leaders: "I want you to act as you would in a crisis. I want you to act as if our house is on fire. Because it is." Speaking on behalf of generations of children, both living and yet to be born, Thunberg demands intergenerational equity of those of us who are in a position to act.

What level of climate risk are we willing to accept on behalf of our children, and on behalf of our children's children?

What level of climate risk are we willing to accept on behalf of *all* children, especially those more vulnerable than our own?

What would it take for us to act as if our collective house is on fire, acting with the same fierce protective instinct that guides us in caring for our families every day?

And how can we cultivate the capacity to stay awake in the face of a crisis we may desperately want to pretend isn't happening?

Chapter 3 Reflection

Key practice: Consider climate risks from a perspective that's both long and wide. As parents, we have a responsibility to consider the well-being of our children and future generations. As ethical humans on this planet, we have a responsibility to consider how climate change may harm vulnerable and marginalized populations.

Questions for reflection and discussion with others:

- How has becoming a parent influenced your perception of risk?

- The chapter describes why our collective response to climate change has tended to be different than our response to other potential threats. Has this been true for you?

- Have you experienced climate change as a direct threat to your or your family's health yet? If so, what has that experience been like for you?

- What is it like to know that children—especially Black children, Indigenous children, and children of color—are more vulnerable to threats from climate change and environmental than any other population?

- What does the concept of "intergenerational equity" mean for you? How might you address intergenerational equity in your own life?

THE EMOTIONAL CLIMATE

"Your grief is a worthwhile use of your time."

—ADRIENNE MAREE BROWN,
Emergent Strategy

SOMEWHERE IN LATE SEPTEMBER 2015, approximately ten weeks and five ultrasounds into my pregnancy, my baby died.

We'd started house-hunting that month. Weeks earlier, when the first ultrasound revealed that our second round of IUI had resulted in the conception of triplets, our small apartment suddenly felt far too crowded. Our cars suddenly felt far too small (if you're expecting triplets, anything other than a minivan technically *is* far too small; there is no sedan on the market that will fit three infant car seats in the back seat). Bart, he'd tell me later, had started shopping for triplet strollers. We channeled our shock into pragmatic action, trying to refine an unwieldy situation into slightly less unwieldy steps: Find a big enough home. Find a big enough car. Find a big enough stroller.

The week of the fifth ultrasound, my calendar was full of coaching sessions, research meetings, and acupuncture appointments, all but the latter of which I was doing remotely given the violent nausea and vomiting I'd been struggling with since mid-August. After a week of throwing up in plastic bags in my office, I'd asked to work from home; none of my colleagues had objected. By September, I could not keep water down without Zofran, a drug often used to help cancer patients fight chemotherapy-induced nausea and vomiting. All of the healthy meals I'd imagined eating during pregnancy were replaced by bowls of dry cereal and weirdly, egg salad (other strange pregnancy yens had included an inexplicable desire to collect snow globes and vintage nineties perfume miniatures from eBay; Bart never questioned me). Each time I vomited—the Zofran helped, but not enough—I understood exactly how women had died in pregnancy in earlier centuries. Had I conceived triplets in 1815, instead of 2015, I surely would have been one of the fallen.

In spite of feeling like being pregnant might literally kill me, I barely slowed down at all. A full calendar and focused shopping agenda distracted me not just from the misery of hyperemesis gravidarum, but also from a decision we'd been asked to make. During the initial ultrasound appointment, after our normally chatty nurse had fallen unusually quiet as she examined my uterus with her magic wand, one of the male fertility doctors had been called into the room minutes later to offer expertise. "You may want to consider selective reduction," he'd said in a voice that sounded like metal scraping against metal. "Your body is only meant for one at a time, you know."

We had signed a release form in July saying that we understood that the risk of triplets and higher-order multiples from the specific cocktail of drugs and procedures we'd chosen was less than 2%. I remember thinking at the time that those risks sounded entirely reasonable. That I'd have jumped off a bridge if there was a 98% chance of survival.

Carrying triplets, we learned quickly, carried significant risks. It was hazardous for me as the mother, almost certainly contributing to the hyperemesis. It was even more dangerous for the babies: triplets are nearly always born prematurely. A significant proportion of triplet births occur earlier than twenty-six weeks, at which point almost all of them will suffer long-term adverse health outcomes, such as permanent brain and internal organ damage; many will die.

Selective reduction, or medical termination of one or more living fetuses, also carries risks. You will read in the fine print about the following possibilities: a ruptured uterus, retained placentas, unintended fetal death, infection, excessive bleeding requiring transfusion, or premature labor may result from this procedure. These risks are rare, as is the risk of conceiving triplets in the first place.

We decided to postpone the decision as long as possible. We Zillowed and CarMaxed and Amazoned. When we told our realtor why we were shopping for a home, she revealed that years ago, she had conceived triplets, too. When she spoke of her two adult daughters, we did not ask what had happened to the third one.

Your body is only meant for one at a time, you know.

When confronted with a harrowing set of circumstances, it's normal to want to shop yourself into oblivion to avoid feeling your feelings. Or to overwork, or overeat, or drink too much, or binge-watch reality television, or create drama in your relationships, or obsessively organize your closet by season and color.

When the truth is truly terrible, it's understandable to engage in elaborate denial fantasies in which nonfiction becomes fiction. When the world no longer makes sense, it makes sense that our brains might cope by lurching precipitously across competing cliffs of incapacitating dread and icy numbness.

These are strategies I am familiar with.

I first learned about the idea of "climate grief" from a Google search. Several months into my own climate awakening, I found myself more and more disturbed by everything I learned, and realized I needed resources for coping. I needed resources for resilience. Most of the search results that popped up for "climate resilience" offered little help on the emotional front. Climate resilience, it turns out, is a technical term. In ecology, resilience describes a system's capacity to absorb stresses and maintain function in the face of adverse external inputs, such as climate change. It also refers to the system's capacity to adapt, restructure, and evolve into more sustainable configurations. The United States government has put together an elaborate resource called the U.S. Climate Resilience Toolkit, which also appeared in my search results. While the toolkit is impressively comprehensive, featuring tools to help users identify potential climate hazards and plan appropriate mitigation and adaptation efforts, it does not offer guidance on how to cope emotionally with the dread-infused sense that the world is falling apart around you as you try to parent young children.

Since internet rabbit holes are one of my favorite strategies for avoiding uncomfortable emotions, I was persistent in my search. Through some passageway of revised search terms and clicks, I stumbled on the website for an organization called the Good Grief Network. These folks, it turned out, were talking about an entirely different type of climate resilience.

Using a ten-step approach, the Good Grief Network offers a framework to help people "build personal resilience while strengthening community ties to help combat despair, inaction, eco-anxiety, and other heavy emotions in the face of daunting systemic predicaments." The first step: *Accept the Severity of the Predicament.* Something inside me shifted as I browsed through the website and took inventory of the ten steps—maybe it was that I felt *seen* in my deep unease about climate change for the first time. Here was a group of people who were not only experiencing the same moments of panic, uncertainty, and grief about climate change as I was, but who were also allowing themselves to fully *feel* these emotions, as I decidedly wasn't. Their approach, I gathered, was working better than mine.

The Good Grief Network was a porthole to the lexicon I didn't even know I'd been missing. There is an emerging language, I discovered, to describe the emotional landscape of humans' relationship with climate change and environmental destruction.

It was *eco-anxiety* I felt when reading reports describing the catastrophic shadow climate change has already cast on food and water security for large swaths of the world, including parts of the United States that people I love call home. It was *eco-anxiety* that kept me awake at night, wondering if my children would have enough to eat in the later years of their lives.

It was *climate grief* I experienced when reading about a dead right whale calf who had washed up on a barrier island in North Carolina, one of the last 400 left of a species whose primary food source—a flea-like animal known as a copepod—has been drastically diminished due to warming ocean temperatures. The idea of environmental grief first emerged in the academic world in the 1980s, thanks to the work of researcher Dr. Kriss Kevorkian. Kevorkian, too, felt deep grief at declining whale populations, and coined the term "environmental grief" in her doctoral dissertation in thanatology.

In 2019, Australian eco-philosopher Glenn Albrecht published a book called *Earth Emotions: New Words for a New World*. Drawing on his own lived experience as well as on older Australian Aboriginal ways of knowing, Albrecht explores a precise vocabulary for humans' emotional responses to the extraordinary scale and speed of ecological and environmental change. "As the threat to humanity of a powerful climatic *global* force of our own making has never before existed," Albrecht writes, "much of what has been written in the past about nature and life is irrelevant to the future we now face." We *need* new words to describe the world that's emerging.

Albrecht's words are surgically precise:

Meteoranxiety: *the anxiety that is felt in the face of the threat of the increasing frequency and severity of extreme weather events.*

Tierratrauma: *acute Earth-based existential trauma in the present.*

Topoaversion: *the feeling that you do not wish to return to a place that you once loved and enjoyed when you know that it has been irrevocably changed for the worse.*

And *solastalgia*, he says, is the word for a specific flavor of distress caused by environmental change. It was solastalgia I felt when I learned that by 2050, the climate of North Carolina is likely to feel like the climate of Northern Mexico, no matter what actions are taken. Solastalgia is the feeling of realizing that the version of home you know and love is slipping away in a slow-motion train wreck, and there's nothing you can do about it. It's the feeling of knowing that once gone, that version of home is never coming back. "It's the homesickness you have," writes Albrecht, "when you are still at home."

September 2015 was the fourth-warmest on record in the contiguous United States, and a band of states stretching from North Carolina to Maine saw above-average levels of precipitation (a cluster of states in the middle of the country, on the other hand, received far lower levels of precipitation than usual). Humidity coupled with warm temperatures, I discovered, make nausea worse.

We had strategically arranged mixing bowls around the house: one by the bedside, one on the coffee table, one near the dining room table, one near the kitchen counter. It's not like I could stand the smell of anything cooking or baking, so they might as well be used to catch vomit. It's called *hyperemesis* for a reason. Some days, when a dose of Zofran wore off, I'd throw up fifteen to twenty times an hour. When the next dose of Zofran kicked in, I'd muster the capacity to send emails, work on a research grant submission that was due the same month as the babies, and review the local housing market.

Also, in between periods of violent vomiting, I found the capacity to panic.

If you're pregnant with multiples and considering selective reduction, there's a somewhat limited time frame to make a decision. It's roughly the same window of time you'd have if you were considering a more common form of termination, what most people would call an abortion: the end of the first trimester, if at all possible, is ideally the last moment to choose which path to take.

I thought of the time I'd made an appointment at the local Planned Parenthood clinic for an abortion in the early days of an unplanned pregnancy in my twenties, a pregnancy that ended days later with a miscarriage.

I thought of what it would be like to choose which embryo to terminate. One was clearly smaller than the other two, but the smallest one also had the strongest, clearest heartbeat on the ultrasound. Was it *that* heartbeat we should end with an injected dose of potassium chloride, or one of the others?

I thought, too, of what it would be like to give birth at twenty-five weeks to triplets who might be permanently disabled by such a premature entry into the world. I imagined watching a two-pound baby die in my arms. How would it feel to know that I could have made a choice that might—just maybe—have prevented that?

We had struggled through months of disappointment, grief, and rumination to bring these lives into the world in the first place. I'd understood that becoming a parent would entail being responsible for a child's life, but it was a lacerating plot twist that less than a third of the way through my pregnancy, we were faced with an impossible decision. The risks of keeping the pregnancy were clear; so were the risks of selective reduction. Both posed long-term consequences to all of us.

How could it be that we were holding our children's fate in our hands so soon?

Environmentalism has long been disconnected from the world of human psychology, and in tandem, human psychology has largely been disconnected from the realm of the environment. The costs of these disconnects have been immense. Decades of environmental messaging around climate change has largely failed to motivate people and governments to take the actions required to mitigate the threats we face. And decades of psychology practice have largely ignored the profound impact the natural world has on our mental, emotional, and spiritual well-being. I remember weeping as a teen when learning about the plight of animals in factory farms, and having therapist after therapist try to convince me to go back to eating meat, rather than acknowledge that becoming a vegetarian was actually an appropriate, sane response to witnessing acute animal suffering.

Rather than being validated, many of us who have experienced emotional responses to trauma in the natural world have had those responses pathologized. We've been told we're oversensitive, assured that things really aren't as bad as we're making them out to be. We've been gaslit and told that we're the ones with a problem, when really, the problem is that the rest of the world has gone numb.

There's a growing recognition that emotional responses to witnessing assault on the natural world are not only reasonable, but increasingly common. The emerging fields of ecotherapy and climate psychology aim to reconcile the gap between environmentalism and human psychology. Preeminent ecotherapists Linda Buzzel and Craig Chalquist state the dilemma their field seeks to address: "It seems both outrageous and irresponsible that so few mental health clinicians connect the epidemics of mental distress in industrial societies with the devastating impact of our own suicidal destruction of our own habitat and ecocide elimination of whole species." Ecotherapists seek to normalize the experience of emotional distress in the face of environmental crisis, whether that distress takes the form of acute emotion or a sense of unsettling numbness.

Like the creators of the Good Grief Network, ecotherapists and climate psychologists also seek to encourage people to *feel* their difficult emotions about environmental trauma and change, rather than to numb out or desensitize. *Accept the severity of the predicament.* "The refusal to feel," writes eco-philosopher Joanna Macy, "takes a heavy toll. It not only impoverishes our emotional and sensory life—flowers are dimmer and less fragrant, our loves less ecstatic—but psychic numbing also impedes our capacity to process and respond to information. The energy expended in resisting despair is diverted from more creative uses, depleting the resilience and imagination needed for fresh visions and strategies." The cost of ignoring our emotions about climate change may literally be the solutions we need to address it.

Accepting the severity of the predicament is not easy work. It's excruciating to bear witness to what's already been lost in the natural world, and excruciating to face what the overwhelming majority of climate scientists tell us is likely to come. The climate crisis is dire, much more urgent than many of us allow ourselves to admit on a day-to-day basis. And while many communities have faced existential threats for generations—Black, Indigenous, Jewish, and queer communities, for starters—many people of European descent have little in the way of inherited resilience in the face of the level of trauma presented by climate change. People like me will need to *learn* how to hold and integrate this much pain. As parents, this pain is magnified when we consider what the coming decades may be like for our children, with so little time left to make collective decisions that will quite literally determine the quality of their future.

It's the inherited resilience and deep wisdom of historically marginalized and oppressed communities that must guide us in navigating the existential threat of climate change. It's ecotherapists, climate psychologists, and environmentally literate coaches, teachers, and spiritual leaders who can help us navigate the day-to-day challenges of this daunting, hard-to-accept reality: *How can it be that this is how it is? How can it be that we're holding our children's fate in our hands so soon?*

When you conceive at a fertility clinic, extra ultrasounds are par for the course. During a "normal" pregnancy, unless there are symptoms to warrant earlier investigation, the first ultrasound typically happens somewhere between six to nine weeks of gestation. When you've been injected with gonadotropins, and when a stranger in a white coat has put another stranger's sperm directly into your uterus, they check sooner.

The first ultrasound showed three distinct amniotic sacs: two that were perfectly on target for gestational size each week; one smaller than the others, but with a mighty heartbeat. Each week the small one grew less than its womb mates, its heartbeat gradually waning. By the fifth ultrasound, the third heartbeat was gone completely. It was like watching a slow-motion train wreck.

Fetal resorption: *the spontaneous disintegration and assimilation of one or more fetuses in the uterus at any stage of organogenesis, which, in humans, is after the ninth week of gestation.*

Vanishing triplet: *when one fetus in a multi-gestation pregnancy dies in utero; it may be resorbed into the mother's body.*

Twins: *two offspring produced from the same pregnancy.*

Somehow, these terms were easier to swallow than *selective reduction* and *medical abortion* and *triplets*. But I do not have language to describe the emotional or somatic experience of knowing that your body is generating life and absorbing death at the same time. I don't have words for the particular sensation of relief at having been liberated from a harrowing decision while knowing the cost of that liberation was a life.

What's the term for watching one future slip away, the future where you're a family of five that drives around in a minivan and uses a triplet stroller, while you're still gestating another future that feels precarious, uncertain, unknowable?

In early 2020, the Seventh Generation corporation released the results of a survey examining generational attitudes towards climate change. The survey assessed the attitudes of 2,000 Americans, split evenly amongst baby boomers, Generation X, millennials, and Generation Z. A significant majority of the millennials (71%) and Gen Z-ers (67%) reported that climate change had negatively impacted their mental health. Perhaps most strikingly, the survey found that four out of five (78%) Gen Z-ers aren't planning to, or didn't want to, have children because of climate change. And seven out of ten millennials surveyed felt the same.

This represents a dramatic generational shift in attitudes towards family building. As recently as 2013, a Gallup survey found that 95% of Americans either had kids, desired and planned to have kids, or wished that they had.

There are a million valid reasons not to want children; climate change is certainly one of them. But when I think about these numbers, I think of all the bereaved parents I have met: the mothers who've lost babies to miscarriage or ectopic pregnancies or stillbirth. The fathers who feel helpless as round after round of fertility treatments fail. The couples who eventually give up attempts to conceive at all, after years of trying. Navigating infertility, research shows, is as stressful as navigating a diagnosis of cancer or HIV. To not have a child in your arms when you desperately want one is a direct threat to our sense of identity, and a devastating personal loss.

We grieve the children who aren't born, too.

Many parents who lose children during pregnancy give their babies names. This can help validate a kind of grief that is often invisible to the rest of the world. We can better articulate a loss that has a name, and better say goodbye to someone we found the language to say hello to. Some parents, in the process of trying to conceive, name the spirits of their babies on the other side. Our unborn, not-yet-born, and no-longer-living children can occupy an extraordinary amount of space in our lives.

What space will these ghost children occupy, I wonder, in the hearts of Generation Z? Will there be a generation of dogs named *Charlotte* and cats named *William* in the place of the children who might have claimed these names in an alternate, non-climate-changed universe?

Born in 2016, my children are at the tail end of Generation Z, a generation that believes that there are only ninety-five habitable years left on the planet. If the results of the Seventh Generation survey can be extrapolated to a larger population, my children are more likely than not to choose not to have children of their own when they come of age.

What's the word for anticipatory grief over the loss of grand-children who may never be conceived?

We are watching one future slip away, while the other one gestates: still precarious, uncertain, unknowable. We are all navigating an extraordinarily complicated relationship with hope. It's deeply sane, and utterly normal, to feel shattered by the reality of climate change. We will face unbearable losses. It's also utterly normal to try to avoid feeling anything at all, as if impulse buying reusable coffee thermoses online could make it all go away. It's agonizing to accept the severity of the predicament, and perhaps even more agonizing to know that our children will one day have to accept it, too. No one—save for our children—could blame us for wanting to wish these dark truths away.

But having a precise vocabulary to describe the nascent experience of parenting in a changing climate may help us rise to the challenge of trying to protect a livable planet for future generations. Expressing our emotions in language helps to validate them, and can help us begin to weave cohesive narratives about the traumatic experiences of our lives. We may, in finding new ways to narrate these emergent experiences, discover words that help us describe unfamiliar sensations of joy as well as unfamiliar sensations of pain.

Soliphilia, Albrecht tells us, describes a "love of the interrelated whole; the giving of political commitment to the protection of loved home places at all scales, from the global to the local, from the forces of desolation."

If our children have to grow up in a world that's fluent in *solastalgia* and *apocalypse fatigue,* may they also grow up in a world that speaks natively of *soliphilia.* If they have to come of age in an era marked by devastating experiences of grief and loss, may they also come of age in an era marked by extraordinary experiences of love.

Chapter 4 Reflection

Key practice: Normalize climate grief, eco-anxiety, and other difficult "earth emotions." They are a sign that we're in relationship with the natural world, and a sane response to what's actually happening. Consider exploring the emerging language of climate distress.

Questions for reflection and discussion with others:

- How have you experienced climate-related distress? Do any of the "earth emotions" described in this chapter resonate with you?

- Have you had to make any difficult choices in your experience of parenthood so far? What parallels do you see between difficult choices in parenthood and the difficult choices we must make in relationship to climate change?

- This chapter draws parallels between the experience of pregnancy loss and climate grief, naming specifically that the futures we lose can occupy an enormous space in our hearts. If you have experienced pregnancy loss, did this resonate with you?

- What is it like to acknowledge that oppressed and marginalized communities have faced existential threats for generations? How might this awareness affect your experience of grief?

- How has becoming a parent influenced your experience of grief?

Part II
POSSIBILITY

STORIES FOR RESILIENCE
IN A LONG EMERGENCY

"Burnt-out people aren't equipped to serve a burning planet."

—Susanne C. Moser, *in All We Can Save*

It's 5:30 in the morning on a Monday, and I've been interrupted three separate times in the writing of this sentence. Once, to watch a child demonstrate a newly acquired gymnastic ability involving a dog leash improbably attached to a chin-up bar in our kitchen. Three seconds later, the other child peed in their underwear. Almost simultaneously, the first child discovered an unacceptable brown spot on their banana that I MUST TAKE OFF NOW. It is late November in the first fall of the COVID-19 pandemic, and the precious hour of early-morning quiet I used to depend on for sanity has been invaded by early rising four-year-olds. No matter how early I wake, they wake too, as if their brains are wired directly to mine. They *know*.

It has been like this for months. I am surviving on coffee, noise-cancelling headphones, and parenting memes.

It was like this several months ago, too, as I tried to write a manuscript for a research study we'd done at my workplace on expressive writing for parents' resilience in the context of

COVID-19. Back in March 2020, when the early days of the pandemic upturned all of the clinical trials we had planned for the year, my colleagues and I put our heads together to brainstorm what we could do during this time, given limited resources and the inability to do any kind of research in person. Several years back, our small team had run a pilot trial on expressive writing for trauma resilience that was both extremely well-received by participants and showed promising results. In the interim, I had trained with our colleague John Evans, a leader in the field of expressive writing and narrative medicine, to become an expressive writing facilitator myself. A writing intervention, we realized, could be administered easily over Zoom. And the theme of trauma resilience seemed painfully relevant.

All three members of our expressive writing research team had young children home from school thanks to COVID-19, and we realized quickly that the pandemic's impact on parents would be distinctly different than its impact on people without children at home. A steady stream of popular news headlines affirmed our suspicions as the year unfolded: *Additional Work Falls on Parents as More People Stay Home. For Working Moms, Pandemic Strain is Unsustainable. Being a Mom is Tough; Being a Mom in a Pandemic is Even Tougher. 'This is Too Much': Working Moms Are Reaching a Breaking Point During the Pandemic. It's Not Just Moms; Pandemic Life is Taking a Toll On Dads, Too.*

And my personal favorite, the headline accompanying a viral photo of an environmental scientist's actual, toy-strewn work environment juxtaposed against the elegant neck-up scene she'd managed to create for a video interview with CNN: *When a Tornado Hits a Toy Store: Photo Shows Reality of Working From Home With Kids.*

This was how two studies emerged: one on expressive writing for COVID-19 resilience in a general population, and the other specifically aimed at parents of children aged eighteen or younger. For the study aimed at the general population, we adapted the six-week intervention that had shown promise in our earlier trial. Writing prompts were tailored to speak directly to the experience of living through the trauma of the pandemic, and included evidence-based practices from positive psychology that could easily be adapted to the form of expressive writing, such as expressing gratitude and savoring positive moments. The writing prompts for the parenting study were similar, but condensed into a four-week intervention with shorter writing sessions each time to accommodate parents' more hectic, COVID-demolished lives. Using surveys administered before and after the interventions, we assessed participants' levels of resilience, perceived stress, and depression. While our sample sizes were limited by our limited recruitment resources, preliminary results indicate improvement in multiple measures in our study populations. In our study for the general population, participants experienced significant improvements in resilience, perceived stress, depression symptoms, and post-traumatic growth over the six-week study period. In our study for parents, participants experienced a significant reduction in perceived stress. These results align with what a growing body of research on expressive writing suggests: that when we face untenable circumstances, putting our emotions into words can help us cope.

Many have described COVID-19 as an unsettling preview of the coming attractions we can anticipate with climate change. The parallels are striking. Like COVID-19, climate change is a global crisis that threatens to harm millions of lives. Both crises exploit existing social inequalities, disproportionately harming Black, Indigenous, and brown lives. Both crises demand racial and socioeconomic justice as a guiding principle of our collective response. Both crises put, or will put, extraordinary strain on the basic infrastructure of societies. The loss of biodiversity associated with climate change directly increases the threat of pandemics, as dwindling animal habitats increase contact between humans and potentially disease-carrying animal vectors. The causes of both climate change and the extraordinary spread of COVID-19 are backed by clear scientific consensus, consensus still facing direct challenge by deniers and the spread of misinformation and conspiracy theories. Both crises ask us to make individual changes and sacrifice for the sake of collective well-being: COVID-19 begs us to act on behalf of our elders; climate change begs us to act on behalf of our children.

And both force us to sit with an uncomfortable question: *will we?* Will we make individual sacrifices for the collective well-being? Will we act on behalf of those who are more vulnerable than we are, even when the threat still seems invisible? And will we act in time?

Like COVID-19, climate change is a long emergency, though climate change will last far longer. Long emergencies require qualitatively different reserves of resilience than more acute, time-limited crises. In a popular article on Medium, science journalist Tara Haelle interviewed resilience expert Ann Masten about the idea of *surge capacity*: "Surge capacity is a collection of adaptive systems—mental and physical—that humans draw on for short-term survival in acutely stressful situations, such as natural disasters. But natural disasters occur over a short period, even if recovery is long. Pandemics are different—the disaster itself stretches out indefinitely."

Months into the pandemic and utterly exhausted by continuing to have to juggle parenting and work without adequate childcare, I felt deeply validated by the idea that my *surge capacity* was depleted.

But I wonder if the idea that natural disasters are qualitatively different than the pandemic will hold in the coming decades, as scientists' predictions that extreme weather events will become the norm begin to unfold. Haelle writes: "Research on disaster and trauma focuses primarily on what's helpful for people during the recovery period, but we're not close to recovery yet. People can use their surge capacity for acute periods, but when dire circumstances drag on, Masten says, 'you have to adopt a different style of coping.'" The dire circumstances of climate change threaten to drag on not just for a few years, but for the rest of our lives. What style of coping will we have to adopt then?

I can already see the headlines:

Additional Work Falls on Parents as More People Stay Home Due to Increasing Heat Waves. For Working Moms, Strain of Frequent Natural Disasters is Unsustainable. Being a Mom is Tough; Being a Mom in a Changing Climate is Even Tougher.

In *Upside: The New Science of Post-Traumatic Growth*, journalist Jim Rendon devotes an entire chapter to the exploration of expressive writing and post-traumatic growth. Expressive writing, he says, is a form of *deliberate rumination*. Unlike the variety of rumination in which you're still awake in the wee hours of the morning worrying about the fact that your husband left the oven on—that's *intrusive rumination*, according to psychology researchers—deliberate rumination involves consciously reexamining and reflecting on a difficult event or circumstance as a way of intentionally processing it. "Talking, writing, and expressing oneself," Rendon writes, "is central to enabling the kind of deliberate rumination and narrative reframing that is required for growth."

One of the most commonly used and well-researched techniques in expressive writing research is the Pennebaker Paradigm, a distinct set of four writing prompts designed to encourage deliberate rumination and perspective-taking about a difficult or traumatic event. Created by researcher James Pennebaker, the paradigm can be adapted to an infinite variety of circumstances. You could use it to write about the death of a friend, a breakup with your partner, an unexpected cancer diagnosis, or the experience of Zoom-schooling your eight-year-old during a pandemic. You could use it to write about climate change. Meant to be followed in a specific order, the prompts can be completed in a single setting, or done over a period of several days. You can spend fifteen to twenty minutes (or longer) responding to each prompt, but research has shown that even two minutes of expressive writing can have therapeutic benefit. These prompts can meet you where you are.

In condensed form, the prompts flow as follows:

Prompt 1: Write about your deepest feelings about a difficult or traumatic event.

Prompt 2: Keep writing about your feelings. Go deeper. Let it all out.

Prompt 3: Now, consider the circumstances from a different perspective—write about this.

Prompt 4: Finally, given everything you've written, write a cohesive narrative about what happened to take forward.

Very often, somewhere between the beginning of prompt 1 and the end of prompt 4, there's a shift. The writer's story changes. In prompt 3, when we're asked to consider what's happened from a different perspective, we're forced to admit that there *is* a different perspective. Even if we're just playing along with the prompt as a creative exercise, it's hard to argue with a new way of looking at things once it's there on the page, staring back at you. In prompt 4, we get to find a way to weave pieces of our original narrative and the nuances of a new perspective together to form a story that's somehow different than the one we arrived at the page with. All of our messy emotions are still with us, and the painful circumstances may not have changed at all, but in writing about them, we've created a sense of spaciousness that might not have been there before.

Writing about difficult events may literally help our brains to organize them, like taking a messy stack of papers strewn about an office, gathering them up, assigning appropriate labels, and filing them carefully back into the proper drawers. Rendon explains:

> "Why does this seemingly simple process work? Pennebaker says that these traumatic experiences tend to remain in the victim's awareness until they are either made sense of cognitively, or they simply fade with time. Making sense of trauma—understanding it and coming to terms with what it means—is a relatively efficient way

of comprehending and accepting adverse experiences…
By talking or writing about difficult experiences,
survivors are forced to translate them into language,
which is particularly important with traumatic
memories…. Writing helps survivors to label the
experience, attaching language to it that allows survivors
to understand and process the event instead of leaving
it as some alert adrift in our neural wiring. Once that's
done, people can assign it meaning, some level of
coherence, and give the event a structure and place in
their lives. Representing the experience with language
is a necessary step toward understanding the experience."

Research also suggests that writing about challenging experiences
in an organized, deliberate manner—such as by responding to
specific writing prompts—is more helpful than doing so in a
disorganized way, such as writing haphazardly in a journal. Many
people find journaling useful, but free-form, prompt-less journaling doesn't necessarily force us to organize our experiences,
explore new perspectives, or create coherent narratives about our
lives. (If you've written "I hate my job and my whole life sucks!"
in your journal nine days in a row without arriving at anything
hinting at a different perspective, journaling may simply be rein-
forcing a story that probably isn't serving you.)

I've personally used the Pennebaker Paradigm several times
throughout the pandemic. It's one of my go-to tools when I'm
feeling utterly overwhelmed by life, and in need of a new way of
looking at things.

My response to prompt 1 generally goes something like this:

Prompt 1: Write about your deepest feelings about a difficult or traumatic event.

This will never end. I'm failing as a mother. I yell at my kids every day. These are some of the most precious years of my children's lives, and I'm spending them angry and irritable far more often than anyone knows. Bart and I are in the same house all the time, but I feel like I haven't seen him in months. I haven't hugged a friend in years. I haven't had a haircut in decades. My children will be permanently traumatized by this. I'm so fucking tired of not being able to go to the playground, the museum, or to take them to preschool. They deserve more than I can give them and I have nothing left to give. My house is a disaster. I can't keep this up. I'm barely holding it together most days.

Prompt 2: Keep writing about your feelings. Go deeper. Let it all out.

Much the same as prompt 1, though usually with more curse words added. Sometimes, entirely curse words. One large paragraph of *fucks*.

Prompt 3: Now, consider the circumstances from a different perspective—write about this.

This sucks, but I'm sure I won't look back on these days and wish I'd spent less time with my kids when they were four. We are struggling, but we are safe and healthy, and so far, everyone we know is safe and healthy. We can't go to the playground or the museum, but we've explored every trail and creek within a two-mile radius, and most of the time, the kids are just as happy to play in the mud in our backyard as anywhere else. I know my other mom friends are struggling too, so at least I'm not alone on that front, and I'm probably not the *worst* mother in the world.

By the final prompt, I've remembered some essential thread of resilience, and sometimes, even a note of self-compassion. I'm able to see something I couldn't see before.

Prompt 4: *Finally, given everything you've written, write a cohesive narrative about what happened to take forward.*

This is a profoundly difficult situation, but we will get through it. It's amazing to think about how many people are working so hard to keep us safe and to keep society running in these extraordinary times: healthcare workers, grocery store workers, postal workers. People have survived far more difficult circumstances than this. My kids are safe and loved, and they are remarkably resilient—Minnie has created art every single day during the pandemic, and I wonder how this art is shaping her. Milo has spent countless hours poring over books about insects while I'm working—will he be a biologist someday? We're all doing the best we can. *I'm* doing the best I can. We're human, and that's enough.

There are, of course, differences between parenting in the midst of an extended emergency like the pandemic and parenting during an acute emergency, like a natural disaster. Similarities aside, pandemics *are* qualitatively different than imminent hurricanes and wildfires. Living in the North Carolina piedmont, I can't describe from personal experience what it's like to haul your children, pets, and a family-sized go bag into a car and drive for miles through apocalyptic tunnels of smoke to outrun a wildfire that may or may not burn your house down in the next few hours. The "big one" hasn't yet hit my town, and I haven't yet had to evacuate my family from hurricane-related flooding. But these accounts of climate-related trauma are increasingly common among American parents, especially for those in geographically vulnerable places like California, Louisiana, Texas, and cities along the east coast.

In an essay from the Washington Post in December 2019, Bay Area psychotherapist Ariella Cook-Shonkoff describes her family's close encounter with a wildfire:

> "In 2017, the climate crisis crept viscerally close to my home. Ash particles descended like snowflakes, and my husband and I fled town with our then-two-year-old, canceling her birthday party at the last minute and heading to a friend's home in the mountains. The following year, my husband, who works closely at the nexus of human health, climate and the environment, invested in air filters for our poorly insulated house. Some days later, informing me that air quality in the Bay Area was worse than in Beijing, he drove our three-month-old to a friend's house on the northwest coast. For another day or two, I stuck it out with my older daughter, showing up at work as usual, trying to convince myself that everything would be ok if I just went through the motions. Eventually, we followed suit."

The stress of Hurricane Sandy, a devastating "superstorm" that wrought destruction from the Caribbean to Canada in October 2012, was so intense that babies born before, during, and after the storm experienced lasting emotional impact. In a study of 380 pairs of mothers and babies in New York, where Sandy made landfall on October 29th, doctoral candidate Jessica Buthmann and Professor Yoko Nomura found that babies whose families experienced higher levels of disaster-related stress (such as loss of electricity or phone service) experienced more negative emotions at six months of age than babies exposed to less stress. Babies whose families had gone longer without support during the crises—such as restored electricity, restored phone service, and financial support—expressed more distress, fear, and sadness. "Although the stress caused by natural disasters might not be preventable," the researchers wrote, "mental health services and other support for expectant mothers and mothers with young children who experience disasters and other stressful events may mitigate their impact."

In the midst of cancelled birthday parties and frantic escapes from toxic air, or while navigating the final days of pregnancy without power or phone service, pulling out a journal to write about your feelings may not be the most practical resilience strategy. Crisis resilience requires, as psychologist Ann Masten explained, access to our "surge capacity": the adrenaline-fueled ability to get things done in an emergency situation.

But the capacity to *choose* the narrative we tell about a circumstance—the capacity we hone in expressive writing—is useful in acute crises, as well.

Child psychologists encourage parents to help their children navigate disaster situations with messages that communicate physical and emotional safety, connection, and resourcefulness: *This is scary, but we're doing everything we can to prepare so that we stay safe. Your feelings are valid. I'm here for you and willing to listen if you need to talk. We'll get through this together. We are connected. We will adapt and find creative solutions for whatever challenges may come.* Children build resilience when they are reminded that their relationship with their caregivers is loving and secure. They build resilience when they know their parents are listening.

As parents, the narratives that help children feel secure and resourced in a crisis may be the same messages we need ourselves: *This is scary, but I'm doing everything I can to prepare so that we stay safe. My feelings are valid. I know how to reach out for help when I need it. We'll get through this together. We are connected. We will adapt and find creative solutions for whatever challenges may come.* Parents build resilience when we tell ourselves stories of safety, connection, and resourcefulness, too.

Both the pandemic and climate change have created, and will create, significant trauma for children and families. Trauma's impact on young children is magnified. A strong body of research tells us that difficult, destabilizing experiences in children's earliest months and years can affect brain development and behavior for years down the road, even well into adulthood. Much of the research on adverse childhood experiences (ACEs) focuses on experiences of witnessing violence, abuse, or neglect, but aspects of a child's environment that undermine their basic sense of safety, stability, and bonding may be considered ACEs, as well.

Some pandemic- and climate change-related traumas will be easy to recognize as traumas. The loss of a loved one to COVID. A parent who reaches their breaking point under intense financial strain and resumes their habit of drinking too much. A devastating hurricane that destroys a beloved school or church. A terrifying evacuation from a wildfire.

But there are other traumas, too, that might fly under the radar. They are the losses we are tempted to sweep under the rug when things seem "fine" on the surface. They are the losses we minimize, telling ourselves that things could be so much worse. These traumas, too, may affect us for years to come.

Six months before the onset of the pandemic, Bart and I found ourselves in a room with a pediatric counselor we'd been referred to for a behavioral assessment for Milo. We'd been struggling for months with escalating conflicts at home: intractable tantrums, power struggles, wild physical behavior, and daily tears—many of which were mine—had become too much to ignore. As the counselor asked us to describe what kind of behaviors we were noticing at home, Milo attempted to swing from the pull cord of the blinds covering a window behind us, nearly knocked over a lamp, and climbed the chairs we were sitting in like they were playground equipment. We were promptly referred to occupational therapy. I remember feeling enormously relieved that a professional had finally validated what I'd secretly been wondering: *Is it supposed to be this hard? Or am I just doing this wrong?*

Sometimes endearing and sometimes maddening, Milo's quirks fall under the umbrella of "sensory processing issues." He needs higher amounts of sensory input than neurotypical children, but also has very particular sensory aversions. In daily life, this means that "hugs" with Milo are more like full-body collisions than tender embraces, and that he prefers wearing his sister's soft, stretchy leggings to most of the "boy" clothes we've received as hand-me-downs from friends. It also means he needs lots of time outside, lots of time climbing and roughhousing, and that an occupational therapy playroom is his idea of heaven. I'm not sure I've ever seen Milo so excited as the moment we went to the playroom for the first time. Full of ropes and swings, giant padded cushions, tricycles, and an infinite variety of colorful toys, he could barely contain himself. Going to the "play doctor" became one of the highlights of our week.

But when the pandemic hit, much of this disappeared. We still had the enormous privilege of access to green space and a wonderful network of local trails, but the amount of time we spent outside was now limited by my work schedule. Living in a townhome, we don't have a fenced backyard where the kids can easily play outside while I work. For months, all the local playgrounds were closed for public health. Weekly visits to the occupational therapy playroom were replaced by weekly Zoom visits with our therapist, and while they helped, they were decidedly not the same. Our downstairs (which also happened to be where I was attempting to work from home) became the playroom instead: Milo raced through the hallway on his scooter, learned how to scale the doorframe and touch the ceiling, and leapt off of couch cushions stacked on the coffee table. There was only so much I could do to intervene while also trying to write manuscripts and sort through data. Milo has managed to remain physically unscathed throughout the pandemic. Our living room is another story.

As the California wildfires blazed through the summer and fall of 2020, I thought of all the Milos stuck completely inside because of wildfire smoke. I continue to think, too, of all the Milos who haven't been born yet. Early research on sensory processing issues suggests that babies born prematurely are at higher risk, and climate change research suggests that rising temperatures will trigger higher rates of premature birth. It would be a harrowing double-whammy to have a child with sensory processing issues and not be able to take them outside because of smoke, heat, or storms. It would be harrowing, as a parent, not to be able to take *any* child outside.

Is it supposed to be this hard? I wonder again, as Milo lobs a frisbee at my head while I'm working at the dining room table. *Or am I just doing this wrong?*

There is a growing movement to explore the idea of story in relation to climate change. Rooted in the wisdom of Indigenous storytelling traditions, modern iterations of this work appear in groups like Our Climate Voices, a youth-led organization that aims to "humanize the climate disaster through storytelling" in storytelling and listening workshops that intentionally center the voices of those most impacted by climate change. Storytelling is also a way of shaping and changing culture. In an essay called "Harnessing Cultural Power" in *All We Can Save*, artist and social justice organizer Favianna Rodriguez calls readers to embrace diverse, creative storytelling as an avenue for social and environmental change:

> "The power of culture lies in the power of story," Rodriguez writes. "Stories change and activate people, and people have the power to change norms, cultural practices, and systems. Stories are like individual stars... When many stars coalesce around similar themes, they form a narrative constellation that can disrupt business as usual. They reveal patterns and help illuminate that which was once obscured. The powerful shine in one story can inspire other stories. We need more transformational stories so that we can connect the dots and shift narratives."

One of the most influential forces in this movement to explore climate change through the lens of transformational stories is undoubtedly scholar and eco-philosopher Joanna Macy, founder of the popular group facilitation framework The Work That Reconnects and author of thirteen books, including *Coming Back to Life: The Updated Guide to The Work That Reconnects*. In *Coming Back to Life*, Macy contends that as bleak as the crises of our time may seem, we *do* have the collective resources we need to opt for a life-sustaining world. "We *can* choose life," she writes. "Even as we face global climate disruption, world-encompassing nuclear contamination, hydro-fracking, mountaintop removal mining, tar sands extraction, deep sea drilling and the genetic engineering of our food supply, we can still choose life. We can still act for the sake of a livable world."

A critical first step of choosing life, Macy says, is choosing our story. In workshops for The Work That Reconnects, one of the guiding principles is the idea that there are three primary stories of our time: Business as Usual, The Great Unraveling, and The Great Turning. Each of these stories offers a lens through which to see the world and current events, and in the sense that each of these stories is presently being told by fiercely devoted storytellers, they are all true.

The story of Business as Usual, Macy says, "is the story of the Industrial Growth Society. We hear it from politicians, business schools, corporations, and corporate-controlled media. Here the defining assumption is that there is little need to change the way we live." *Everything is fine. No need to worry about economic or environmental disruption; they're just temporary difficulties. We'll recover, we'll profit, and everything will be back to normal soon.*

The story of The Great Unraveling offers a different perspective. This, Macy tells us, "is the story we tend to hear from environmental scientists, independent journalists, and activists. It draws attention to the disasters that Business as Usual has caused and continues to create." The Great Unraveling is backed by data, by terrifying reports about climate change, and by the accumulating evidence of catastrophe wrought by extreme weather events and other forms of ecological destruction. *Nothing is fine,* this story goes, *and here's the evidence to prove it. We're running out of time, and things are only going to get worse. We're fucked.*

The third story, The Great Turning, "is the story we hear from those who see the Great Unraveling and don't want it to have the last word. It involves the emergence of new and creative human responses that enable the transition from the Industrial Growth Society to a Life-Sustaining Society. The central plot is about joining together to act for the sake of life on Earth." *Things are not fine, but the story isn't over yet. We can and will find creative solutions to the challenges of these times. We will work together and leave no one behind. Whatever it takes, we will choose life.*

Each time I am reminded of these stories, I feel the same shift that I find on the pages of my journal in responding to a writing prompt that invites me to see my pain from an alternate perspective. Half of the battle of getting unstuck from a painful situation is realizing that there *are* alternate perspectives, and remembering that we always get to choose which perspective we embrace. The three stories of our time are also, essentially, the three basic stories we can tell about the private wounds of our individual lives. We get to choose how to narrate our own trials and heartbreaks.

I am still learning, day by day, to choose the stories that help me to choose life.

Late in the first fall of the pandemic, as another wave of COVID-19 breaks, I break too. On top of the baseline chaos of continuing to work from home, Milo's tantrums have escalated again to the point of bringing me to tears on a daily basis. We are back to the same struggle that sent us looking for professional help a year earlier, and I don't know how to help him anymore. The story inside my head, more often than not, is a story of great unraveling: *I am exhausted, and this keeps getting worse. I don't know how to help this child. I'm failing as a mother. I don't know how to keep doing this.* I know I should make time to write in my journal, to take this knot of emotion through the familiar quartet of prompts that always helps, but the twins keep waking up during the early morning hours I used to be able to guard for myself. In the midst of pandemic life, carving out any time alone is a struggle.

On the recommendation of a close friend, I go to the website for Hand in Hand Parenting. My friend has been telling me about Hand in Hand for months, sharing how helpful their parenting model has been for her family, but I've been too overwhelmed to follow up with her counsel. (Also, according to the dominant narrative in my head, I shouldn't *need* more support; shouldn't I be able to handle my own kid?) Now, though, I'm desperate, and I finally reach out for a consultation with a Hand in Hand expert. I'm assigned to a consultant whose own child has had struggles similar to mine, and in that moment, it feels like I've been personally assigned an angel.

The consultant's first email makes me cry: *I'm so glad you reached out to get the support that you deserve,* she writes. The reminder that *I* deserve support, too, feels like a lifeline. We schedule our session for the following week, during one of my precious windows of childcare.

During our conversation, the consultant asks about my history with Milo, all the way back to his conception and birth. I tell her everything. I tell her about the infertility struggle, the violent vomiting for nearly six months of my pregnancy, the traumatic decision about whether or not to terminate, the loss of the triplet, the twins' first nine days of life in the NICU. I tell her about how hard it was to tandem nurse, and how we couldn't easily carry the twins around in a baby carrier. I admit, for the first time, how jealous I was of the babywearing singleton moms who got to hold their one-at-a-time babies close to their hearts for months. I tried to be a babywearing mom, too, but I just couldn't make it work with twins. I had always wondered if Milo's intense physical clinginess in his toddler and preschool years was related to this: when his tantrums are at their worst, he insists that we carry him around like a baby.

She listens. She tells me she can see how hard I've been working, how much I love these children, how I am a *good mom*. These words, too, make me cry.

Then, she offers me a reframe: "In the Hand in Hand model," she says in a gentle voice, "tantrums and crying are seen as a form of *healing* for a child. Crying is a healing process. It's a physiological way of releasing trauma and tension." She suggests, in a way that somehow manages to be free of any hint of shaming, that Milo's tantrums are his way of trying to release the trauma of his earliest moments: the harrowing pregnancy, his first days of life spent in the NICU, being born a multiple. On top of this early trauma is, of course, the present trauma of the pandemic. He is working through this, too. In the Hand in Hand Parenting model, an escalating series of tantrums or behavioral struggles can be viewed as an *emotional project*. When children are caught in a deeply rooted hurt that threatens their sense of safety, they need to work through this pain in repeated releases of emotion. The consultant offers me a strategy called *staylistening*. *Staylistening*, the Hand in Hand model says, means listening all the way through your child's hurt. One meltdown at a time, if we as parents can stay present and attentive to their pain, it will gradually drain away.

The reframe gives me an alternate story about what's happening: Milo isn't simply a difficult child with a diagnosis I can't manage; he's working through an emotional project. In his own unique way, with his tiny body and four-year-old brain, he's doing his best to work out some really, really big feelings about really, really difficult things that have happened. He is trying to heal. All I need to do is to stay present and listen.

The moment I begin to take this story in, I can feel that it will be life-giving for our family. This is a story that honors what is painful while also honoring what is possible. In the tucked-away part of my heart that has felt inadequate and wounded at nearly every stage of motherhood, a great turning is underway.

Although the most difficult moments of parenting can feel profoundly isolating, I know that I'm not alone. There are countless other families working through their own versions of trauma, many facing challenges far more painful than my family will likely ever face. As the pandemic has, climate change will almost certainly yield child and family trauma on a massive scale. These traumas will not be evenly distributed, but portioned along lines of social, racial, gender, and geographic inequity. Some traumas, like the acute disruption of a natural disaster, will be easy to recognize; some, like the developmental trauma of a difficult pregnancy or premature birth, may take months or years to unfold. Nearly all of us will feel some level of impact, and those who are parenting young children in these years will be the front-line responders for the pain that climate change inflicts on our families on top of the pain of everyday human life. We will need robust strategies for resilience in order to thrive.

There is no one-size-fits all approach to cultivating resilience, and the resilience strategies that carry us through one season of life may need to adapt as we move through different stages of parenthood. But there are common through lines in the resilience practices that, I've found, help the most. Three of these through lines are *emotional expression, connection,* and *conscious storytelling.* Our capacity for resilience depends on our ability to fully feel and express our deepest emotions about the wounds of our lives in the presence of a safe and compassionate witness, whether that witness is the page of a journal or the ear of a devoted listener. Resilience requires connection, the connection we might feel in the presence of a listener, in a cohesive family unit, or in solidarity with a beloved community. Resilience depends, too, on our ability to choose life-giving narratives about the circumstances we face. Parenting is hard; parenting in the midst of global crisis and personal trauma is harder. But this doesn't have to be the last word: if we can stay deeply present with pain, both ours and our children's, we can find our way together into stories of great turning, and from these stories, a universe of possibility emerges. From these consciously chosen stories, new futures can be born.

I keep a quote from eco-philosopher Susan Griffin at my desk to remind me of this:

> *"No one can stop us from imagining another kind of future, one which departs from the terrible cataclysm of violent conflict, of hateful divisions, poverty, and suffering. Let us begin to imagine the worlds we would like to inhabit, the long lives we will share, and the many futures in our hands."*

Chapter 5 Reflection

Key practice: Recognize that the stories we tell about the world shape the world we live in. Practice bringing awareness to the stories that you're hearing and telling about climate change, and practice choosing the stories that feel life-giving and possibility-generating.

Questions for reflection and discussion with others:

- How did you and your family experience the stress of COVID-19? What parallels do you see between COVID-19 and climate change?

- This chapter introduces Joanna Macy's "Three Stories of Our Time" model. Which of the three stories have you tended to gravitate towards the most? What story do you tell most often about climate change?

- What practices help you cultivate resilience during difficult times?

- Which relationships help you feel resilient?

- How might you acknowledge and honor the inherited wisdom and resilience of oppressed and marginalized communities in your own journey to cultivate resilience?

- What stories about climate change are—or would be—most life-giving for you? For your children? For the collective?

IMAGINING THE MANY FUTURES IN OUR HANDS

"Fear is a short-term spur to action, but to make changes over the long term, we must have hope."

—KATHARINE HAYHOE
Climate scientist and chief scientist for
The Nature Conservancy

FOR A COUPLE OF years after the twins were born, I taught yoga at our local fertility clinic, the same one where I'd conceived triplets in the summer of 2015. Each week, a small cohort of students in various stages of their own fertility journeys would practice yoga with me in a humble conference room with brownish-grey, low-pile carpet and a whiteboard that was often covered with complex medical terminology and drawings of abnormal sperm. Once, I came in to find a drawing of a sperm with a happy face on it. The students took it as a good omen.

Each Monday evening, as I'd prepare for class, I'd linger in a hallway that stretched from the front desk to the conference room. The hallway was lined with pictures of babies. There were too many babies to count: babies of all shapes, sizes, and colors; screaming and smiling babies; singletons and multiples; elegant, posed newborn photos and delightfully un-posed candid shots; photos from holiday cards and photos with heartfelt thank you notes attached. Each one of these pictures was a tiny, infant-sized triumph of vision over challenging circumstances. The pictures were there to encourage the patients, virtually none of whom arrive at the fertility clinic because they think it will be fun to build their families with advanced reproductive technology. But they're also there to encourage the clinicians, who are on the front lines of helping the patients hold onto hope for their futures in the face of what sometimes seem like impossible odds. I have spoken with women who have endured harrowing ectopic pregnancies, repeated miscarriages, multiple stillbirths, and complex diagnoses that made the odds of conception slim. I remember a woman who conceived in her thirties with donor eggs after losing all of her own frozen IVF embryos, a couple who conceived with donor sperm after the man's childhood cancer treatment left him infertile, and several couples who conceived their babies with reciprocal IVF—a truly astonishing medical miracle in which eggs from one partner are fertilized with donor sperm and implanted in the uterus of the other partner.

In every painful family-building story, there are moments when it seems like the happy ending will never come. Moments when it would be easier to give up. Moments when the repeated heartbreak and disappointment of another miscarriage or another failed round of fertility treatment seems like too much to bear. For some people, the physical, emotional, and financial toll of trying to conceive *does* become too much and giving up trying to conceive is an act of radical—if heartbreaking—self-preservation.

But much of the time, people who really, really want families can find a way to build them, even if the family that ultimately manifests looks nothing like the one originally pictured. People find ways to bring their dreams of nurturing children to life. And while there's no minimizing the grief that can accompany choosing not to continue family building in the traditional sense, I have also seen people at this fork in the road find ways to cast new visions for their futures, visions where they are childfree and thriving.

I remember lingering at the wall of babies when I was a patient at the fertility center, too. And I know the power of a single, compelling image to offer hope in difficult times. I give partial credit for my own family to a photo taken in December 2014. Just a few months after Bart's azoospermia diagnosis and in the middle of a holiday season in which every pregnancy announcement, round belly, and baby shower made me cry, I visited my friend Ruth, whose eight-month-old twins were conceived with fertility treatments and born several weeks early that spring. Ruth's path to motherhood hadn't come easily either, and her understanding offered a safe space in this raw season of my life. In a photo from the visit, I'm holding Ruth's twins, enamored with their round, perfect cheeks, and in awe of their resilience after such a rough start to life. I printed out the photo and put it on my vision board that New Year's Eve.

No vision board makes promises; no dream of the future comes with guarantees. One of the reasons infertility is so intensely stressful is that it can feel life-threatening: it threatens the basic architecture of the future we'd always imagined for ourselves. When people dream of having a family, they dream not just of the joy of holding babies, but also of the joy of cheering at soccer games and dance recitals, of hard-earned graduations, of walking a daughter down the aisle at her wedding, of rosy-cheeked grandchildren. Infertility threatens a lifetime of future memories. Anyone who has arrived at the doorstep of a fertility clinic is counting on a mix of science and faith to bring their dreams to life in the most literal sense, and there's always a possibility that these forces won't pull through with a baby.

But sometimes—a lot of the time—they do.

When you're in the midst of what feels like a hopeless situation, it can be helpful to see images of hope. But when it comes to climate change, most of the stories and images we receive about the future are anything but hopeful. The "great unraveling" narrative positions humans in permanent opposition to the natural world, as if it's human nature—no pun intended—to cause harm to the environment.

It isn't easy to tell stories about hopeful versions of the future when this story of humans' inherently destructive nature is so all-pervasive. In *All We Can Save*, an essay called "Wakanda Doesn't Have Suburbs," by climate reporter Kendra Pierre-Louis, explores how the fictional African country from the Marvel film *Black Panther* offers one of the few mainstream visions that starts with the assumption that humans can live in harmony with the earth. "*Black Panther's* vision of Wakanda," Pierre-Louis writes, "rejects the oft-repeated story that we humans and our environment are natural enemies. Instead, it tells a story in which humans have become technologically sophisticated while maintaining a flourishing relationship with their surrounding environment."

Pierre-Louis's essay joins an emerging literature exploring *positive* visions for the future in the context of climate change, rather than simply offering stark warnings of how bad it's going to be. The opening chapters of *The Future We Choose: Surviving the Climate Crisis*, by Christiana Figueres and Tom Rivett-Carnac, offer two striking visions of the future: one describing the world we're creating, and the other describing the world we must create. The world we're creating, Figueres and Rivett-Carnac describe, is heading for frightening uncertainty: "We don't know how habitable the regions of Australia, North Africa, and the western United States will be by 2100. No one knows what the future holds for their children and grandchildren: tipping point after tipping point is being reached, casting doubt on the form of future civilization." But the world we *must* create, they say, holds other possibilities:

"We are making communities stronger. As a child, you might have seen your neighbors only in passing. But now, to make things cheaper, cleaner, and more sustainable, your orientation in every part of your life is more local.

Things that used to be done individually are now done communally—growing vegetables, capturing rainwater, and composting. Resources and responsibilities are shared now. At first you resisted this *togetherness*—you were used to doing things individually and in the privacy of your own home. But pretty quickly, the camaraderie and unexpected new network of support started to feel good, something to be prized. For most people, this new way has turned out to be a better recipe for happiness."

The Future Earth, by climate journalist Eric Holthaus, offers another "radical vision of what's possible in the age of warming." Decade by decade, Holthaus describes the next thirty years as if they've already happened, and as if we were collectively able to do what it took to avoid the worst potential climate outcomes and build a more just, equitable world. A key focus of Holthaus' vision of the future is the transition from endless-growth capitalism to a more regenerative, circular economy. "For us to get where we need to go," Holthaus describes, "we need to become a society with a cultural focus on repair and maintenance, rather than innovation and efficiency." Holthaus interviews economist Kate Raworth, author of the 2017 book *Doughnut Economics*, and describes how a circular (or "doughnut") economy could support humanity's well-being *and* respect the finite boundaries of our natural resources. In a circular economy, there is no waste; there are only resources in the wrong place. The byproducts of every natural and industrial process become fuel for another cycle. Holthaus writes: "A society that eliminates the concept of waste, Raworth told me, will no longer treat its members as disposable."

That's the future I want for my children, and for all children: a future where people and resources are no longer treated as disposable.

As a coach, I'm drawn to the process of visioning. Most coaching relationships start with some version of a visioning exercise, where the coach asks the client to imagine the future or a specific desired outcome in vibrant detail: *What do you* really *want? If you could create exactly the future you want for yourself, what would that future look like? Who would be there with you? What would an ordinary day feel like? What sights, sounds, smells, tastes, and experiences would be part of this future? What makes this vision matter to you?*

In my experience, most clients find the process of visioning expansive, even if it feels tentative and a bit audacious at first. It requires a specific kind of daring to imagine exactly the future we want for ourselves and to abandon—even just for a few minutes—all of our preconceived ideas about what is or isn't possible. Some clients need the support of the word *permission* to relax more fully into a visioning exercise: *If I gave you full permission to dream of the future you most deeply desire, and permission to let go of all of the reasons you think that future can't happen for just the next few minutes… what might that future look like?*

It's not unusual for tears to well up at this part of the process, and laughter is often present as well. When a client has some kind of emotional response to the vision they've described for themselves, I know we're getting somewhere. A well-explored vision provides a solid foundation for the process of change. It's an anchor to return to again and again as the initial excitement of forging a new habit or path inevitably shifts to the less-glamorous phase of actually showing up for the work. Old ways of being rarely go down without a fight. On the days when the old ways seem to be winning, it's a compelling vision of a different future that keeps us from the temptation of giving up or giving in. When training student coaches, mentors often give the advice: *Don't rush through the visioning stage. Everything else will be harder if you do.*

I have been thinking a lot lately about my own personal vision, what I want for my future and for my family's future. Climate change throws a bit of a wrench into the kind of visioning process that I'm used to. In the vision I'd create if all limitations vanished with the wave of a magic wand, there is no climate change. In this fantasy world, there are stable, reliable seasons—there will *always* be stable, reliable seasons. Natural disasters are rare, sea levels are low and constant, and the weather is not an issue of justice or politics.

I'm a dreamer, but I'm also a realist: I can't un-know what I know about climate change. There are many potential collective futures ahead of us, but climate change will be a defining feature of all of them. There is no magic wand, no scientific silver bullet, that will alter this truth. It takes courage to vision under any circumstances, but it requires even more courage, I've found, to cast a vision for a vibrant future in the face of unavoidable limitations.

So I'm practicing envisioning what it might look like to thrive in a climate-changed future, what it might feel like to live abundantly in a circular economy, in the ordinary moments of my future life. I am daring to imagine that life in the next decade could look something like this:

> *It's 2030. We live happily in a modest duplex or triplex, sharing a community garden with a diverse, intergenerational cohort of neighbors. We live near family and friends, grateful for a close-by network of childcare support. Our home is close enough to farmer's markets and grocery stores to walk or bike to get most of the food we need on a regular basis, and we enjoy sharing a community-supported agriculture box with neighbors every week. We enjoy a plant-rich diet and love sharing food with our friends and neighbors. There is a fluid exchange of loaves of freshly-baked pumpkin bread, mason jars full of squash soup and homemade sauerkraut, and summer baskets of cucumbers and tomatoes. The kids help us compost our*

food scraps, and we use our matured compost to feed the garden. Each home in the neighborhood is outfitted with rainwater collection equipment and solar panels to conserve water and energy. Though setting up this equipment required some initial investment, it was supported by government subsidies so that all households in our community could benefit. Now, our water and energy bills are more manageable than they were before.

We find other ways to adapt to reduced energy use and changing weather. In the winter, we stay warm with blankets, cozy socks, and chunky hand-knit sweaters, rather than hiking up the thermostat. When the temperatures soar in the summer, our phones alert us to dangerous heat and air quality conditions, offering clear guidance for how to stay healthy and safe. School hours adapt to allow children to spend much-needed time outside early in the mornings. During heat waves, we check on elderly neighbors as a norm, and local governments have clear plans for keeping vulnerable populations safe.

Hurricanes come with increasing force, as we knew they would. We have a well-organized hurricane emergency kit that's stocked with everything we might need for weathering a few days of power outages or even an emergency evacuation. In our community, the local government subsidizes hurricane emergency kits for people who might not have the means to purchase supplies on their own, and everyone is connected to mutual aid networks that help to ensure community needs are met during times of crisis and times of stability. Preparing for hurricane season is part of our yearly rhythm, both individually and collectively. It's not exactly fun, but it reduces anxiety to know that we're as prepared as we can possibly be for the worst. Local communities are better prepared for hurricanes than they used to be, as well, and local climate adaptation plans include robust support for emotional resilience. Parents and teachers can take free community classes on how to support children through anxiety around natural disasters, and a trauma-sensitive approach to both parenting and teaching has become the norm.

Emotional well-being is a central focus of all school curricula now. The twins go to a racially and socioeconomically diverse public school that's staffed with enough well-trained counselors and social workers to support all students. Students learn about climate change, but not without the emotional support to process what they're learning in a way that builds resilience. Classes on climate change and the environment are focused more heavily on solutions than on problems, and all children spend plenty of time outside in school learning to connect with nature directly. Teachers know that children won't learn to protect what they don't love. Alongside history and math classes, students learn about how to be engaged citizens of democracy. They learn about racial and environmental justice. They're taught to be positive changemakers, assessed on their ability to think creatively and strategically about real-world issues, rather than their ability to regurgitate rote facts. In this new model of education, neurodiversity is welcomed as a gift, rather than a problem. Children who think differently are exactly what the world needs in this moment in time.

Parents have far more support on the emotional resilience front, too. As natural disasters come and sea levels rise as scientists predicted they would, climate anxiety and grief are as common and widely acknowledged as postpartum depression. But there is a wealth of resources to help. Alongside free community classes to help parents learn how to support their children, parents can participate in support groups for themselves. Climate grief is no longer an elephant in the room; it's a normal part of conversation. Collective grief rituals help individuals and families honor difficult losses, freeing up emotional space for continued participation in climate solutions. A strange side benefit of parenting in a climate changed world is that our parenting has become more emotionally literate: because we've been forced to confront climate anxiety and grief, we're getting better at navigating other kinds of anxiety and grief, as well.

Many parents have embraced climate action as a normal part of responsible parenting. Acknowledging that it's a privilege to have the time and space to do so, many parents now belong to local and national climate action groups that encourage continued government action to protect the environment. These action groups explicitly recognize the importance of addressing racial, socioeconomic, and intergenerational justice in all forms of environmental activism. Black, Indigenous, Latinx, youth, LGBTQ+, and female voices are centered. Parents have become a force in seasonal getting-out-the-vote efforts, significantly boosting participation in local elections and primaries, and children happily join the cause: putting stamps on postcards to voters, baking cookies for voter registration events, making vote-encouraging signs with crayons and markers. Recognizing the long-term economic importance of having a livable planet, employers offer far more flexibility in hours and work location than they did before, and this makes it much easier for parents to participate in democracy and climate action efforts. It makes it much easier for us to parent, as well.

There's been a collective movement to embrace "low-carbon happiness." We buy less. Far, far less than we used to. Recognizing that capitalism and a consumerist culture lie at the root of climate change and environmental destruction, people have slowly begun to shift away from the gluttonous levels of shopping that had been the norm for the first two decades of the 21ˢᵗ century. We buy nearly all of our clothing used, and have learned how to mend and upcycle clothing; the satisfaction of renewing an outdated garment by hand is far better than the quick hit of pleasure mindless shopping used to be. Used and handmade gifts are the norm for holidays and birthdays now, and the social pressure to move away from endless heaps of plastic and fast fashion have forced all companies to adopt more ethical, sustainable practices. When we buy anything new, we know that it's been produced with respect for the earth's resources. Instead of deriving happiness from things, we've collectively rediscovered the joy of less. Less air travel and jet-setting mean more time to explore local adventures, and deeper relationships with place. Less hustle to earn money to buy things we don't really need means more time to connect with the people we love. Our homes, and our hearts, are more spacious.

Life is vastly different than it was a decade ago, and there's no doubt that the decade has come with its share of heartbreak as we felt the impact of the global warming that was already set in motion. There's no bringing back what has been lost. But what has been gained is invaluable, too. Somehow, one day a time, we've become the parents our children needed us to be: parents who showed up when it mattered the most. Parents who helped to bring a future worth living for to life.

This vision is iterative and fluid, and it's one I find myself returning to for inspiration in the moments when a positive mindset about the future feels harder to hold onto. When I find myself ruminating on all that will be lost in the future, I sometimes need a reminder that much of value is still to be gained. While the process of bringing new versions of ourselves to life with behavior change can use both negative and positive visions for the future as fuel, positive visions have an important role. It's often a vision of what we *don't* want that tells us that something in our lives has to change, but it's usually a vision of what we *do* want that's more effective at actually motivating us to make changes.

The context of climate change, however, may require that we build a bridge between negative and positive visions of the future by cultivating emotional resilience *before* we can begin to dream of what we want. In the introduction to *A Field Guide to Climate Anxiety*, author and professor Sarah Jaquette Ray describes an experience in her college environmental studies classroom in which she asked students to visualize themselves thriving in a climate-changed world. After they envisioned the positive outcome of all of their collective efforts to promote positive change, they would break down their imagined future into a doable, actionable strategy. To her surprise, the visioning exercise failed:

> "This exercise was supposed to be empowering, to free them from the immobilization we all feel in the face of a problem as enormous and intractable as climate change. But it bombed, and in a way I hadn't anticipated. The students *could not visualize the future*. When I asked them about their ideal future state, I heard crickets. When I pushed them to answer, they confessed that they couldn't even form a mental picture of the path ahead, much less a future they could thrive in."

Before this experience, Ray describes measuring her success as an educator by her students' ability to "see *more* problems in the world." She had assumed, as most environmental messaging does, that giving her students information about the problems of the world and a critical academic lens through which to analyze them would lead to action. But without the emotional resilience to withstand and metabolize what they had learned about climate change and the state of the world, the students were too traumatized to imagine anything other than a continuation of the story of great unraveling.

I have seen traditional visioning exercises fail in coaching, as well. In the aftermath of terrible or repeated disappointment—another miscarriage, another failed IVF cycle—it may not feel possible in that moment to imagine a different, more hopeful version of the future. Even a wall of babies may not help. When hope has gone missing, a different kind of support is needed. In the context of fertility, this support often looks like taking an intentional break from family building. It looks like extra sessions with a good therapist, spending time outdoors, traveling, watching comedy specials on Netflix, baking dense quick breads, and mid-afternoon naps. It looks like learning to knit, reading escapist fiction, having living room dance parties to nineties pop music, and conversations with the friend who always knows how to make you laugh. It looks like practicing rest and practicing joy.

These strategies are good medicine for climate despair, too. When grief for the world becomes too much to bear, stepping back from the work is what allows the work to eventually continue. "Radical imagination," author adrienne maree brown suggests in *Emergent Strategy*, is a muscle that can be cultivated. When visioning feels hard or even impossible, rest may be needed before this muscle can be used. Rest *will* be needed as we build the strength to imagine a positive future. Restorative, regenerative self-care practices are not an optional luxury; they are essential for resilience and long-term success. If we do not care wisely for our muscle of imagination, we will not be able to use it to craft the future our children and grandchildren deserve.

So when despair, anxiety, or a sense of numbness make it difficult to envision thriving in a climate-changed future, the wisest approach may be a counterintuitive one: take a break from trying to dream about what's to come and refuel by reconnecting with who and what you love in the present. Hug someone you adore. Move your body in a nourishing way. Bake your grandmother's gingerbread. Watch a favorite television show. Take a walk through the forest. Come back to your imagination practice when you feel renewed.

It is too late, the most recent science tells us, to achieve the best-case scenarios for the future that were still possible a decade ago. That future is dead to us. No matter how much we may want them, we will not get future seasons that closely resemble the seasons of our childhood. The summer of 2050, when my children will be thirty-four, won't feel like the summer of 1990, when my mom was thirty-four, or even the summer of 2017, when I was thirty-four. No amount of hoping, praying, or scientific intervention will bring those summers back—at least not during our lifetimes. This is a terrible loss, and it's a loss that some will feel far more acutely than others. There are future memories we will never get to live.

But it is not too late to imagine a future where we can thrive.

We build the muscle of visioning in our everyday lives, weaving the fabric of our most private dreams. It's the vision of what we want in a partner that allows us to recognize that partner when they walk in the door. It's the vision of what might make us happy in our work that allows us to steadily craft careers that bring us to life, guiding us to say yes to opportunities that move us closer to that dream and no to opportunities that take us farther away. Sometimes the visions closest to our hearts are also the most mundane: I am practicing, day by day, being a calmer parent. On a good day, that vision of calmer mothering can help me keep my cool during even the fiercest of preschooler tantrums. On a bad day, I try to remember to bake cookies and take a walk.

In order to cast bold, radical visions for a positive, climate-changed future, we're going to have to cast bolder, more radical visions for our personal lives. The future our children deserve requires our dreaming muscles to be strong. To create a world whose fundamental architecture is sustainable and just, radically loving and compassionate to all, we're going to have to find ways to envision these values in the intimate spaces of our own lives.

On the last day of 2020, the end of the year my friend June describes as "the longest decade ever," I decide to try making New Year's Eve vision board collages with the twins. They're restless after the excitement of Christmas, and it's been a few years since I've done a vision board myself. Minnie is vibrating with excitement at the prospect of an art project. I gather a stack of old magazines and catalogs, allot sheets of cardboard, Elmer's Glue, and age-appropriate scissors to everyone, and attempt to explain what a vision board is by way of example: I've dusted off two previous vision boards, including the one from New Year's Eve 2014. In the middle of the board is the photo of me holding my friend Ruth's twins.

"Is that us?" Minnie asks, a little confused.

"Not exactly," I tell her. "That's another set of twins who were born before you were. But I put this picture on my board because I wanted babies, and seeing this picture gave me hope when hope felt hard. I looked at this picture because I hoped you and Milo would come."

Minnie knows, at a four-year-old's level, that it wasn't easy for us to conceive. She knows she and her brother were conceived with a sperm donor; she knows they lost a triplet sibling. She is satisfied with my answer, responding with a smug look that says, *of* course *we came. We were always meant to be here. It was always meant to be like this.* Her faith in the future is infused with a sense of inevitability: *of* course *my visions will come to life.* She practices her radical imagination with her art every day.

I'm starting to suspect that my most important job as a parent is to meet my daughter's radical imagination with my own. It's to practice envisioning the world she and all children deserve, and letting that vision teach me, day by day, how to do my part in bringing it to life.

Chapter 6 Reflection

Key practice: Practice envisioning a thriving future. If your children are young, allow their natural ability to dream inspire you to build your own muscle of imagination.

Questions for reflection and discussion with others:

- What, if anything, did you dream of when you imagined becoming a parent?

- In the past, how have you related to the process of envisioning what you wanted for the future? Does this come easily to you, or feel difficult?

- What practices help you to cultivate the inner resilience that is needed to be able to dream about—and work towards—a thriving future? How do you relate to the idea that rest and joy are essential to our capacity for sustainable climate work?

- How might climate change impact your personal vision for the future? What might it look like for you and your family to thrive in a climate-changed world?

- What might it look like for *everyone* to thrive in a climate-changed world?

Part III
PRACTICE

HOW TO TALK ABOUT CLIMATE CHANGE (OR, WHAT NOT TO SAY IN A MOMS' GROUP)

"Talking about climate change is what builds social and political pressure for radical action. It's also a radical personal step itself in a world that treats conversations about climate change as taboo, even in the company of friends."

—ERIC HOLTHAUS, *The Future Earth: A Radical Vision for What's Possible in the Age of Warming*

ABOUT A YEAR AFTER the twins were born, my mother gave me a humorous book called *Welcome to the Club: 100 Parenting Milestones You Never Saw Coming.* I knew I would like this book when I randomly flipped to the milestone described in Chapter 41: First Time the Sleeping Technique That Some Book Promised Would Solve All of His Sleeping Problems Doesn't Solve Any of His Sleeping Problems. (By this point in motherhood, I had thrown away all of the parenting books I had so carefully curated before actually becoming a parent, because (a) most of the advice in them did not apply to twins; and (b) even the advice that *did* purport to apply to twins was not working for us. We had also, by this point, forgotten to use 80% of the "baby milestone" cards that singleton moms post in cute pictures on Instagram. They are still sitting in a sad pile somewhere under our bed.) *These* were milestones I could relate to, like First Time Your Child Bleeds While You're Trying to Cut Her Nails; Baby's First Constipation; and First Time a Stranger Gives You Aggressive, Unsolicited Advice on How to Raise Your Child.

I'd like to add another milestone to this brutally realistic list, to be filed under the "Interactions With Other Adults" section: First Time You Say Something You Think is Relatable in a Parenting Group and None of the Other Parents Can Relate.

Once, in the nascent stage of my climate awakening, I was in a moms' group that met regularly in a friend's home. A circle of six or seven mothers was arranged on chairs, couches, and the floor, and as the group usually began, we were taking turns sharing how we were doing. Most of the time, the group offered a refreshingly safe space for authentic sharing about the difficult parts of motherhood, but for me, that day felt different. I had been learning about the impacts of climate change on children's health and was struggling with intense waves of anxiety. When it came time for my turn to share, I decided to be honest. I don't remember exactly what I said, but it was something along these lines: *I'm depressed about climate change. The World Health Organization predicts that 80% of deaths due to climate change will be in children under age five. I'm worried about our children's futures. I'm worried that there might not be a livable planet left by the time they're our age. I panic a lot. I'm having trouble sleeping at night.*

It was as if the air had been sucked out of the room. (Let it be said that no one has ever accused me of being the "fun" one at parties.) The other women shifted in their seats, their body language letting me know I had crossed an unspoken line. My sharing had been a little *too* honest. A few women nodded kindly, but no one said *yeah, me too;* no one offered any comments that would take the discussion further. When it was clear that there would be no additional response to my sharing, the next woman rescued the awkward silence with her own contribution. She was annoyed at her husband for wanting so much sex. (This, I discovered, is a popular topic of discussion in moms' groups.) The group dynamic had been revived, but I felt isolated and confused: was no one else in this progressive, highly educated group of mothers worried about climate change? Or did they just not want to talk about it?

An April 2020 report from the Yale Center for Climate Communication revealed that more than six in ten Americans say they "never" or "rarely" talk about global warming with family and friends. Only a third say they talk about global warming "occasionally" or "often," and this represents a significant increase over the last five years. The same report revealed that seven in ten Americans believe that global warming is happening, and two in three Americans are "worried" or "very worried" about it. In Durham County, North Carolina, where I live and say awkward things in moms' groups, climate beliefs and concerns are higher than the national average: 70% of Durhamites, according to Yale's data, are worried about global warming.

Here is another paradox for parents to wrestle with: we *are* worried about climate change, but most of us are still not talking about it with our peers. There is a gap between our values around climate change and the way we talk about it, and this gap leaves many of us feeling more isolated than we really are.

We may not talk about climate change because we don't want to *think* about it. Even those among us who have fully accepted the overwhelming scientific consensus about climate change may wish to put our heads in the sand and pretend that none of this is actually happening. Naming the enormous elephant in the room carries risk. We risk, in talking about climate change, having to *feel* about climate change. We also risk having to act. The more the difficult truth about climate change is openly acknowledged, the harder it becomes to reconcile our extractive, materialistic lifestyles with our values. Emotional processing and behavior change both require capacity at a time when many of us—especially parents of young children—already feel depleted.

There's a cost to not talking about climate change that reaches far beyond feelings of personal isolation—consequences extend to our personal and collective action, as well. This is closely related to what social scientists call "social norms." There are two distinct kinds of social norms: *descriptive norms,* which describe what we believe other people are doing, and *injunctive norms,* which describe what we think other people expect *us* to do. Descriptive and injunctive norms can be distinct, but often overlap.

Research reveals that social norms have an incredibly powerful influence on behavior. Parents are no exception: we take and act on cues from other parents, even when we believe we're acting independently. A 2016 study examined the impact of social norms on parents' reading behavior at home with their children. One group of parents at an elementary school received an intervention with information about the reading behavior of the majority of other parents; a control group of parents at a separate elementary school did not receive this information. Seven months later, researchers compared rates of completion for a home reading challenge. Over three-quarters of parents in the intervention group completed the reading challenge, while less than half of parents in the control group did. A follow-up survey revealed that parents in the intervention group did not believe the social norm had been a motivating factor in their completion of the challenge. Parents did not believe that they had been influenced by what they were told other parents were doing, in spite of clear evidence that the social norm intervention had worked.

Perceived social norms may have a greater influence on our actions than actual threat. If you have ever worked in an office building when a fire alarm went off, you know that most of us will look to our office mates, not the sound of the alarm itself, to decide whether or not it's urgent to leave the building. If the majority of our colleagues (especially if that majority includes the boss) are sitting at their desks carrying on with their work as if nothing is happening in spite of the blaring alarm, it will feel awkward to run out of the building to safety. If we can't actually see flames yet, we might interpret others' inaction as an indicator that the alarm is just a drill, even if the building is about to burn down around us.

What we talk about, and how we talk about it, has a direct influence on how we *act*. Social norms also guide our conversational interactions with others, heavily influencing what topics are perceived as appropriate to talk about in particular contexts. In the context of a moms' group, libidinous husbands are perceived as a "normal" and acceptable topic of conversation. Existential climate dread and frightening statistics about child mortality, not so much.

Yale's data suggests that just under half of Americans perceive injunctive social norms for taking action on global warming, though this norm may not yet be very strong. Thirty percent of survey respondents indicated they believed it is "moderately" important to their friends and family that they take action to reduce global warming, while only 17% said their personal action is "very" or "extremely" important to their loved ones. An even smaller cohort of respondents perceived a descriptive norm, reporting that their friends and family make "a great deal of effort," "a lot of effort," or "a moderate amount of effort" to take action to reduce global warming. Just under half of us, these numbers suggest, see our family and friends responding to climate change's metaphorical fire alarm at all. And less than 10% of us see our loved ones making a concerted effort to put out the fire.

Climate scientist and mother Katharine Hayhoe believes that talking about climate change is one of the most important tools we have in addressing it. In her 2018 TED talk, Hayhoe describes the troubling reality of escalating climate disasters that two-thirds of Americans don't talk about, and that much of the media doesn't talk about, either:

"It's a vicious cycle. The planet warms. Heat waves get stronger. Heavy precipitation gets more frequent. Hurricanes get more intense. Scientists release yet another doom-filled report. Politicians push back even more strongly, repeating the same sciencey-sounding myths. What can we do to break this vicious cycle? The number one thing we can do is the exact thing that we're not doing: talk about it."

But not just any kind of conversation around climate change will be effective, Hayhoe continues, noting social science research that has shown that people's beliefs around climate change are closely linked to their social identities. This research reveals that in the United States, beliefs about climate change are more closely linked to sociopolitical identity than any other single factor. A challenge to these beliefs is a challenge to an entire, tightly-constructed identity—not a simple debate over facts. If your social identity is built around the rejection of a certain set of facts, Hayhoe says, arguing over those facts will be perceived as a personal attack. That personal attack will create further division, rather than building a bridge for meaningful discussion. This may help explain why many environmentalists' approach of sharing alarming statistics about the climate crisis hasn't worked with a certain segment of the American population, largely those who align with a conservative political identity. When presented with facts that contradict our beliefs about who we are and how the world works, our instinctive response is to dig in our heels with defensiveness, not to listen to what's actually being said. Sharing more scientific data with people whose social identity is committed to the *rejection* of that data is an ineffective way to talk about climate change.

Another ineffective way of talking about climate change, as I've learned from numerous firsthand failures, is the "disaster framing" approach described by researcher Per Espen Stoknes. The segment of the media that *is* talking about climate change overwhelmingly uses this approach, and it's the approach often used by environmentalists, activists, and anyone who has a clear grasp of how dire the widely agreed-upon scientific reality of climate change actually is. Disaster framing tells the story of climate change as a story of great unraveling. This is the approach to conversation I used in the awkward moms' group incident: where we talk about how the world is falling apart, how it's getting worse every year, how we're terrified about the future, how we're running out of hope. Even in a group of people who may privately share your concerns, this approach to climate conversation tends to trigger an instinct to shut down. Instead of engaging in discussion, your audience will shift uncomfortably in their seats while they inwardly panic and try to think of a way to change the topic. *Enough about climate change. Let's talk about something less depressing, like our postpartum sex lives!*

Hayhoe presents an alternate option to talking about climate change: an approach grounded in values and connection, rather than data. "The most important thing to do," she says, "is instead of starting up with your head, with all the data and facts in our head, to start from the heart, to start by talking about why it matters to us, to begin with genuinely shared values." And one of the most effective ways to tune into shared values in a conversation is to ask questions, and then, to listen. Learning to listen is simple, but not necessarily easy. In my professional role as a mentor to student coaches, I often share what I call the "banana trick" with students who are struggling to talk less and give their clients room to speak. Imagine, after asking your client a single, powerful question, that you've taken a bite of a banana and *literally cannot keep talking.* Some especially loquacious students have employed actual bananas for this experiment, and report that it's surprisingly effective. The Alliance for Climate Education advocates for a *stop talking* approach to climate conversations, as well. Here's how they describe this strategy in a four-minute educational video called "The Secret to Talking About Climate Change":

> "First, think about all the things you want to say about climate change. And don't say them. Really. You see, if you just start going off on how bad climate change is,

people are probably going to shut down. They may feel attacked and put up their guard. It doesn't matter how eloquent your words are. If the other person's not listening, there's no point. So here's the secret to talking about climate change: listen. Listen to the other person. I know it sounds weird, but it's the most important part. You may think the goal is to convince the other person of your perspective, but that's going about it all wrong. The goal is just to have an actual conversation, and that only happens when people listen."

When it comes to conversations about difficult topics, I know a thing or two about "going about it all wrong." I am an accomplished veteran of bad conversations about social change. I started young. At age fourteen, I crossed paths with a series of PETA brochures and became an ardent vegan and animal rights advocate overnight. Along with two friends as accomplices, my first gesture of activism was to put a sign with the words "MEAT IS MURDER!" on our high school's opinion board, which was a centrally located bulletin board for posting items meant to foster collective discussion. We had decorated the sign with bright red, magic marker blood dripping from the letters for emotional effect, imitating PETA's graphic, in-your-face style. You could technically say that discussion was generated, as the next day, the varsity boy's lacrosse team posted a counterargument that included a brutish defense of Bojangles fried chicken biscuits. But though the blood-red sign was in the style of activism PETA modeled for me, the outcome wasn't quite what I'd hoped for. I don't think anyone on the lacrosse team stopped eating meat that day.

Like the climate scientists who have hammered us for years with alarming statistics about global warming trends, I have, historically, approached conversations about social and environmental change with the belief that others will surely be swayed by the data and intense emotion behind my convictions. I have bungled tense conversations about animal rights, racial justice, gender and LGBTQ+ equity, the death penalty, gun control, and reproductive rights with statistics and tears, rather than listening. More often than not, these conversations have left me feeling isolated and ineffective. One thing I have learned: it is painful to bear witness to a terrible truth, but it is more painful to think no one else cares because you couldn't talk about it effectively. Skillful, connected conversations about social and environmental justice are deeply important because of the role they play in shifting social norms and bringing about change. They're also important to our sense of belonging and mental health.

There's a catch to this, however: as important as it is to work towards discussions about climate change that feel skillful and connected, there's also danger in assuming that a messy, uncomfortable, or even stalemated conversation equates to a faulty approach. Important parallels can be drawn between conversations about climate change and conversations about race, and many of these parallels relate to white privilege. There is privilege in avoiding conversations about difficult topics because we perceive them as primarily affecting others. Many white parents are finally waking up to the importance of having conversations with white children about race. Parents of Black children have always had these conversations, because for their families, it's a matter of survival. What's at stake in the absence of hard conversations about police brutality and systemic racism, for parents of Black children, is literally their children's lives.

Race plays an important role in our perceptions of and conversations about climate change. In the United States, Hispanic/ Latino and Black Americans are significantly more likely than white Americans to report being alarmed or concerned about global warming. They are also more likely than white Americans to take action on this concern, with Yale's survey data suggesting that 40% of Hispanics and 39% of Blacks would be willing to join a campaign to try to convince elected officials to take action to reduce global warming. Only 24% of white survey respondents indicated the same willingness. Many Black and Latino parents already understand that climate change, as an amplifier of systemic injustice and racism, is a matter of survival for their children, too.

There is also white privilege inherent in the assumption that good conversations are "comfortable" or "nice," and that there is a single "right" way to talk about difficult topics. The root cause of climate change is the same toxic, extractive, patriarchal white supremacy culture that has trained those of us who are white to turn away from disruptive conversations about systemic oppression in favor of maintaining the status quo with our silence. This, too, is a problem with our willingness to listen: if the only voices we're listening to about climate change or racism are white voices, we aren't really listening at all. The deep listening required for difficult conversations about climate or social change must extend past conversations with our white, climate-denying Uncle Earl or the other parents in our social groups, and include listening deeply to the voices of those who are most vulnerable to climate impacts. If we're really listening to those who are most vulnerable to the impacts of climate change—to Black communities, Indigenous communities, and communities of color, to the youth activists who know their generation will bear the brunt of the climate impacts previous generations caused—some of our conversations may well become *more* difficult and disruptive as our understanding and skill increases, particularly for those of us who are white.

Addressing racism and systemic oppression is critical in our collective response to climate change (and has always been critical, its importance long preceding our collective awareness of global warming). Environmentalist Leah Thomas, known on Instagram as Green Girl Leah, noticed the striking silence of environmentalists in the wake of George Floyd's murder in May 2020, in spite of the well-documented links between racism and environmental injustice. In an interview with *W Magazine,* she noted:

"I am not buying that environmentalists didn't know," Thomas said. "It's that they didn't care, frankly, or their privilege allowed them to say 'This isn't affecting me. Therefore I'm going to look away.' I didn't hear much from people that I had gone to marches with to advocate for salmon and other endangered species. There just didn't seem to be a connection when it came to endangered Black and brown lives."

Along with a group of other eco-activists, Thomas created the Intersectional Environmentalist platform, a website and social media movement dedicated to dismantling systems of oppression in the environmentalist movement. The website features stories from a diverse community of environmentalists and a podcast called *Dismantled,* promoting a different kind of conversation about climate justice than has typically been seen in the mainstream (and predominantly white) environmental movement. For those of us who are white, learning how to have skillful conversations about climate change also requires us to learn how to talk about racism and systemic injustice. These conversations require practice, and they also require us to take an anti-racist approach that actively disrupt the status quo that harms Black communities, Indigenous communities, and communities of color every day. Conversations that disrupt the norms of white supremacy are often messy and uncomfortable because we're doing them *right,* not because we're doing them wrong. These conversations might look like asking our workplaces to take a clear stand in support of racial justice, like challenging racist stereotypes perpetuated by the media, calling for an end to police brutality, or pointing out the voices of color that are missing from our social and professional circles. They might also look, for white people, like quieting our own voices in certain contexts so that marginalized voices can be centered.

Good conversations about climate change and social justice don't always *feel* good. They take practice, requiring discernment, reflection, and humility. They call us to account for what we *don't* say, as much as for what we do. As a listening tool, silence can be used wisely to deepen understanding and connection. But the silence of the conversations we avoid speaks volumes, too.

As parents, we naturally want to protect our children from bad news about the world. Yet at the same time, we know we're tasked with preparing them to *live* in a world where climate change and painful social and environmental inequities are part of the fabric of reality. The context of talking about climate change with our children can feel like especially sensitive and nuanced territory, often requiring even more discernment than our conversations with adults. Instinctively, we know that a fear-based approach to discussion doesn't feel right to use with children, but in the absence of practice with other strategies, many parents feel lost in approaching climate conversations with their kids.

Our role in conversations with children is a little different than our role in conversations with other adults. With adults, the goal of a discussion about climate change might be to raise awareness and encourage active engagement with the issue. With our kids, we might have the same goals, but we also bear the added responsibility of nurturing their mental, emotional, and spiritual well-being. We want our children to *love* the natural world, rather than to fear it.

Unfortunately, much of the messaging around climate change that's currently part of school curricula across the United States is still grounded in the data-centric, disaster-framed approach that science communication experts are finally recognizing as ineffective. Months ago, I took a course on teaching climate change in the classroom from a nationally recognized organization to better understand what's currently being taught about climate change at the elementary and high school levels. The course left *me* feeling anxious and frightened about climate change, and there was a striking absence of any attention to emotional resilience in the curricula offered. With children, teaching emotionally difficult subjects without careful attention to resilience may do more harm than good. I have no doubt that there are extraordinary science teachers across the world who are finding ways to center emotional resilience in their climate curricula, but this approach is not yet the norm. Until it is, parents' skill in conversations about climate change with their kids remains more important than ever.

The strategies we use to talk about climate change with our children must be age-appropriate and child-appropriate, tailored to our children's temperament and developmental level. Rowanbank Arts and Education, an Edinburgh-based organization that offers arts-based environmental education for children, suggests an approach they call the "Natural Flight of Steps." Informed by a Swedish Forest School method called *Skogsmulle*, which aims to help children grow closer to nature through outdoor learning, the Natural Flight of Steps sees human connection to nature as a process. I met Rowanbank co-founder Lucy Power on a group call led by Parents for Future, a U.K.-based parents' climate action group, and asked about the Rowanbank approach. At the first step, children simply enjoy connecting with nature without any kind of learning agenda. The next step invites children to spend time observing in nature, then at the third step, caring for nature. The fourth and final step engages people—children and adults—in campaigning to care for the natural world.

"Often with environmental education you expect people to already be on the third step, to care for nature," Power told me in an email, "but often they've never spent enough time on the first two steps—that important and crucial time simply enjoying nature and observing it. More and more children are disconnected from their natural environment and don't spend time in nature at home or at school. Spending time enjoying the natural world and observing the seasons change, that's the fundamental foundation." Rowanbank's offerings include a traveling, acrobatic Forest Circus that transforms local green spaces in Scotland into magical forests and fun, interactive climate change and renewable energy workshops in schools. They train educators in the forest school approach, and put on outdoor performances including aerialists, hula hoopers, stilt walkers, puppets, and musicians for children from underserved areas. A far cry from the data-centric, disaster-framed approach to climate education that I encountered in the U.S.-based course I took, Rowanbank's model focuses on cultivating a sense of wonder and delight in the natural world. Power shared a David Attenborough quote with me in our email exchange: "No one will protect what they don't care about, and no one will care about what they have never experienced."

Not everyone can send their children to forest schools—often, schools centered around outdoor learning experiences come with a private tuition price tag that's out of reach for many. But there are lessons from the "Natural Flight of Steps" approach that can be adapted to any school setting and any family. At the first step, we might take our very youngest children outside to play in muddy puddles and leaf piles, bask in the warmth of spring sunshine, and delight in the discovery of dandelion puffs. At the second step, we might invite them to notice how the leaves change color in the fall, to watch a tadpole's evolution into a frog, or observe a seed's miraculous growth from sprout to full flower. The third step might include reading children's books about the environment that tell the stories of young earth protectors, and engaging children in everyday earth-care actions. Young children love to be helpers, especially when helping is fun, and can easily participate in things like composting, picking up trash while out on walks, buying food from local farmer's markets, and growing a home garden. Finally, at the fourth step, we might invite them to join us in environmental activism: making colorful protest signs, walking alongside us at a march, or writing letters to politicians and companies.

After learning about Rowanbank's method, I reflected on my own approach to talking about climate change with my young children. I've spoken with them about climate change before, in part because it has become part of my work, and in part because I don't want their first exposure to climate change to be the common core curricula in an American public school. I want them to hear about it from me first, in a context where I can be there to help them process emotionally; I don't ever want them to feel blindsided by it. Also, I think about climate conversations with children in much the same way as I think about conversations about racism: if Black and brown children aren't too young to experience it, white children aren't too young to learn about it. Shielding white children from difficult conversations about topics that Black and brown children can't avoid only serves to deepen racial inequities and injustice. But in the context of climate change, I wonder now if I've sometimes asked my children to jump to the third step of caring about nature before spending enough time on steps one and two. I wonder if *I've* spent enough time lately on steps one and two, knowing that with any progression of learning, sometimes moving backwards is a necessary precursor to moving forwards. At the very least, learning about Rowanbank's approach reminds me that spending time enjoying the magic of nature isn't a distraction from the work of protecting the planet, it's actually *foundational*. It's a foundation that adults need to nurture for ourselves as much as for our children.

Over a year after the awkward moms' group experience, I started reading *A Field Guide to Climate Anxiety*. I quickly realized it was a book I wanted to *talk* about. After posting a casual inquiry on my Instagram account to see if anyone wanted to join me in reading it, a small, intimate book group was born. Instead of looking away from our climate distress, we looked towards it together, naming honestly how we really experienced climate anxiety; one climate book turned into the next. These conversations weren't medicinal just because of the sense of isolation that dissolved when we named our messy feelings out loud, but also because we started discussing strategies for cultivating resilience and participating in climate solutions. I realized that the conversations *themselves* were a practice for cultivating climate resilience, and saw in a new way how talking about climate change may really be one of the most important forms of activism we can engage in. Sometimes the conversations will be difficult and disruptive, requiring us to face painful truths about ourselves, about others, and about the state of the world. But sometimes, the conversations will remind us at exactly the right moment that we aren't alone, that the world is full of people who care deeply, and that we are far stronger in community than we are apart.

Skillful conversations about difficult subjects matter more in our parenting than we might realize, especially in a changing climate. In *Our House is On Fire: Scenes of a Family and a Planet in Crisis*, Greta Thunberg's family recounted the story of their experience of Greta's climate awakening. "She was slowly disappearing into some kind of darkness and little by little, bit by bit, she seemed to stop functioning," her parents wrote. My own parents might have written the same thing about me as I, in my teens and early twenties, slipped into a dark hole while learning about the horrors of the factory farm industry and the complex social, environmental, and human rights toll of eating meat. Just as Thunberg developed an eating disorder in the throes of her climate despair, I gradually stopped eating as well, dropping out of college in the second semester of my freshman year to enter rehab for anorexia.

I have been recovered from my eating disorder for nearly a decade, but I still remember the deep bruise of isolation and confusion I felt for years in the heavy shroud of my own early environmental despair: *Why isn't anyone else talking about this? Why doesn't anyone else seem to care?* In Thunberg's story, I saw not just my own disaffected teenage self, but also my children's *future* teenage selves. Climate change, research shows, is already having a devastating impact on many teenagers' and young adults' mental health; this trend is highly likely to continue in the coming decades as extreme weather events become increasingly frequent and intense. The next generation is paying attention to what we talk about, and how we talk about it. Our children are listening to the conversations we choose to have with them, with our peers, and with people in positions of power. They are watching the ways our conversations acquiesce to, or consciously disrupt, problematic social norms. What conversations will we be forced to have about climate change with our children in the future if we don't talk about it now, when it matters the most?

I'm still learning, one conversation at a time, how to lean into difficult conversations about things that matter. I'm still learning how to talk about racial justice in ways that are effective, but also intentionally disruptive. I'm still learning how to talk about animal welfare in ways that are honest, but not alienating to the people I love. I'm still learning how to talk about climate change in a manner that conveys the reality of an overwhelming scientific consensus, but that also builds connection and resilience. I'm still learning how to tell the truth in moms' groups.

Talking about climate change isn't easy, whether with other adults or with children. It's a skillset we'll have to practice again and again, with as much attention to how we listen as to how we speak. Our approach will inevitably evolve as we evolve, both individually and collectively. We won't always get it right. But as parents, we have a responsibility to our children and to *all* children to keep trying.

Chapter 7 Reflection

Key practice: Practice having brave conversations about what matters most. Remember that many of the most effective conversations begin (and end) with listening.

Questions for reflection and discussion with others:

- What kinds of conversations do you notice about climate change in your social and professional circles? Are there places in your life where climate change might not be a comfortable topic of conversation?

- This chapter talks about social norms as a powerful influencer of human behavior. What social norms do you notice in terms of pro-environmental behaviors in your social and professional groups?

- What has been your personal experience with navigating conversations about difficult topics, like climate change and racism? Do you tend to avoid these conversations, or to lean in? How do you measure whether a conversation has gone "well"?

- What has been your experience with talking to your child or children about climate change?

- What kinds of conversations about climate change have you avoided? What has been, or might be, the cost of this?

CLIMATE SOLUTIONS AT HOME

"A vibrant, fair, and regenerative future is possible—not when thousands of people do climate justice activism perfectly but when millions of people do the best they can."

—Xiye Bastida, *in All We Can Save*

A FEW WEEKS BEFORE THE twins' fourth birthday, I asked them what kind of cake they wanted. In a dilemma I could have seen coming, they insisted, of course, on *two* kinds of cake: a superhero cake for Milo; a princess cake for Minnie. Feeling stretched for time already and not being an especially talented cake decorator, I considered my options.

We could pay someone else to make the two cakes, but this was during the earliest days of the COVID-19 pandemic, and paying someone else to make the cakes would both cost more than I wanted to pay and felt risky on the public health front. I looked to the internet for inspiration and immediately regretted it, feeling a familiar surge of inadequacy as I scrolled through Pinterest's response to "superhero cake" and "princess cake" ideas. (Unless you are an expert cake decorator, I cannot recommend Pinterest for children's birthday cake ideas. It will only deflate your confidence.)

In a stroke of what I considered to be parenting genius, I decided to offer to let the twins decorate their *own* birthday cake, each taking on half. This would (1) let me off the hook on the decorating front, saving me from being personally responsible for a cake that looked like a Pinterest fail; and (2) delight the twins, who leapt at any chance to decorate anything.

When I proposed this idea to the twins, they were elated, even managing to agree on a dirt cake base. I ordered small superhero and princess figurines from the internet, and picked up a large bag of gummy "earthworms" and Oreos from the grocery store.

On the morning of their birthday in early March, we got to work on the cake. I had prepped the base the night before, assembling alternate layers of crushed Oreo "dirt" and coconut cream, and washed the figurines so they'd be safe—well, safe enough—to put on top of the cake. Milo lost interest in decorating after the first few minutes, having found the Flash figurine and deciding to play with it rather than put it on the cake. Minnie decisively took charge of the cake project, and curious to see what she'd come up with, I gave her free reign.

She took on the task of decorating with intense concentration. Minnie carefully placed all of the superheroes lying down on their backs, side by side in a line that stretched the full length of the 9x11 pan: Batman, Superman, Green Lantern, and several unidentifiable plastic comrades all felled in a bed of sugary dirt, teeming with gummy worms. She arranged the Disney princesses in a dignified, upright train, led by Mulan and flanked by Belle from *Beauty and the Beast*. With eight lit birthday candles, four for each of them, the overall effect was that of a line of female warriors walking through a graveyard of fallen, comically over-muscled macho men. It was an undeniably feminist scene, the birthday cake version of Jungian sand tray therapy. It was a vignette straight out of the depths of my psyche.

It was a proud mom moment.

The week of the twins' birthday, which happens to be International Women's Day, there was a slew of articles about the research collated by Project Drawdown, a nonprofit organization devoted to helping the world reach "drawdown." Drawdown, scientists say, is the potential future point in time when greenhouse gases in the atmosphere stop climbing and start to steadily decline. It's the possible moment in the future when we start to *reverse* global warming, rather than simply slowing the progression of what many have already accepted to be an inevitable march towards catastrophic planetary decline. Project Drawdown's approach is rooted in rigorous scientific review and focuses on the *solutions* to climate change, offering a perspective that's both grounded and explicitly hopeful. Rather than simply focusing on what Project Drawdown cofounder Paul Hawken describes as the familiar climate "proverbs" (consume less, be energy efficient, change your lightbulbs)—maxims that are useful, but seem wholly inadequate to address the magnitude of the problem—Project Drawdown details a framework of a hundred substantive, already existing solutions to address global warming. The solutions fall into three broad categories: (1) reducing sources of greenhouse gas emissions; (2) supporting carbon sinks; and (3) improving society through global efforts to address health and education. Combined, their research suggests, these solutions can bring us to the point of drawdown.

We already know what to do to reverse climate change, Project Drawdown tells us. The technology exists. And some of the solutions are both counterintuitive and shockingly simple. One of the top hundred solutions, according to the project's research? Educating women and girls.

In a global context, when girls have access to education and reproductive health services, they earn higher wages and are able to contribute more to economic growth. This helps to protect their families in the case of damage from natural disasters, such as hurricanes or other storm-related flooding. During times of drought- and flood-related food scarcity, women with higher education are more likely to spend more money on feeding their children than men do, helping to prevent malnutrition in children. Education can help women better understand the risks of climate change, and to better prepare their families and communities for responding to natural disasters. A harrowing summary of a 1991 cyclone disaster that killed 140,000 people in Bangladesh showed that the death rate among people aged twenty to forty-four was seventy-one per thousand women, while only fifteen per thousand among men. Women, researchers explained, were more likely to be homebound looking after children and elderly relatives. Wearing saris, their movement was restricted, making it physically more difficult for them to escape a deadly tidal surge. Educating women and girls will help mitigate the impact of climate disasters both directly and indirectly, potentially having a profound ripple effect throughout families and communities.

Educating women and girls may also help mitigate carbon emissions. When women have more years of education and access to high-quality reproductive health services, they have fewer and healthier children. Research suggests that having one fewer child is one of the most impactful lifestyle choices families can make to improve their overall carbon footprint. Though the science is clear, this position remains controversial. The population control approach to environmentalism has been rightfully criticized as racist, classist, and sexist, as environmentalism with shades of eugenics. Project Drawdown's website explicitly states—and I strongly agree—that family size should be a personal decision, not something policed by policy or social stigma: "People's choices about how many children to have should be theirs and theirs alone. And those children should inherit a livable planet." Project Drawdown suggests, instead, that we focus our efforts on educating and trusting women to make the best decisions for their families—and making sure women are in positions of leadership. When women are in leadership roles in both their lives and their communities, everyone benefits.

While gender disparities in education are significantly more pronounced in the Global South than in the Global North, disparities in leadership (and in some places, access to reproductive health care) still abound in high-income nations. In the United States, while women now earn more than 57% of undergraduate degrees and 59% percent of master's degrees, they are still underrepresented in leadership roles in nearly every professional sector. Politics is no exception: as of a report from August 2018, women represented only 18% of U.S. state governors and 23% of the mayors of the largest hundred American cities. These disparities are significantly more pronounced for women of color. Yale's research on climate change beliefs suggests that women, and Black and Hispanic/Latino Americans, are demographically more likely to care about climate change than white men, who hold the vast majority of leadership roles in politics and nearly every other sector.

Research from Australia's Curtin University has also shown that countries with more female politicians pass more ambitious climate policy, and it's not just because countries that elect more women tend to be more supportive of environmental protection. Economics professor Astghik Mavisakalyan led an analysis of the legislatures of ninety-one countries that compared the percentage of seats held by women with each country's climate policies. The analysis considered a variety of potentially confounding variables, including national education levels and general political orientation, and researchers found that none of these factors could adequately explain the link between female political leadership and climate policies. When it comes to environmental policy, gender representation in leadership matters.

Between 2020 and 2050, Project Drawdown's research estimates that addressing gender equality on a global scale could result in the equivalent of diverting 85.42 gigatons of CO_2 from the atmosphere. (A gigaton, in case you were wondering, is one billion metric tons—it's a *lot*.) And parents are ideally positioned to support this effort in our everyday lives, with our own children. Feminist parenting isn't the kind of climate action that can be checked off of a to-do list like switching to LED lightbulbs or installing solar panels, and it's not the kind of action that comes with immediate gratification. It's a long-haul commitment to the process of parenting for the future, with plenty of mistakes and learning along the way.

In practice—and as a mother imperfectly attempting feminist parenting myself, may I emphasize the word *practice*—feminist parenting looks like talking to children openly about gender equality and women's rights. It looks like talking openly about gender, and challenging the still overwhelmingly prevalent societal assumptions that gender and biological sex are the same thing, and that gender can only be expressed in a binary. It looks like teaching your children, through your own example, how to share your pronouns when you meet someone new. In households where parents are in a heterosexual partnership, it looks like hard conversations to promote gender equity at home, so that the balance of domestic labor and income-generating labor doesn't fall without questioning along stereotypical gender lines. Feminist parenting looks like teaching children of any gender about body boundaries and consent from a young age, and by having frank, factual conversations about menstruation, sex, and reproductive health. It looks like engaging in critical conversations about media stereotypes and expectations about what women's (and men's) bodies should look like. It looks like embracing diverse role models, and directly challenging the norm that says that *thin, white, young, cisgender, able-bodied,* and *conventionally feminine* is the only acceptable version of beautiful. It looks like talking about race and intersectionality alongside discussions of gender equity, and naming that they're inextricably intertwined. It looks like sharing examples of powerful female leaders, environmentalists, and climate activists, from Greta Thunberg and Jane Goodall to Xiye Bastida and Wangari Maathai.

And if you're me, it looks like celebrating your son when, in one moment, he insists on stealing your makeup bag and jewelry because he "wants to be beautiful," and in the next moment, has changed into a Miles Morales Spider-Man costume and is trying to fly off the couch. It looks like reading *Good Night Stories for Rebel Girls* at bedtime, to both of your children's delight. It looks like making a mental note to engage in conversation with your daughter after she constructs a birthday cake that looks like a scene from a feminist battlefield, realizing that she's watched as many superhero cartoons as her brother and may have gotten the message that *power* and *domination* are the same thing. It means making a mental note to question your own internalized assumptions about power, as well.

This work isn't simple or easy, especially in a world in which gender disparities are still the norm. But every effort we make to raise children of any gender—male, female, nonbinary, trans, gender-fluid—who can champion women's leadership and empowerment is part of one of the most impactful climate solutions available. It's one of the most powerful ways we can parent for the future every day, from our own homes.

In the context of public health, one of the ideas you'll encounter frequently in discussions of climate change is that there are significant "co-benefits" of climate action for human wellness. It's critically important for our collective health to take action on climate change, but it turns out that several of the actions we can take on a personal level to help the planet have immediate benefits for our own well-being and happiness. Replacing gas-guzzling car transportation with forms of active transport, such as regularly walking or biking to work, makes us healthier, reducing our risk of chronic diseases linked to sedentary lifestyles and boosting mental health. Eating a plant-rich "planetary diet" reduces the carbon emissions and deforestation associated with animal agriculture, and reduces our risk of a wide range of diseases associated with consuming animal products. Living more simply by reducing mindless overconsumption and waste can help us to embrace what some call the "low-carbon happiness" movement, which challenges the assumption that human health and happiness requires high carbon activities. Educating and empowering women and girls have profound co-benefits beyond the climate, too.

Many of the solutions within the Project Drawdown framework align with the idea of co-benefits for our personal happiness and well-being, and several deal with the intimate terrain of how we eat and manage our food. Changing the way we eat can have a profound impact not only on our health, but also on the planet. The single most impactful solution, second only to the high-impact work of empowering women and girls, is reducing global food waste.

Roughly a third of the world's food, I learn from Project Drawdown, is never eaten. A few years ago, this estimate would have been about right at our house. Between two toddlers and two exhausted adults, an embarrassing amount of food got thrown away after being forgotten in the refrigerator. (Also, an embarrassing amount of food got thrown under the table by a certain picky eater and consumed by the dog, though I doubt this technically counts as "waste.") Wasted food means wasted resources: wasted seeds, water, energy, land, fertilizer, labor, and money. Wasted food means methane emissions when the last few servings of last month's squash casserole begin to decompose in a landfill because they got hidden behind a large batch of lentil soup, and you didn't find them until a layer of mold had started to grow. On a global scale, food waste is responsible for about 8% of our collective greenhouse gas emissions. In low-income countries, food waste tends to happen unintentionally, occurring early in the supply chain as food goes to waste on farms, rots in storage, or spoils during the distribution process. In higher-income countries, food goes to waste much further along the supply chain. In households like yours or mine, food goes to waste because we reject bruised bananas at the grocery store (knowing our picky toddlers won't eat them), or because we simply buy and serve more than we can actually eat. Food goes to waste because we don't plan well—or perhaps as is more often the case for busy, worn-out parents, because we struggle to find the bandwidth to plan and organize well.

Also, in the United States, most of us don't compost our food.

While recycling has been widely adopted across the country, composting has not yet become the norm in most places. In 2018, the EPA reported that the national rate of paper and paperboard recycling was 68.2% percent, having jumped significantly from 42.8% in 2000. The rate of composting food and other organic municipal solid waste was, however, just 4.1%. Many cities and towns offer recycling services to make recycling easier for residents, and in some places, recycling is mandatory for both commercial entities and individual citizens. In the United States, few cities offer free services to help residents manage organic food waste, and few offer incentives to individuals who do compost. A notable exception: in Vermont, a gradually rolled out law called Act 148, the Universal Recycling Law, fully banned all food scraps from municipal waste collection in 2020, making Vermont the first state in the country to enact a mandatory composting law. Act 148 requires waste haulers to offer food scrap collection to customers, and lawmakers expect that Act 148 will help boost Vermont's recycling and composting rate to 60%.

When sustainable behaviors are easy, they're far more easily adopted on a broad scale. When they require significant effort that isn't supported at the community level, adoption rates are low.

While my town offers excellent recycling services, composting is not yet mandatory or supported by the local government. The city is exploring changing this, though. A 2019 survey of Durham residents assessed interest in municipal composting services, and found that close to half (47%) had attempted to compost on their private property (35%) or by using a composting service (12%). Compared with national averages, these results make Durham a very compost-friendly place. Here, even without yet having local government support, food composting is mainstream behavior, a socially normal thing to do.

Though I didn't give it much conscious thought at the time, this social norm probably had a lot to do with our own decision to try a composting service in the summer of 2018. We'd seen a truck bearing a "CompostNow" logo drive through our neighborhood each week for several months before finally deciding to give it a try. I'd always assumed that you needed a yard to compost, and had assumed our tiny townhome backyard was too small for a compost bin, but noticing the compact composting bins that appeared on several of our neighbors' front steps each Wednesday morning piqued my curiosity. For a reasonable monthly fee, we discovered, the CompostNow service would pick up a four-gallon bin of food scraps each week and replace it with a clean one. Over time, we'd earn credits that could be used to request compost ready to use in a garden, or we could choose to donate our compost to community gardens supporting local food security initiatives.

We filled our four-gallon bin to the brim every week, and at the beginning, I remember being shocked by the weight of it. With each week's haul of food scraps weighing over fifteen pounds, I couldn't believe we had been throwing this much food away. Over the course of two years, our weekly CompostNow bins managed to divert nearly 1,700 pounds of food waste from local landfills, enough to produce 840 pounds of compost, avoid over 200 pounds of methane released at the landfill, and offset nearly 5,000 miles driven by car. After Bart built a set of raised beds in our tiny townhome backyard, feeling inspired by our composting success and by the stack of books on home gardening I'd bought in a panic about climate change-related food insecurity, we requested gallons of accumulated compost to help nurture a tentative first attempt at a backyard vegetable garden. We grew kale and chard, cucumbers and tomatoes, basil and cilantro. We grew an incredibly prolific row of okra that stretched taller than I knew was possible for okra to grow, bested only by the output of a fig tree Bart had planted a few years earlier. The first summer we used compost in the garden, we had enough figs to share with several friends and neighbors, and made the best fig jam I have ever tasted.

It wasn't just the satisfaction of seeing a concrete measure of the impact of our diverted food waste that made me so happy about composting—it was being able to gift a jar of our home-grown, homemade fig jam to a dear friend. It was watching the twins joyfully shred leaves of kale and chard from the garden and eat them as they ran around in the backyard, and seeing their enthusiasm for the worms and pill bugs they'd find in the rich soil. It was their unbridled delight at the progress of every single sprout, and how they'd cheer on every single flower and vegetable. It was the taste of roasted okra with sea salt, of fresh tomato-basil sandwiches, and salads made with greens grown a few feet from our home. It was knowing that any compost we didn't use in our own backyard would be used to help feed someone else in our community who needed food: a hungry child, an underpaid day laborer, a mother down on her luck. It was the satisfaction of giving my children something I hadn't had growing up: a sense of deep connection to their food. A sense of respect for the time and resources it takes to grow what we eat, a respect that's nearly impossible to cultivate in the aisles of a grocery store. It was the reminder that what we mindlessly throw away can be transformed into something life-giving. Composting, too, offers unexpected lessons in parenting for the future.

You don't, as I discovered, have to have a huge backyard to start composting. Even if there aren't composting services available in your local area, it's possible to start composting with an airtight under-sink bin for food scraps or even a small bin on your kitchen counter. Google "countertop composting," if you're curious; it's a thing. And composting certainly isn't the only way to reduce food waste at home; thoughtful meal planning can help. Shorter, more frequent grocery trips can help. Learning more about food storage and preserving can help. One of my own non-composting efforts to reduce food waste has been to start learning about preserving and fermenting, transforming vegetable scraps into pickles and sauerkraut. Reducing waste, I've found, often inspires creativity—and sometimes the solutions are delicious.

Third on Project Drawdown's list of most impactful climate solutions, according to carbon reduction/sequestration impact, is embracing plant-rich diets. Because I've been a vegetarian since I was a teenager and my husband became a vegetarian before we were married, embracing a plant-rich diet hasn't required much behavior change effort for us as a family; it has always been our family norm. But even though awareness of the environmental and health benefits of plant-rich diets has increased over the past few decades, the world's consumption of meat and dairy products has skyrocketed over the past fifty years. Social scientists attribute this to multiple factors: rapid population growth means there are more people to feed, and rising global incomes mean there are more people who can afford to eat meat. The increase in consumption of industrial meat has had a significant impact on the health of both our planet and our bodies.

Meat production on factory farms is profoundly destructive to the environment, contributing directly to deforestation, climate change, and human rights abuses. The devastating Amazon rainforest fires that made headlines in the fall of 2019 were started by Brazilian farmers using slash-and-burn tactics to clear land for cattle ranching and growing industrial animal feed. Deforestation releases billions of tons of greenhouse gases into the atmosphere and destroys forests' ability to absorb carbon, accelerating climate change and pushing ecosystems close to dangerous tipping points. Industrial meat production is also linked to land-grabbing from Indigenous communities. In places like Brazil, Indigenous communities are at the front lines of protecting forests, often putting their lives and welfare at risk to do so. Protecting Indigenous land tenure is also one of Project Drawdown's top hundred climate solutions, as protecting Indigenously owned forests means protecting important carbon sinks and reducing carbon emissions from deforestation. "Beyond carbon," Project Drawdown's website says, "Indigenous land management conserves biodiversity, maintains a range of ecosystem services, safeguards rich cultures and traditional ways of life, and responds to the needs of the most vulnerable." Many of Project Drawdown's climate solutions, it turns out, are interrelated.

The good news is that while meat consumption has grown overall, attitudes towards reducing personal meat consumption are gradually changing. In 2015, a nationally-representative survey of 1,115 U.S. adults suggested that two-thirds of Americans reported reduced consumption of at least one type of meat over the last few years, with the most reductions seen in red and processed meat. Health and cost factors were noted as being important reasons for reducing meat consumption, while most in this survey weren't motivated by environmental or animal welfare concerns. In the

United Kingdom, a 2016 survey found that nearly 30% of Britons reported having reduced meat consumption in the past twelve months, with women (34%) being more likely than men (23%) to reduce their meat intake. Health concerns were also the most frequently cited motivation for reducing meat consumption in this survey. These concerns are well-founded, as collectively, our consumption of meat and dairy products far exceeds nutritional recommendations, and demonstrably contributes to high rates of chronic disease. Long-term consumption of red and processed meat is associated with increased risk of mortality, cardiovascular disease, type two diabetes, and colorectal cancer. Eating less meat is undoubtedly good for the planet, but it has immediate benefits for our bodies, as well.

Project Drawdown defines a *plant-rich diet* as "the individual dietary choice: to (1) maintain a 2250 calorie per day nutritional regime; (2) meet daily protein requirements while decreasing meat consumption in favor of plant-based food items; and (3) purchase locally produced food when available." In Europe, the concept of the "planetary diet" has been steadily gaining momentum, with an understanding of a healthy diet as one that considers social well-being alongside physical nutrition. In 2019, a group of leading scientists from around the world came together to discuss whether it would be possible to feed a future population of 10 billion within healthy planetary boundaries. Their conclusion, published in the EAT-Lancet Commission report, was that this *is* possible—but not without radical transformation of our collective eating habits, making food production more efficient, and reducing food waste. A planetary health plate, according to the EAT-Lancet report, should consist by volume of approximately half a plate of vegetables and fruits, with the other half consisting primarily of whole grains, plant protein sources, unsaturated plant oils, and (optionally) modest amounts of animal protein.

Neither a plant-rich diet or a planetary diet mandate going entirely vegetarian, or suggest that animal-based food sources must be eliminated completely. There is widespread recognition that food is inextricably tied to culture and social identity, and that changing eating habits takes time. What's critical to our successful response to climate change, according to these models, is a significant *reduction* in our collective consumption of animal products, and getting food in ways that are more efficient and less wasteful.

Just as composting holds unexpected lessons, so does eating a plant-rich diet. Choosing to reduce or eschew consumption of animal products can be a way to challenge the largely unchecked cultural assumption that the only person whose well-being matters when it comes to the way we eat is the person at the top of the food chain. Conventional approaches to nutrition rarely consider the well-being of the humans and animals who contributed to getting a particular meal to our table. Eating a plant-based meal can be a way of acknowledging that bodies other than our own—the bodies of people who will be hit hardest by climate change-related food insecurity, of people in Indigenous communities devastated by deforestation, of immigrant slaughterhouse workers and people living near farm waste facilities, the bodies of animals factory farmed to become food—that these bodies matter, too.

How different would our world be, I often wonder, if we lived as though others' bodies—especially those that do not look like ours, and those that have not yet been born—mattered as much as our own? What would it mean for the future to raise a generation of children with this kind of respect for others?

We're not completely plant-based at our house in this season, eating some eggs, and occasional dairy when it's baked into treats from our local coffee shop or farmer's market. As someone who used to struggle with restrictive eating, this approach to a planetary diet feels balanced to me, though I've also gone many happy years without eating animal products at all. What's more important to me than that my children follow a perfectly plant-based diet on their own as they get older is that they understand that what and how we eat has an impact on others. That how we consume *anything* has an impact on others. The way we eat isn't truly a "personal choice," as it's so often treated; it's a decision that has tangible consequences for others, even if those others are people and animals we may never meet. Making lifestyle choices with others' well-being in mind as much as your own is a way of adapting to and parenting for the world the future needs—a world

driven by collective care, by radical compassion, by an understanding of our unavoidable interdependence.

For us, eating a plant-rich diet means hearty bowls of lentil
soup and black bean chili, spicy vegetable curries and Buddha
bowls, tempeh "bacon" sandwiches and fresh salads with
homemade lemon-tahini dressing. It means dense plant-based
burgers with sweet potato fries, roasted cauliflower "steaks," peanut
butter-banana smoothies, rich loaves of homemade banana bread,
and frequent batches of chocolate chip cookies. The best thing
about vegan baking, I tell the twins, is that you can always lick
the bowl without worrying about food poisoning. Without fail,
licking the bowl is their favorite part of every family baking project.
We're extraordinarily lucky to have the economic privilege of eating
well, and fortunate that both Bart and I truly enjoy cooking. We'd
eat this way even if there weren't benefits for our health and the
planet, simply because it's delicious.

And, because, let's be honest—I like to lick the bowl after
baking, too.

A strong critique of the idea that climate solutions start at
home is that the "personal responsibility narrative," as critics call
it, is a distraction from the real causes of climate change, and
thus, a distraction from the work that most needs to be done to
address it. A 2017 study showed that just a hundred companies are
responsible for 71% of global carbon emissions, and a wealth of
research—including the conclusions of Project Drawdown—agrees
that no amount of personal lifestyle change will be enough to fix
the problem of global warming without large-scale systemic change.
In an article for *Sierra*, the national magazine for the Sierra Club,
editor Jason Mark writes:

"A larger—and more pressing—concern about the personal
responsibility mantra is the way in which it obscures the culpability
of fossil fuel giants and other industrial actors in fueling the crisis.

To insist that individuals must make some behavioral changes only serves to let the real bad actors—the carbon barons, the banks, the right-wing ideologues who have promoted climate science denial—off the hook. See, for example, BP's recent campaign asking people to calculate their individual carbon footprint. Such concern trolling is little more than the climate-and-energy version of the bottling industry's long-running (and well-documented) campaign to encourage personal recycling: just as the beverage and consumer product companies have sought to place the responsibility for the plastic pollution crisis on individuals, the energy industry is trying to put the onus of climate action onto ordinary people."

In combination with the phenomenon of greenwashing, in which companies use slick marketing tactics to persuade us that an organization's products, aims, and policies are more environmentally friendly than they actually are, the personal responsibility narrative not only convinces us that we're directly at fault for the problem of climate change if we don't trade our gas-guzzling SUV for a plug-in Prius, but also convinces us that we've fully done our part if we do. If we eat a plant-rich diet, compost, ditch single-use plastic, drive a Prius, install solar panels, trade fast fashion for used clothing, and use only LED light bulbs, this narrative tells us, we can check "did my part for the planet" off of our to-do list.

The personal responsibility narrative *is*, in many ways, a distraction from the critical work of climate activism and political engagement. And yet.

Mark continues: "...here's the thing: when you choose to eat less meat or take the bus instead of driving or have fewer children, you are making a statement that your actions matter, that it's not too late to avert climate catastrophe, that you have power. To take a measure of personal responsibility for climate change doesn't have to distract from your political activism—if anything, it amplifies it."

I agree. And from a behavior change perspective, it makes sense to embrace the small steps we can take to be more climate-friendly at home. Successful long-term behavior change is the result of an accumulation of small wins that build our sense of self-efficacy over time. As our confidence grows, we're more likely to engage in more challenging actions, like joining a climate action group, showing up for a nonviolent direct action protest, or learning how to lobby for political change. Our personal behavior changes *prepare* us to engage in collective action.

Individual behavior changes also have a profound effect on social norms. As noted in the previous chapter, research suggests that social norms are one of the most powerful influences on human behavior, with multiple studies showing that what our neighbors are doing has a far greater impact on adoption of environmentally-friendly behaviors than educational campaigns or even financial incentives—in short, we respond to peer pressure. What we do at home matters not just because of the impact our personal actions can have in terms of our carbon footprint, but because our social networks can quite literally magnify the impact of our behavior, especially when tipping points are reached. According to social scientist Damon Centola, when 25% of a population embraces an idea, social change accelerates like a catalyst has been added to a chemical reaction. The key ingredient for conversion to new ideas, Centola's work has shown, is the strength of our social ties. In other words, having a cohesive network of friends and family who know each other makes it more likely that your personal sustainability efforts will spread "contagiously" within your social circles. Well-organized moms' groups may be a far more potent agent for environmental and social change than many of us have realized.

For parents, engaging in climate action at home is also a way of preparing our children to live in a future that will likely be very different than the reality in which our generation came of age. Many of the highest-impact changes we can make in our households—eating a plant-rich diet, reducing food waste, reducing car and air travel, switching to green energy—will make it easier for our children to thrive in a world where these practices will *need* to be the norm. They're climate mitigation strategies, but embracing them early is also a form of climate adaptation. Although the work of parenting is wildly undervalued in our society, I'd argue that the work we can do now to help our children prepare to adapt to a rapidly changing world is one of the highest contributions parents can make to the collective effort to address climate change. As parents, we need to be thinking beyond the solutions whose impact on greenhouse gas emissions can be measured in gigatons—we need to be thinking about what kinds of skills our children will need to thrive in the coming decades. Parenting for the future in our everyday lives isn't just about sustainability in the classic sense; it's a radical reconsideration of what kinds of knowledge and ways of being will be useful in a future world that may be very different from the one we know now.

On a practical level, that might look like embracing more mindful consumption patterns: teaching our children how to compost, reuse, up-cycle, mend, and share will prepare them to live in a circular economy that distributes resources more equitably and efficiently. Teaching our children to be actively anti-racist and gender-inclusive will help them to embrace our collective differences as a beautiful expression of the biodiversity we desperately need to protect. Creating opportunities for our children to build strong relational ties with local classmates, friends, and neighbors will strengthen community resilience during the natural disasters we'll inevitably face. Helping children cultivate emotional resilience and normalizing the skills needed to metabolize grief and trauma will be far more valuable in the decades ahead than the ability to ace standardized tests through rote memorization. Nurturing our children's sense of wonder and love for nature will fortify their capacity to fight for the planet in the coming years. Encouraging their innate creativity and imagination may allow them to generate innovative solutions to climate challenges we can't even see yet.

These are climate solutions that *must* start at home, within the intimate domain of our family lives. And while we mustn't let ourselves be fooled or distracted into thinking that the "personal responsibility" level of change is enough to adequately address the problem of global warming—quite simply, it isn't—let's also not be fooled into discounting the actions we take at home, or dismissing the importance of the way we parent. Your actions matter more than you may think they do.

In *The Parents' Guide to Climate Revolution,* mother and veteran climate activist Mary DeMocker writes:

"Most importantly, what I have learned is that a sustainable ecosystem and climate requires sustainable parenting. To me, sustainable parenting means that we don't just pour our loving attention into our own children for eighteen years, preparing them for success in college and the job market. It means putting on the climate lens for every interaction so that we can prepare them to thrive in the natural world that sustains their lives—and in the democracy that shapes the quality of those lives. Sustainable parenting means taking the well-being of *all* children into account—not just our own—when deciding how to live in the world and what to model around the ethical use of the world's resources. Finally, to me, sustainable parenting means loving our children for their whole lives. That requires acting in ways that let them feel our love now and that ensure they'll feel it after we're gone, when they are thriving in the world we've pulled back from the precipice."

We know what is needed to pull the world back from the precipice. The science is clear, and the solutions are already available to us. We can start participating in those solutions today, the very next time we interact with our children. And as DeMocker says, this is a way of loving our children for their whole lives—a way of casting our love into the future, hoping that it might be felt for generations to come.

This year, for the twins' birthday, Minnie is asking for a "top cake," which I interpret from her elaborate hand gestures to mean a tiered layer cake. The "fluff part," she tells me, must be chocolate, with vanilla frosting decorated with strawberries and blueberries. Strawberries and blueberries are significantly less complicated than last year's request for superheroes and princesses; I am relieved. Milo, being more concerned about the Spider-Man toys he's anticipating for his birthday, is happy to go along with Minnie's desired cake idea. We don't have the springform pans required for a layer cake, but instead of impulsively buying them from Amazon like I would have in the past, this year, I'll borrow them from a neighbor, offering a slice of cake in return. It will be a tiny gesture in the direction of the world I hope will someday be the norm for all of us: a moment of mindless consumption averted, a borrowed cake pan, a shared piece of plant-based birthday cake, a small investment in connection and community. As frightening as the prospect of a changing climate is, the future won't, I have a feeling, be all bad.

Chapter 8 Reflection

Key practice: Remember that big changes start with small shifts. The climate actions we take in our everyday lives can help promote positive social norms, spread important ideas, contribute to adaptation and resilience efforts, and build confidence in our ability to influence larger systems and communities.

Questions for reflection and discussion with others:

- Did it surprise you to learn that educating women and girls is one of the top climate solutions, according to Project Drawdown's research? How have you related to gender in your own parenting?

- What's your personal experience with food waste? Have you ever experimented with composting or other ways to reduce food waste in your household? Does your local community offer support for composting efforts?

- Have you ever experimented with moving towards a plant-rich diet? If so, what's gone well? What have you found challenging?

- What would shift in the way you relate to food if you were to embrace a "planetary diet"—a diet with the health of the planet in mind, as much as your own health?

- There are strong, valid critiques of the "personal responsibility" narrative around climate change. And, as this chapter addresses, many of the things we can do to address climate change at home are also ways of preparing our children to live in a future that will have to adapt. What might it mean for you, on a very practical level, to "parent for the future" at home?

EMBRACING ACTIVISM IN PARENTHOOD

"You cannot say that you did not know. All that remains is to consider what you will now do."

—RUPERT READ, *Parents for a Future: How Loving Our Children Can Prevent Climate Collapse*

"BEING AN ACTIVIST IS an aspiration," my friend Alaya tells me, "but I have a story that what I'm doing doesn't count as activism."

We've been engaged in an extended back-and-forth conversation over Marco Polo, talking about our lives as mothers and how we want to show up for our values during the most care-intensive years of parenting. Like me, Alaya has two small children. Like me, she's been trying to find her way towards her values around the environment in the midst of a life that's full of snack requests and the seemingly endless rollercoaster ride of tending to big emotions in small bodies. Like me, she *used* to consider herself an activist, but had trouble seeing herself in this identity after becoming a parent. In college, Alaya was the president of the student environmental club at her campus, active in trainings with the Student Environmental Action Coalition, and showing up at marches for social and environmental justice. That was her introduction to activism: working alongside other student activists, engaged in direct, grassroots efforts for change. A decade later, now a mother of two, her deep care for the environment can't as easily be translated into showing up for on-the-ground protests.

In my early twenties, I took a summer trip to France to learn more about the French response to the HIV/AIDS pandemic. I'd become deeply interested in the HIV/AIDS crisis after taking a service-learning class in the spring of my sophomore year. The class had involved a series of lectures on the epidemiology and social justice aspects of the pandemic, alongside a practical requirement of volunteering at an AIDS care home. I felt deeply compelled by everything I learned in the lectures, but more compelled by everyone I met at the care home. My favorite resident was a man named Tony: within the first five minutes of our acquaintance, I'd been informed of his status as a former prize-winning drag queen in Kentucky. His Southern Baptist family had disowned him years earlier when they found out he was gay. Frail and not responding well to antiretroviral treatment, Tony wore a lush pair of false eyelashes to the care home's group breakfast each day. I still remember the hushed whispers of the other residents one morning when I arrived to volunteer, and the deep sadness in their voices as they told me Tony had passed away.

I was thinking of Tony as I sat in the back row of a tucked-away lecture hall in Paris, trying to follow the proceedings of an ACT UP meeting with rusty, intermediate French. ACT UP, or the AIDS Coalition to Unleash Power, is an international grassroots political organization whose aim is to end the AIDS pandemic. Started in the late 1980s, amidst the frightening early days of the AIDS crisis in New York City, direct action has always been a significant part of ACT UP's approach. Many of the activists at the meeting were wearing black t-shirts bearing pink triangles and succinct, unequivocal catchphrases: ACTION = VIE. SILENCE = MORT. *Action equals life. Silence equals death.*

Looking around the room, it wasn't hard to imagine that everyone there had lost someone they loved: a partner, a brother, a lover, a friend. They were planning a "die-in" demonstration, in which activists would line their bodies in the streets in a striking, nonviolent visual protest, demanding the attention of the media and people in power. They were motivated by anger at the lack of resources offered in response to a disease that at that point in time was still largely considered to impact mainly gay men, but it was clear to me that they were also motivated by love. People they loved had died. People they loved were living with a deadly virus, and people they loved were at risk. I'm sure many of the activists themselves were HIV-positive, hoping their actions would buy them more time with their loved ones. They were willing to put their bodies quite literally on the line for the cause they cared about.

So this, I remember thinking at the time, *is what it means to be an activist.*

How we see ourselves—our sense of personal identity—has a lot to do with how we behave. The habits and norms of our everyday routines are far more grounded in *who we think we are* than in any perceived limitations. I lace up my running shoes and run several mornings a week, even in terrible weather, because I have thought of myself as a runner for over twenty years. I identify strongly with the idea of being "a runner." I identify equally strongly as "not a gym person," and accordingly, haven't set foot in a gym in well over a decade. I could join a gym at any time, but to do so would challenge my belief that I'm not the kind of person who does that. If I wanted to create the habit of going regularly to the gym, I'd have to first be willing to update my identity: I'd have to find a way to see myself as a "gym person."

In the book *Atomic Habits,* author James Clear describes the idea of identity-based habits: "To change your behavior for good," he writes, "you need to start believing new things about yourself." Rather than focusing simply on the outcome you want, as most approaches to behavior change do, it's key to understand what type of person could get this outcome. Clear says that the recipe for success in sustainable behavior change includes two key steps: (1) deciding the type of person you want to be, and (2) proving it to yourself with small wins.

If you want to lose weight, Clear suggests, assume the identity of someone who moves every day, and prove it to yourself with the small wins of buying a pedometer and gradually increasing your daily steps. If you want to be a better musician, become the sort of person who plays their guitar for an hour every day, and start with the small win of just five minutes of daily practice. If you want to be a better partner, become the kind of person who devotes time and energy into cultivating their relationship, and begin by asking your partner out on a date. Taking on the identity of the person who could achieve the outcome you want leads to small actions that help you to reinforce that identity. Eventually, those small actions become solid, sustainable habits.

If you want your children to inherit a livable planet, what kind of person would you have to become to contribute to that outcome?

It will be harder for us to see ourselves as "activists" or "change-makers" as long as we're holding onto the story that only certain kinds of action "count." This story is reinforced by images we see in the media. If you conduct a Google image search for the phrase "climate activist," or "environmental activist," you'll see almost exclusively pictures of marches and street protests. You'll see rows of images of Greta Thunberg with a megaphone and youth holding signs like "Planet Over Profit!" and "There is No Planet B!" It's notable that the faces in these images are overwhelmingly white, overwhelmingly young, and portray a very specific version of activism. Activism, these images tell us, is bold, direct, and public. It's loud, overtly disruptive, and media-worthy.

You will not see the mundane, unglamorous, behind-the-scenes tasks of organizing, making protest signs, or donating much-needed money to environmental causes. You won't see phone calls made to politicians from kitchen tables or emails sent to the CEOs of fossil fuel companies by hands that are also holding writhing children. You won't see hard, patient conversations with a climate-denying uncle or equally hard, patient conversations with a frightened child who's just learned about climate change in school. You will not see, in an internet search or on the evening news, images of exhausted parents who are doing the very best they can to show up for their values in a world that largely fails to support parents and families. If we don't see people we identify with in a certain role, it's going to be harder for us to imagine ourselves in that role. Representation matters.

I decide I'm going to become the kind of person who helps to protect democracy and get out the vote.

This decision starts with another conversation with a friend. In the early months of my climate awakening, my high school friend Erica comes over with her two daughters for coffee and a playdate. Her older daughter is just a few months older than the twins, and while the three of them play in my living room, Erica and I talk while she bounces her younger daughter on her lap. She's an environmental lawyer who works on cap-and-trade policies, which address climate change by putting a cap on allowable carbon emissions, and creating a market for them by letting companies buy and sell allowances that let them emit a certain amount. Erica has been a vocal advocate for climate solutions for years—she'll know, I think, what the most effective approaches to climate action are. So I ask her: "What do you think is the *single* most important thing everyday citizens can be doing to combat climate change?"

I'm expecting an answer that has something to do with her work in carbon policy. Maybe lobbying government officials and asking them to support carbon pricing legislation? Maybe boycotting companies that aren't actively reducing their carbon emissions? Maybe, even, limiting family size to reduce overall carbon footprint?

Her answer is far simpler.

"Honestly," she says, "the most important thing people can do is vote."

Many of the sweeping systemic changes that will be needed to address climate change will only happen with the support of local, state, and federal governments, and they can only happen with elected officials who support strong environmental policies (and who are held accountable for their campaign promises). As recently as 2016, up to a *third* of the members of the United States Congress were climate change deniers, according to the Center for American Progress Action Fund. In 2016, the list of high-ranking climate-denying politicians included then-Senate Majority Leader Mitch McConnell. A report released the day the twins were born showed that 63% of Americans were represented by a climate-denying politician, in spite of the fact that 67% of Americans supported climate action. (The percentage of Americans supporting government climate action has since increased significantly; in December 2020, the Yale Center for Climate Communication reported that three in four registered voters—75%—supported U.S. participation in the Paris Climate Agreement, while support varied by party.)

Only 58% of voting-eligible Americans voted in the 2016 election. Post-election analyses revealed that Trump, an anti-science politician who called climate change "mythical" and a "hoax," was elected by little more than a quarter of eligible voters. In 2017, Trump appointed climate denier Scott Pruitt to lead the Environmental Protection Agency, and over the course of his presidency, rolled back over a hundred environmental protections, including withdrawing the United States from the Paris Agreement. Post-election analyses also revealed the extraordinary extent to which the Trump campaign went in 2016 to keep voters—specifically, Black voters—from turning out at the polls. A disinformation campaign waged by targeting 3.5 million Black voters with negative Hillary Clinton ads on Facebook could well have swung the 2016 election: "The secret effort," *The Guardian* reported, "concentrated on sixteen swing states, several narrowly won by Trump after the Black Democrat vote collapsed."

As actor Samuel L. Jackson put it in a Biden campaign ad before the 2020 U.S. election: "If your vote didn't matter, they wouldn't be trying so hard to take it from you."

Voting *does* matter. Democracy matters. It matters for every aspect of our lives, and it matters immensely when it comes to protecting the planet.

Throughout most of my adult life, I'd been the kind of voter who showed up to the polls every four years and cast a ballot for the presidential election, often forgetting primaries and midterms. It wasn't that I didn't think voting mattered; it was that I assumed *other* people thought voting mattered, too. It was that, thanks to white privilege, I didn't fully understand the extent to which racist voter suppression was still rampant, especially in the southern United States. It was that I figured it was someone else's job to help protect democracy, and that I could afford to focus on other things: my family, my career, my own priorities. It was, quite honestly, that I took the right to vote for granted.

For me and many others, the 2016 election was a sobering reminder of what happens when you assume that protecting what you take for granted is someone else's job. (It was also a sobering reminder of the specific dangers of unchecked white privilege to our collective well-being.)

The first small win in my endeavor to become the kind of person who protects democracy was filling out an online form of interest to become a precinct official for Durham County's Board of Elections. It had never occurred to me before to do this, but I heard about the idea from an activist I follow on Twitter. A few days after submitting the interest form, I received an email asking me to come in for an interview. In a windowless office tucked in the entrails of a building on one of the side streets of Durham's busy downtown, a woman named Rebecca asked me about my professional background, about my administrative and computer skills, and most directly, why I wanted to get involved in Durham's elections.

"Because elected government should represent the will of the people," I said, using as neutral a tone of voice I as could muster, "and because I'm concerned about election interference." Rebecca nodded her head in agreement; I was hired. I'd receive my election day assignment several weeks before the next election.

Five months later, after attending an extensive half-day training on Durham County's election policies and procedures, I worked my first election as a precinct assistant. It was a local election I might have forgotten to vote in myself a few years earlier, focused only on the mayor and city council seats. Assigned to a voting district a few miles from my home, our election day polling place was in the fellowship hall of a Baptist church. One of the other members of our election day team was a former coworker whose presence immediately put me at ease, and I took my place at the ballot table next to a grandmotherly, more experienced election worker who took me under her wing. Our job was straightforward: give people their ballots, and make sure the number of ballots given out precisely matched the number of ballots received in the voting tabulator machine. Over the course of a fifteen-hour day, we served over 800 voters. The mood was buoyant and cooperative, our bipartisan election team working seamlessly together to make the day run smoothly. Each time a first-time voter came in to vote, the entire team stood up and cheered. There were voters of every background, voters in running clothes and wheelchairs, voters with walking canes and voters with babies on their backs. Many of the voters thanked us for being there, assuming we were volunteers, in spite of the fact that all Durham County election workers are paid. It didn't take me long to decide that this was a job I'd have happily done even without compensation—the sense of collaboration and community was a powerful antidote to the political depression I'd been feeling since the 2016 election.

Each time someone thanked me for handing me their ballot, I realized that showing up for the election meant that *other* people saw me as someone who was protecting democracy. This was another win, another step in the direction of becoming the kind of person I wanted to be.

There were also moments that were… not exactly wins. The week before the March 2020 primary election, just days before I'd work my second election day as a precinct assistant, I'd piled the kids in the car to bring them with me to cast an early primary vote. I'd been talking up voting for weeks: trying to explain at an almost-four-year-old's level how important it is to vote. How it's kind of like raising your hand when someone asks a question: *who do you pick to be in charge?* I tried to convey that voting for good people is a way of helping people who need care, and a way of protecting the earth. I tried to explain that not everyone has always had the right to vote. Both kids seemed to be paying attention, but Minnie was especially enthusiastic.

I was feeling a rare moment of confidence in my parenting as we drove up to our early voting site at a local Unitarian church, sure that my weeks-long civics lesson was the reason Minnie seemed so excited about this outing. Both twins seemed slightly confused as we walked through the indoor polling station, but I chalked this up to the newness of the venue. Milo knocked over a plastic chain link barrier guiding the voting line, and a precinct official glared at us. He was characteristically hyper, darting around between the handful of other early voters and touching things he wasn't supposed to touch. Minnie, on the other hand, was unusually quiet. She seemed to be looking for something.

The whole process took about five minutes. Anxious to get Milo out of the voting room before he could do more damage, I slid my ballot into the tabulator machine, gratefully accepted the extra "I Voted!" stickers for the kids, and tried to usher them back to our car in the parking lot.

"We did it! We voted!" I exclaimed, trying to regenerate the enthusiasm we arrived with. "And look, you got *stickers!*"

The stickers were an adequate reward for Milo. But Minnie still looked confused and disappointed, her lower lip wavering. I asked her what was wrong.

"Where are the *boats?*"

In that moment, it dawned on me that my skills as a preschool civics teacher needed more work.

There were tears. I tried to explain that we'd had a miscommunication. I'd said we were going *v-v-v-VOTING*, not *b-b-b-BOAT-ING*. I tried to empathize with her disappointment as she sobbed in protest that "voting isn't *EXCITING!*" There was no convincing her in that moment that voting was anything but a pale, limp excuse for the sailing expedition she had been expecting. She felt betrayed, livid, refusing to get in the car. She would *NEVER*, she screamed loudly in the parking lot, *go voting again!*

But she would, thankfully, accept the promise of a cookie from our favorite coffee shop. I managed to get her in the car with a shamelessly manipulative reminder of how much she likes chocolate chips. We'd have to talk about voting again another day.

After the voting/boating fiasco, I tried to find other ways to get the kids involved in my voting efforts. I'd written several batches of postcards to voters for the 2016 election and for the high-profile 2018 midterms, and enjoyed how tangible and introvert-friendly this form of outreach was. At four, the twins were old enough to help me put stamps on the postcards, having had plenty of practice with stickers by now. If going to vote in person wasn't exciting for them, I figured, a project involving stacks of colorful postcards and sticker-like stamps might have more appeal.

It did. We started working on postcards to voters for the November 2020 election in July, working in batches of ten to twenty at a time. While the kids watched *Peppa Pig* or *The Octonauts* on television, I'd write the addresses and messages on the postcards while watching *The Bachelor* or *Outlander* on my laptop, calling them over when it was time to apply the stamps. Both of them loved this, especially Minnie. She'd stick out her tongue in concentration, trying to make sure each stamp was aligned exactly right. Many of the postcards we wrote were heading to other swing states, and each batch offered an opportunity to show the twins where the states were on a U.S. map and to re-explain why we were working so hard for this. By the end of October, we'd written over 600 postcards to voters in Georgia, Pennsylvania, Florida, and North Carolina. When not writing postcards, I'd try to squeeze in shifts of phone and text banking, and the twins would greet me with enthusiastic, slobbery hugs after each shift was done. Every time we'd go out for a walk on our neighborhood trails, they would remind everyone we met to vote, and Minnie helped me to decorate the letters V-O-T-E in colorful sidewalk chalk near our front steps—they were among the first letters she learned to recognize on her own. She'd draw sunny, rainbow-filled scenes of crayon stick figures telling people to vote. "These people are doing something *important*, Mom," she'd say.

There were many moments, moments I hid from the twins and almost everyone else, when I was terrified that our collective efforts to get out the vote would fail. That, in the face of massive voter suppression and disinformation efforts, they wouldn't be enough. Moments I wondered if we'd lose our chance to elect a president who could address climate change at a critical moment in history, and potentially lose one of our last remaining chances to avert the worst manifestations of climate catastrophe. More than anything else, it was my kids' faith in me—a faith imparted from my own determination, and borrowed back when my confidence faltered—that kept me from giving up.

While the spark of the modern environmental justice movement is often credited to the 1982 protest in Warren County, North Carolina, just sixty miles from my hometown, Indigenous communities and communities of color have advocated for environmental protection for generations. These communities' significant contributions to the environmental movement, such as the fight for land sovereignty and food justice, are often erased by the media and by white-led environmental organizations. In spite of the fact that historically (and presently) oppressed communities will be hardest-hit by all aspects of climate change, the vast majority of climate action groups are still led by white individuals. The vast majority of environmental funding goes to white-led organizations, often leaving organizations focused on environmental justice to operate on meager budgets. In recent years, there has been a swell of interest in climate action among parents as media coverage of climate change has increased. This is an exciting and much-needed trend—and for those of us who are white parents, freshly on board with the climate movement, it's important to acknowledge that parents from oppressed and marginalized communities have been fighting for their children's right to a healthy, livable planet far longer than we have.

One of the earliest groups in the United States to focus specifically on parents and climate change was Climate Mama. Founded in 2009 by veteran climate activist Harriet Shugarman, author of *How to Talk to Your Kids About Climate Change*, Climate Mama offers education and workshops about global warming to climate-concerned parents and grandparents. Mothers Out Front has mobilized over 35,000 moms in their movement to fight for a livable climate for all children, with an agenda focused on environmental justice, civic engagement, and clean energy. With state campaigns currently active in California, Massachusetts, New York, and Virginia, Mothers Out Front has played an active role in protesting gas pipelines and encouraging local get-out-the-vote efforts. Moms Clean Air Force, a sister organization to the Environmental Defense Fund, enacts a national mission to protect children from air pollution and climate change through state branches and targeted online action campaigns that make it easy for mothers to send messages to politicians about environmental justice and policy. Science Moms is a nonpartisan group of climate scientists and mothers, founded to help climate-concerned mothers take confident action on behalf of our children's futures. Many of the climate activists in mainstream climate organizations like Citizen's Climate Lobby, the Climate Reality Project, and 350.org are parents as well, citing their children as their driving motivation for action.

Parents for Future, formed in 2019 in response to the youth-led Fridays for Future movement, extends the mission of supporting parents to engage in climate action around the world. In just two years, the Parents for Future network has formed chapters in over twenty-three countries, promoting intergenerational activism as a tool for climate justice. Our Kids Climate, a sister network to Parents for Future, was founded in 2015 by a group of parent climate activists in Sweden who wanted to bring the perspective of concerned parents to the Paris Climate Agreement. Our Kids Climate has a network of fifty-eight parent groups across twenty-three countries, and has recently partnered with Parents for Future to offer fellowships to parent climate organizers around the world; at least half of the fellowships will be given to parent organizers in the Global South. These organizations work with parents across multiple continents, from the United Kingdom to Nigeria, Mexico, India, and Australia. One person at a time, they are helping parents and families find ways to engage directly in climate action in a way that honors the unique perspectives and lived reality of parenthood. They're modeling what it means to embrace the identity of "activist" as a parent, breaking down collective action into doable, concrete steps. They're also offering climate-worried parents an invaluable sense of community, normalizing difficult climate emotions in a world that still largely avoids talking about them. (A list of climate action communities can be found in Appendix F.)

While approaches to climate advocacy vary in parent-focused environmental groups, a common theme is strong. These parent activists are motivated by a fierce, unconditional love for their children and a belief that the "climate generation" we've given birth to deserves a better future than the one we're currently on track for. These parent activists also know that activism doesn't have to look the same as it used to in earlier seasons of our lives, or as it might for people who aren't caregivers of small children. These are parents who know what the ACT UP activists I encountered years ago in Paris knew: that action equals life, and that silence carries consequences we cannot afford to risk. These are parents who have found a way to update their stories so that "activist" and "parent" aren't mutually exclusive roles, but identities that enrich and strengthen each other. We may be better activists *because* of our children, rather than in spite of them. And we are undoubtedly better parents when we take action to advocate for the future our children deserve.

In my experience, getting involved with an action group is one of the very best ways to combat climate distress. It's harder to hold on to the belief that your actions don't matter when you're surrounded by others who have decided to show up for the cause. It's easier to face the hard moments—moments of being felled by climate grief, or a stab of existential despair, or the haunting fear that your efforts might never be enough—in community with others who aren't strangers to this kind of distress. If I could go back in time to 2018, meeting the version of myself who spent months in a climate change-induced panic, the one piece of advice I'd give myself would be to join a climate action group or civics engagement community sooner. I'd have spent far less time feeling so alone.

My new friend Julia and I meet over Zoom one day, our conversation spanning across five time zones. She's a fellow coach based in London, working with a group of mothers in the United Kingdom to form a climate action group, and I've reached out to connect and learn more. She tells me about her "penny drop" moment with climate change, the moment she realized she had to take action. One of her closest mom friends, a woman she met in a mother's group after her child was born, sent her a New Yorker article about "the other kind of climate denialism." The other kind of climate denier, Julia explains, is someone who thinks that someone else will take care of climate change. That it's a problem, but not an *everyone must drop everything and run* kind of problem. Something bad, but something that can wait. The other kind of climate denier might be a mom who thinks she can't be an activist until her children are older, because of a story about activism that isn't compatible with early motherhood. "I realized when I read the article," Julia explained, "that *I* was that kind of climate denier."

Before my own "penny drop" moment with climate change— the month that three of my fertility coaching clients worried out loud that maybe they weren't getting pregnant because the babies didn't want to come—I had been that kind of climate denier, too.

I look up and read the article, struck instantly by how author Rachel Riederer describes the same visceral, physical reaction I had to reading David Wallace-Wells' *The Uninhabitable Earth* early on in my own climate awakening. ("The problem is worse, much worse," that book begins, "than you think." It does not get more cheerful from there.) Riederer explores a range of attitudes towards climate change. One is the "climate truth" approach taken by Wallace-Wells and Margaret Klein-Salamon, author of *Facing the Climate Emergency*, that offers no sugar-coating or optimistic frame to stories about climate change, choosing to report in brutal detail exactly how bad many scientists think things are going to be. Another approach, promoted by John Fraser, a psychologist who has studied burnout among environmentalists, recognizes the possibility that for many people, "doomsday reporting" tends to lead to paralysis and inaction, sabotaging our response to the very problem we desperately need to address. Fraser's approach, Riederer explains, "takes a relentlessly positive, solutions-oriented attitude." A third perspective, championed by climate psychologist Renee Lertzman, rejects the idea that there must be a dichotomy between doomsday reporting and manufacturing hope to avoid terrifying people too much. "What works really well," Lertzman tells Riederer, "is when people feel they are invited and inspired to be part of something constructive, combined with having the safety to grapple with the magnitude of things."

I've listened to Lertzman speak before, and her approach is the one that resonates most with me. It's the one that, for me, feels most supportive of the long game of action that the magnitude of the climate crisis will require. We *do* have to face the harrowing truth about climate change, and we must find a way to engage with extraordinarily difficult factual realities without burying our heads in the sand. Yet we also need to do so in a way that allows us to build resilience and stay connected to joy, especially as parents. We can't afford to let any form of climate denialism rob our children of their future, but we also can't let our climate anxiety rob them of the chance to have connected, emotionally healthy parents in the present.

There is no single right or perfect way to engage in climate activism, especially as a parent. For some parents, activism might start out with the small wins of gradually making environmentally friendly changes at home; for others, it might look like signing up for the email list of a local climate action group. It could look like programming your senators' names in your phone contacts and setting up a reminder to call them about climate change each week, or finding out how to be a precinct official in your local election. It might look like writing postcards to voters and politicians, engaging your children in making colorful protest signs to take to a climate march, asking your employer to join a composting program, or starting a book club with other parents at your child's school to talk about climate change and the environment. It might look like broadening discussions about climate change in movements to address racial justice, gender equity, or to transform health care; there is no issue or sector that won't be profoundly impacted by climate change. Often, the sweet spot in activism is the place where your natural talents, interests, and resources intersect to meet a collective need. If there's an aspect of climate change you're especially curious about, or a particular skill you can offer, start there.

Over time, small wins in the direction of a new habit or identity accumulate; gradually, small wins expand into confidence in taking bigger risks, more daring leaps of faith. Becoming a parent climate activist won't be without moments of disappointment and failure, but it also won't be without moments of joy and celebration. For us, the outcome of the 2020 U.S. presidential election was all the sweeter because of how hard we'd worked as a family to contribute to the effort to get out the vote. Along the way, I began to understand for the first time in my life what it felt like to be part of a powerful collective movement: not an individual with the weight of the world on my shoulders, trying to save the planet by myself, but a small instrument in an enormous orchestra of people, each showing up to play their unique part. There is no more beautiful music than this.

And there is no more *needed* music than this: our children *need* parents who are actively working to build their confidence as activists in the climate movement. Our children need parents who hold their representatives accountable for climate action, who are students of and advocates for environmental justice, who write postcards and organize community discussions. Our children need parents who show up on the front lines of nonviolent direct action protests, even if they've never attended a protest before in their lives. Our children need parents who are willing to start small, and then think—and *act*—big. Our children need parents who fully grasp the gravity and possibility of this moment in time, and who are willing to do whatever it takes to become the kind of people who can meet this moment with the ferocious love of those who know that everything is on the line.

Making climate action a high-priority habit is a vote of hope for the future, an acknowledgement that indulging in pessimism is a luxury we cannot afford. It's a way of promising a generation of children that we won't give up on them, and for some, a way of reminding ourselves that it's never too late to update our stories about who we think we are and what we believe ourselves to be capable of. Parents have an extraordinarily important role to play as activists in the climate movement, and parents all over the world are waking up to their potential to effect powerful change. Ultimately, climate action is an expression of love for our own children and for *all* children. It's sacred, transformative work. And it's a responsibility we can't look away from.

Chapter 9 Reflection

Key practice: Align your beliefs about yourself with the world you want to see.

Questions for reflection and discussion with others:

- How do you relate to the word or idea of "activism"? What stories do you hold about what activism means, or what "counts" as activism?

- How has becoming a parent shifted your capacity for engagement with the social and political issues you care about?

- How might your sense of identity need to shift in order for you to engage in an active response to climate change?

- The chapter references a *New Yorker* article about "the other kind of climate denialism"—the kind that thinks that it's someone else's job to take care of the problem of climate change, or that the problem can wait. How might this kind of denialism be showing up in your own life, or in your social and professional circles?

- Would you consider joining a climate action group? What barriers or limitations might be present? How might you overcome them?

- What's the boldest climate action you could imagine taking part in? What would it take to become the kind of person who could take that action?

GRIEF AND LOVE

"Grief and love are sisters, woven together from the beginning. Their kinship reminds us that there is no love that does not contain loss and no loss that is not a reminder of the love we carry for what we once held close."

—FRANCIS WELLER, *The Wild Edge of Sorrow: Rituals of Renewal and the Sacred Work of Grief*

IN THE FALL OF 2018, after my grandmother's death, after our post-funeral trip to the beach with the kids, there was a stretch of time when I did not know if I would ever be able to take them back. Memories of the kids' elation at streaking across the sand and splashing in the warmth of the late-summer ocean curdled as I learned more about sea level rise in a self-imposed immersion of books and online classes about climate change, realizing that the face of the North Carolina coastline would change rapidly within their lifetimes. In a few decades, the coastal town that generations of my family had loved might not look anything like the town I remembered from my own childhood. I wasn't sure if *I* would ever want to go back. The landmark I treasured most, my grandmother's home, was already gone, though not because of global warming.

It was my first experience of *topoaversion*, the emotion that philosopher Glenn Albrecht describes as *the feeling that you do not wish to return to a place that you once loved and enjoyed when you know that it has been irrevocably changed for the worse.* I knew it wouldn't be the last. That winter, we had one snow day. It was a day that should have been delightful, enjoying the rare wonder of central North Carolina snow with two three-year-olds. In many ways, it was delightful, at least for the twins. They opened their mouths to the sky to eat snowflakes like they were candy, tried to make snow angels in a meager dusting of snow, and waddled around in puffy coats and mittens like two small, cheerful penguins. For me, the joy of the moment was soured, once again, by my anxiety about global warming. I was acutely aware that my kids might be among the last generation of children to experience gentle snow in central North Carolina outside of freak winter storms, and debated whether to spend the whole time outside taking pictures, or to put away my phone and just be present with the kids. I took pictures. I told myself that I wanted to document the occasion, like the thousands of other moments from the kids' childhood I'd documented through my iPhone. But in truth, watching the snow through a camera lens offered a tiny layer of protection. I'd been out in the snow—there was evidence in dozens of photos—but I hadn't put my phone away for long enough to really fall in love with it, in the way that's only possible when you're fully present.

It's the same way you stop calling your best friend as often when you know they're about to move away. It's the same way part of you freezes when finding out someone beloved has terminal cancer, uncertain whether to let yourself feel the unbearable flood of how much you love them, or to start gradually pulling away so it won't hurt as much when they're gone.

Solastalgia: the homesickness you have when you are still at home.

If you have ever pulled away from someone you loved as you realized you were losing them, you already know that this doesn't make it hurt any less when they're gone. It hurts *more,* in fact, to be left with all that went unsaid, undone, knowing you had a chance and missed it.

Throughout my twenties, before marriage and children, I used to drive down to the North Carolina coast a few times a year and spend time with my grandmother. Nestled in a quiet Wilmington neighborhood a fifteen-minute drive from the beach, her home was a safe, dependable haven during a turbulent decade of my life, a lifeline to the calmer days of childhood. Sometimes, I'd go to the beach to cast wishes for the future, writing down hopes and dreams on scraps of paper that I'd fold and bury at the line between dry and damp sand, knowing they'd eventually be carried away by the tide. Other times, I'd bury grief and heartbreak, writing letters that were never sent on pieces of paper torn from my journal. At twenty, I said goodbye to a friend who took her own life in my second year of college. At twenty-four, I said goodbye to a first love after a breakup, finally accepting that she was never going to love me the way I wanted to be loved. At twenty-six, I released the crushing shame of an unplanned pregnancy and the heartbreak of my first miscarriage into the ocean, never telling my grandmother what had happened. If she ever suspected, she never let on. The earlier in the morning I could make it to the beachfront, the better. Fewer fellow beachgoers offered more privacy for these intimate rituals. And I loved watching the sun rise over the water.

I never once thought about sea level rise during these trips. Like my grandmother's house, I thought the coastline I loved would remain steady and constant, able to recover from any hurricane, any disturbance. I thought it would always be there the way I remembered it.

It's February 2021, nearly a year into the COVID-19 pandemic. I decide to make a solo day trip to the beach; I'm desperate for time alone. Aside from short trips to the grocery store, weekly three-mile walks, and a handful of solo hours at my parents' house during their pandemic travels, I haven't been *truly* alone—as in, not within earshot of any child or adult who could potentially request my attention—in well over 300 days. For a highly sensitive introvert, this has been like being deprived of an essential vitamin. I'm starting to develop a form of introvert scurvy from too many months of pandemic togetherness.

My parents' pandemic travels have been made possible by an unusually creative solution to the public health dilemma of public restrooms. Months earlier, after a trip to the mountains punctuated by anxious, masked, and hurried stops at highway rest areas, fearful of picking up germs from strangers, they bought a used Honda Element that had enough room in the back to install a camping toilet. In a stroke of engineering genius involving a complex system of bungee cords, windshield covers, and towels, they managed to put up removable "curtains," and a way to secure a roll of toilet paper and bottle of hand sanitizer. It's a truly impressive system, if you prefer functionality over aesthetics. Bart and I had also attempted one restroom-less trip to the mountains, and while using the camping toilet in the backseat of a car is awkward, it's decidedly less awkward than circling the parking area of a public rest area until you can find a relatively secluded spot near the woods.

I call it the "Toilet Car." My dad prefers to call it the "Model T."

On a chilly, cloudy Monday morning, I borrow the Toilet Car, saying goodbye to Bart and the kids with promises to bring back takeout for dinner. I'm heading for the coast.

In *The Future We Choose,* authors Christiana Figueres and Tom Rivett-Carnac describe three key mindsets required to meet our current crisis. "In order to open the space for transformation," they write, "we have to change how we think and fundamentally who we perceive ourselves to be. After all, if what's at stake is nothing less than the quality of human life for centuries to come, it is worth digging down to the roots of who we understand ourselves to be." Transformation is possible, but only if we're willing to abandon our death grip on the status quo and adopt radical new ways of thinking and being. The mindset shift that stands out to me the most is what Figueres and Rivett-Carnac describe as *stubborn optimism*. Stubborn optimism isn't pie-in-the-sky denial of how critical a moment we face when it comes to climate change. It doesn't ignore that in order to avert mass catastrophe, urgent and immediate action within the next ten years of our lives (and for the rest of our lives) is necessary. It doesn't paste a Pollyanna veneer over grief. But it also doesn't indulge our tendency to fall limp with apocalypse fatigue, or let doomsday climate narratives have the final say. "In the face of climate change," Figueres and Rivett-Carnac write, "we all have to be optimistic, not because success is guaranteed but because failure is unthinkable... Optimism is not the *result* of achieving a task we have set for ourselves. That is a celebration. Optimism is the necessary *input* to meeting a challenge."

Successful change or transformation, whether for individuals or entire societies, requires faith that change and transformation are possible.

For parents, stubborn optimism is also what makes it bearable to watch our children fall in love with a changing world. It's what gives us the ability to withstand a four-year-old's delight in the snow of a faltering winter, or their glee in making sandcastles on a beach whose shoreline is shrinking. Stubborn optimism acknowledges anxiety and grief, but sees them through the lens of a story of great turning: *yes, things are bad, but what a privilege it is to be alive in this precise moment in history, just in time to turn it around.*

The last time I visited my grandmother's house was in the summer of 2017, a few months before my mother made the decision to bring her to Durham so she could be closer to us during what would likely be the final months of her life. Since the twins had been born, my grandmother's health had begun to fail, and every trip to Wilmington had felt like it might be the last chance to see her. She was frail, but lucid during the visit. I remember her telling me how glamorous she felt in the light blue dressing gown my mother had bought her, and how it matched the aquamarine color of her eyes.

This time, almost four years later, my mother has given me a bag of freshly baked banana bread to give to my grandmother's old neighbors, and as I drive towards their street, I'm focused on this mission. I tell myself I can leave as soon as the bread is handed off, that I don't have to stay if it's too painful. The street is still lined with magnificent magnolias and majestic live oaks, but my body knows something is different as I approach the cul-de-sac where my grandmother's house used to be. On the same stretch of road where my heart used to swell in anticipation of seeing my grandmother, a new sensation arises, unfamiliar and unwieldy. It's a feeling that doesn't fit comfortably within the boundaries of my skin.

I'd packed Kleenex to prepare for this moment, but it turns out I don't need it. At the moment I'd expected tears, there is only shock. My grandmother's house has been replaced by a barren, sandy lot. By an absence that is both outsized and surprisingly humble: how could so many years of memories have been contained on such a small plot of land? I'm not sure what I was expecting, but somehow, it wasn't this. I park in the adjacent driveway, still on a mission to deliver banana bread.

I knock on the neighbors' door, having called ahead of time and reaching only voicemail, and after a few moments, a familiar figure emerges at the door. I've known Connie since I was ten and as nervous as I am, it is so good to see her face; I haven't seen her since my grandmother's funeral, almost three years earlier. We chat across the awkward six-foot distance that still feels so foreign and strange, even twelve months into the pandemic, asking about each other's families and how we've been faring during this difficult year. Connie puts on a mask and insists that I come in; she has some things she wants to show me. Her kindness and warmth thaw my instinct to run away.

When confronted with heartbreaking destruction in the natural world, whether it be from the devastation of extreme weather events or the wounds of fracking and clearcutting, many of us reflexively look away. At best, we may pull out our credit cards to donate to a cause or call our representative in Congress to ask them to stop the building of an oil pipeline or the rollback of another environmental protection. These actions are helpful—and necessary—but they don't force us to confront our grief about what has been lost. They don't require actual *relationship* with the natural world, nor do they require us to be in relationship with our grief.

Writer Trebbe Johnson explores our relationship with broken places in her book *Radical Joy for Hard Times*. Referencing the work of prominent ecotherapists Sarah Anne Edwards and Linda Buzzel, Johnson acknowledges that the grief we feel about environmental changes is not a one-time loss that we eventually learn to move on from; it's more akin to living with a chronic, degenerative illness, one we know will worsen throughout our lifetimes. For those of us who are parents, it's like living with a chronic, degenerative illness that's genetic, knowing we've passed it on to our children. We know *they* will be living with environmental grief throughout their lifetime, as well.

Environmental grief—like the grief many feel with infertility or pregnancy loss—tends to be disenfranchised. It's often unseen, unacknowledged, and unvalidated by our social norms, and we have few resources or collective rituals for metabolizing it. As anyone who has ever experienced disenfranchised grief knows, the loss is only made *more* painful by its lack of visibility to others. But when it comes to broken places, Johnson says, there are practices we can engage in to honor both our grief and the specific beauty of brokenness. One of these practices is gazing: looking with love, openness, and receptivity at a landscape, image, or being that we might otherwise look away from in shame, horror, or sadness. Johnson describes her experience of sitting vigil for a clear-cut forest:

"Being willing to gaze at the broken forest, we discovered that what we had feared would be too painful to bear was not. The first sight had packed a powerful punch, but as the reality of the place seeped into our consciousness, we were able to settle down into what it offered. The forest's past blended with the details of its present existence. And we saw that it did exist. Existence had not ended with clear-cutting. What was before us in all its waste and clutter and decay was a forest—not a pretty one, but touching in many unexpected ways. By confronting that existence, we recognized our own abilities to face truths that not only didn't incinerate us but enlightened us about all kinds of matters in our personal lives. We had simply shown up and been willing to see, and we were seeing things we had never expected."

In order to gaze at a broken place, you have to stay long enough to *see* it.

The first thing Connie shows me is a china cabinet. As soon as she tells me it used to belong to my grandmother, I can picture exactly where it was in her house. Connie spent hours, she tells me, refurbishing the cabinet's tigerwood frame after my grandmother died. She shows me one of my beloved great-aunt's paintings, a pair of red fabric chairs that had belonged to my grandmother, and an antique ironing board that had belonged to my great-grandmother. It's deeply moving to see so many artifacts from my family's history in this home that neighbored my grandmother's for so many decades; it's like visiting a still-living sister when one sibling has passed, and seeing a striking, comforting family resemblance. There's a moment in our conversation when Connie pauses and goes upstairs, returning with a small wooden box painted on four sides with tea kettles.

"Do you like it?" she asks. "It used to belong to your grand-mother. It was one of the things she especially liked."

I can picture exactly where my grandmother kept the box, too. In her den, a small hiding place for tea bags and Reese's peanut butter cups. I gratefully accept it. I'll take it home and fill it with tea bags and chocolates, too.

Connie tells me the neighborhood lost twenty-three trees during Hurricane Florence; the loss of my grandmother's house isn't the only reason the cul-de-sac looks bare. She tells me a pair of small children across the street play in the empty lot, and that this is one of the things that brings her joy when she looks out the window and feels sad.

Play, Johnson says in *Radical Joy for Hard Times*, is a way of creating beauty and giving back to broken places. I am beginning to be able to imagine bringing my children back here. I know they would delight in playing in the lot, too.

There is only one thing missing from the visit: Carlton, Connie's husband. I have known Carlton for the entirety of my life. He first met my grandmother when she was a teacher at his Wilmington middle school in the 1950s, his own parents having been neighbors to my grandparents first. Carlton is at the beach, and will be back later in the morning. I've been planning to take my lunch to the beach anyway for a chilly winter picnic, and tell Connie that I'll return in the afternoon for a second visit.

One of the myths about climate optimism is that it's a mindset one can arrive at as if to a sunny destination with a one-way ticket. I've seen many climate workshops headlined with the encour-aging charge to *"Move from anxiety to action!"* But to me, this is an oversimplification of the reality of climate engagement. I'm active *and* anxious. I'm optimistic *and* heartbroken. My love for the planet, for people, and for my children is the reason I grieve the irreparable damage done to the environment. It's the reason I worry, daily, about natural disasters, food insecurity, and the people who are already being left behind as the world begins to respond to climate change. But this love is also what compels me to act. It's what reminds me, daily, that failure is not an option. It's what holds me accountable in the moments that I'm tempted to look away, to slip into the "someone else will take care of it" genre of climate denialism. As long as I am connected to this love, I will have to find a way to hold space for all that it requires of me. This love insists that I feel both hope *and* heartbreak. That instead of looking away, I stay.

There will be no moment within our lifetimes where we'll arrive safely on the other side of the threat of climate change, no moment when we get to go back to life as it was. Life will not ever go back to the way it was; all of us will have to learn how to allow optimism and grief to coexist. "The next twenty years will be a period of deep uncertainty and tremendous risk, no matter what," writes author Roy Scranton in a *New York Times* op-ed about climate change. "The first thing we need to do is let go of the idea that life will ever be normal again." Even if the very best-case scenarios were to play out in the coming decades, there will be sorrow along the way. There will be losses that haunt us in the spirals of ever-gentler winters and ever-warmer summers, and losses that stab us with the acute fury of wildfires and hurricanes. There will be quieter, more intimate losses, too. For some of us—for me—there will be wanted children we choose not to bring into the world. There will be travel we choose to forgo. There will be migration, altered career plans, and the pain of watching our children learn to live with a level of uncertainty many of us never had to face in our own youth.

But heartbreak, too, offers gifts. There is still beauty and possibility in broken, dying places. In clear-cut or wildfire-singed forests, in hurricane-ravaged coastal land, in empty lots where beloved houses once stood. I think often of the way a caterpillar's body dissolves completely in a chrysalis, its latent imaginal cells coming to life to orchestrate a dramatic process of metamorphosis. The birth of a butterfly necessitates the death of a caterpillar.

Caterpillars, as I learned during our summer of raising swallowtails, spend the last few days of their lives in a rampage of gluttony and waste-making. You can tell that a caterpillar is almost ready to form a chrysalis by the level of excrement it produces, a detail conspicuously absent from the classic children's book *The Hungry Caterpillar*. Throughout the short season of voracious consumption, the caterpillar's imaginal cells lay dormant, holding all of the information that will soon be needed to direct an extraordinary transformation. Once the chrysalis is formed, the caterpillar's body dissolves into an unrecognizable cellular soup, and the imaginal cells come to life. At first, they act independently as single-celled organisms, gradually growing and dividing into small clusters called discs; they are even regarded as invaders, attacked by the caterpillar's immune system. The caterpillar *resists* the process of transformation. Small imaginal cell clusters grow in size, gradually joining with other imaginal discs to form ever-larger clusters that use the raw organic material in the chrysalis to form the anatomic structure of a butterfly. Within a matter of weeks, the butterfly is ready to emerge.

It's an imperfect metaphor, to be sure. We cannot know, in this messy, turbulent time, exactly what will come next. Unlike the predetermined fate of a caterpillar, the fate of humanity is—at least to my knowledge—more a matter of choice than destiny. But it's a metaphor that brings me comfort just the same. I like to imagine that the small clusters of the climate movement around the world, already rapidly expanding and joining together, hold the imaginal architecture of the future. That we are waking up just in time to arrest the world's gluttonous consumption and waste-making, alert and ready to create something entirely new.

A certainty, amidst all that remains unknown: in order to make way for whatever is coming next, we are going to have to let the caterpillar version of the world pass away. We are going to have to let go of the idea that the world will ever be that version of normal again.

Wrightsville Beach is cold and windy, and a large fleet of pelicans is diving for fish in the water. It's cloudy; the sky and the water are nearly the same shade of greyish blue. I spread out a striped, green blanket on the sand and eat my lunch. In February, beachgoers are sparse: there's a couple walking a black dog, a man looking for seashells, and in the distance, a surfer braving the winter ocean in a wetsuit. Johnnie Mercer's Pier, an iconic local landmark, stretches into the water just a few hundred yards away. The original pier was demolished in 1996 by the dual assaults of Hurricanes Bertha and Fran, but a hurricane-resilient concrete replacement was built in 2002. From a distance, the concrete pier looks almost the same as the wooden pier I remember from my childhood.

One of the most personal losses of climate change, for me, is the absence of a third child. Growing up, I never wanted three children, but ever since the loss of our triplet, it has felt like someone was missing from our family. For much of the last four years, I'd held on to the possibility that we might try again to conceive, in spite of the numerous obstacles to doing so. I'd held on to maternity and baby clothes, just in case. In my own personal ontology, I'd imagined that we could invite the triplet's spirit back into physical form again in another pregnancy, that a third child would somehow complete the trio that broke during my pregnancy. I'd been saving a name for her; I'd been sure that it was a *her.* I've realized only recently how much I'd disenfranchised my *own* grief about the loss of the triplet with this hope for another baby. I'd been telling myself the same callous cliche I'd counseled so many others not to say to someone after a pregnancy loss: *don't fret so much about this one; you can always try again.*

The decision not to try again didn't happen in a particular moment; it unfolded over time, punctuated by episodic surges of doubt and hormonal longing. Climate change wasn't the only reason we chose not to try again, but it factored prominently. It was a decision that was hard to speak aloud once I realized it had been made. There are few things more intimate than the choices we make around building our families, and few decisions more loaded with social, cultural, and emotional baggage than the choice to have or not have a child—even a third child. Climate change has heightened reproductive anxiety for many, a trend that is likely to increase. Though it's rarely spoken of aloud, I know there are others grieving children who will not be born, many of whom are already parents. There will be more of us in the future.

Something about the ocean invites grief with open arms. Maybe it's the wide expanse of the landscape that encourages a heart to open, or maybe it's that, as author Isak Dinesen wrote, "the cure for anything is saltwater—tears, sweat, or the sea." I've come here today not just to say goodbye again to my grandmother, but also to my third baby, the one who will never be part of my life in physical form. I write her a letter.

I address it to her by name: I tell her how much she is and will always be missed, and how profound of a difference she made in her fleeting trip to earth. I tell her I remember the sound of her tiny heartbeat. I tell her I will always wonder what she would have looked like: blonde and blue-eyed like Milo, or brown-eyed and brunette like Minnie? Would she share Minnie's love for art and music, or Milo's delight in spiders and superheroes? *You would have loved your brother and sister*, I write—*they are a handful, but they are really the best.* I tell her I hope she can understand why I've closed the door on trying again. It's complicated, but in large part, it's because I want the future to be a place where Minnie and Milo might feel safe choosing to have their own children, and having fewer children now is one small contribution I can make to that future. Maybe, I tell her, she can return decades from now through one of them. We would so love to meet her.

After an hour, my hands are too cold to write legibly; I've forgotten to bring my gloves, and more pressingly, I've left the Kleenex in the car. I pack up my journal, my beach blanket, and hastily gather a few promised seashells to bring home to the twins. As I'm driving off the Wrightsville Beach island, I see a sign with her name on it: *Haven.* It feels like an acknowledgement from the universe that, as raw as today has been, I've done something right by coming here.

Carlton is thrilled to see me when I return, and I am just as thrilled to see him. It felt easier to drive into the neighborhood this time, the visit with Connie having soothed my sense of dread. Carlton, too, has things to show me: he's photocopied his notes from my grandmother's ninetieth birthday celebration, a newspaper article of my great-grandmother from the 1970s, and a photo of my grandmother on Wrightsville Beach in the early 1950s, looking glamorous in a black one-piece bathing suit. Johnnie Mercer's Pier—the original wooden one—is in the background of the photo, and I realize that it must have been taken very close to where I'd been sitting today. The three of us share memories of my grandmother and memories of her house. I'm so deeply grateful for their kindness in spending this time with me. It's a ritual of remembrance I hadn't known I still needed so much.

I hate to leave, but I've promised Bart and the kids that I'll be back in time for dinner, and it's getting late. Still masked, we do a round of COVID-distanced self-hugs that don't come close to the real thing, but I promise I'll return soon. When my grandmother was still alive, she'd stand in her doorway and wave until I was out of sight every time I'd drive away and head back to Durham. This time, Connie does.

During our last "normal" day before the pandemic, the day before the twins' fourth birthday in early March, we took a day trip to Wrightsville Beach. We'd headed straight for the coast on that visit, not stopping at my grandmother's neighborhood; I hadn't been ready to see it yet. The twins had been thrilled to see the ocean and have a picnic on the sand with their favorite superhero figurines—at the time, The Flash and Batgirl. Minnie talked for months afterwards about the excitement of eating Whole Foods pizza and chocolate chip cookies on the beach. We'd set up camp that day near Johnnie Mercer's Pier, and both kids had relished running back and forth between the concrete pillars. I remember being both happy and nervous that day. The twins' delight was contagious, but I'd still felt tender and anxious about being at the coast after my grandmother's death, and after all I'd learned about climate change. I'd still wondered if letting them come to love the North Carolina coast was the right thing to do as a parent. I still wondered if they'd come to resent me someday for letting them love a world that would only break their hearts.

The sea level of North Carolina's coast is eleven inches higher now than it was in the 1950s, when the photo of my grandmother at the beach was taken. Climate scientists say that the water level is now rising an inch every two years. By the time the twins are my age, the water level will likely be at least another sixteen inches higher. In the coming decades, Wilmington and Wrightsville Beach will be at extremely high risk for coastal flooding, both during hurricanes and the daily swell of high tide. Climate resilience and adaptation efforts are already well underway at the coast, but there's no doubt that the face of the built coastal landscape will change dramatically during the 21st century. I am heartbroken that the Wilmington of the future may not resemble the Wilmington of my childhood. I am stubbornly optimistic that coastal residents—with the support of a growing, imaginal network of climate activists around the world—will do whatever it takes to protect the places and the people they so fiercely love. *I* will do whatever it takes to protect the places and people I love. More and more, I am seeing others rise to the same commitment. I no longer feel alone.

Throughout the long months of the pandemic, I've asked the twins many times what they most want to do when it's safe to travel as a family again. *Go to the beach again!* they say, without fail. Minnie is dreaming of another picnic on the sand and splashing in the water, Milo of finding seashells that once housed tiny creatures.

We'll go, I promise them. *We'll go as soon as it's safe.* Finally, it's a promise I can make without hesitation.

Chapter 10 Reflection

Key practice: Go beyond binary thinking. Practice holding space for grief *and* love, beauty *and* brokenness, anxiety *and* optimism, and everything in between.

Questions for reflection and discussion with others:

- Have you ever had an experience of "topoaversion"? How do you typically respond when faced with images or in the presence of broken places?

- What is it like for you to sit with the idea that life will never go back to "normal" again?

- What climate change-related losses are or will be most personal for you? How might you honor these losses in a tangible way?

- How do you cultivate joy and beauty during difficult times?

EPILOGUE

"I love this world, and I don't want to live in space."

—MINNIE, *age 5, on a spring day*

WHAT DOES IT MEAN to be a good—or good enough—
parent in a changing climate?

I can't possibly answer this question for anyone other than myself. As a white, socioeconomically privileged North American, I'm squarely among the demographic that has contributed most to the root causes of climate change, environmental destruction, and systemic oppression, while being harmed the least. This directly informs the level of responsibility I feel to be actively engaged in climate solutions on a daily basis. I have benefited throughout my life from the exploitative mining of fossil fuels, and I live on land stolen from Indigenous Americans. Many of the belongings in my home—computers, iPhones, and absurd amounts of plastic toys—are the spoils of an extractive, wasteful economy that has abused the planet; disproportionately harmed Black, Indigenous, Asian, and Latinx communities; and will injure future generations even more as the planet continues to warm. My children will have larger carbon footprints than most other humans on the planet, by simple fact of their being U.S. citizens. Their birthday is just a week before the United States' "Earth Overshoot Day," the day when, if everyone on the planet consumed like the average American, the ecological resources consumed would exceed what the Earth could regenerate in a year. Their birthday is in early March.

One of my coaching colleagues, a passionate climate activist and veteran coach named Eve, asks groups of climate-concerned coaches to reflect on the following question: *what is mine to do?* What resources do I have to offer? What part of the climate movement can I most effectively contribute to, within the finite bounds of my time, energy, strengths, and money? How can I influence systems of power? In her presentations, Eve often shares a poem called *hieroglyphic stairway,* by Drew Dellinger. The poet is awake at 3:23 in the morning, troubled by the insistent questions of his yet-to-be born great-great-grandchildren. *What did you do when the planet was plundered?* they ask him in dreams. *Surely you did something when the seasons started failing?*

What did you do once you knew?

Eve models her own answers to these questions, working tirelessly alongside her colleagues in the Climate Coaching Alliance to bring climate change to the forefront in the field of coaching. I have witnessed so many others model their own answers to these questions as well. I've seen academic colleagues shift their research trajectories completely, pivoting from years of work in other areas to focus on climate change. I'm awed by the fierce dedication of scientists, environmental justice advocates, Indigenous land protectors, journalists, voting rights activists, teenage climate strikers, and parent climate organizers around the world, all working for climate justice and sustainable solutions at such a critical moment in time. While tech billionaires plan their escape route to Mars, ordinary citizens are showing up every day to protect the planet the rest of us still want to call home. I'm inspired, too, each time I see someone embracing a plant-rich diet for the first time or stepping outside of their comfort zone to attend a meeting in a local climate action group. Meaningful answers aren't always visible and grandiose; sometimes, they are humble, tentative first steps.

I have spent the last three years trying to figure out my own answers to these questions in the context of early parenthood:

What does it mean to be a "good enough" parent in a changing climate?

What is mine to do?

What did I do once I knew?

One day at a time, I'm learning how to let the reality of climate change and a love for the future inform nearly everything in my life. It has informed a decision to shift career paths and go back to graduate school to study public health and climate change in my late thirties, to get more involved with several climate action groups, and to talk about climate change with nearly everyone I meet. It inspires me to stay engaged in my local elections and get-out-the-vote efforts, to buy far less than I used to, to keep up the composting, and to learn more about gardening and every-day permaculture. It requires me to be a continuing student of racial justice, and to learn how to be accountable for the way I show up not just for future generations, but for the oppressed and marginalized communities who are living and breathing on our planet *now*. Climate change informs the way I parent, too. Each time I practice *staylistening* when a child has a tantrum, instead of reacting in frustration, I know I'm helping them to cultivate the emotional agility and resilience their future will require. It invites me to cultivate my *own* emotional agility: to care more tenderly for the waves of climate grief and anxiety that still come, and that will probably always come. It inspires me to love the natural world bravely, with the wide-eyed awe that comes so easily to my kids.

There is no single "right" answer to these questions; what is mine to do may be different from what is yours to do, as you and I have different lives. But what is *ours* to do together is simple: as parents, our job is to love children. Our job is to love children so much that we see *all* of the world's children as our own, all worthy and deserving of a livable planet. Our job is to love children so bravely that we are willing to remake the world for them, to participate with all of our inner and outer resources in moving towards a way of being that is sustainable, just, and equitable for all. Our job is to love children so deeply that we cannot help but be moved to adore and protect the natural world that is their home, and to do so with the courage and fortitude this moment in time demands.

Our job, simply, is to love children so fully with our hearts and our actions that years from now, when our own children or grandchildren or great-great-grandchildren ask us, as poet Drew Dellinger does—*what did you do once you knew?*—the answer we give will be one that we're proud of.

Epilogue Reflection

Key practice: Let love be the inspiration behind your climate action. There's no better way to love your children, and children around the world, than to show up to protect their right to a livable future.

Questions for reflection and discussion with others:

- What does it mean to you to be a "good enough" parent in a changing climate?

- How do your social, cultural, and geographic identities inform your own sense of responsibility around climate action?

- What is yours to do in response to the climate crisis? How might you use your unique circumstances (your resources, strengths, connections, privilege) to contribute to positive change?

- How do you want to be held accountable for showing up for those who are most vulnerable to climate threats—both those who are yet to be born, and those who are alive today?

- What do you want to be able to tell your children someday in response to the question: What did you do once you knew? How can you begin to act on that answer today?

APPENDIX A:
THIRTEEN KEY ACTIONS FOR CLIMATE-CONSCIOUS PARENTS

Now that you've finished the book, chances are, you might be wondering: *now what?* Many parents struggle with what to actually *do* about climate change once they've realized it's something they need to act on. While each of us has a unique role to play in the climate movement that will depend on our individual strengths and resources, here are a few steps I'd encourage every climate-conscious parent to take.

Actions to take in the next one to three months

I. **Join a climate community.** If you're reading this book, there's a good chance you've experienced climate distress, and you know how isolating these emotions can be. Finding a group of people who can hold space for conversations about climate emotions and/or work together to take climate action is one of the best things you can do for your mental health when it comes to climate distress. You might join a climate action group, like Citizen's Climate Lobby or Parents for Future, or join a group devoted to navigating climate grief, such as a Good Grief Network circle. You might start your own climate book club, or join a sustainability committee at your workplace. If the first group you try isn't exactly the right fit, keep trying. Ideally, you'll find a group that intentionally centers the voices and leadership of those most impacted by climate change, a group where you feel safe to be exactly who you are *and* challenged to grow and to act. And if you can find or create this community locally, even better—strengthening local ties is one of the most important ways to build climate resilience at the community level. (For a list of climate action communities, see Appendix F.)

2. **Imagine a better future.** What kind of future do you want? For yourself, for your children, for all children, for the world? When it comes to climate change, we've tended to focus on what we *don't* want for the future, or to engage in magical thinking that ignores the actual magnitude of the climate crisis. Individually and collectively, we need to practice using what adrienne maree brown calls our "radical imaginations" to cast visions for the kind of future we *want* to inhabit, in a way that also acknowledges the challenges we face. You might practice envisioning a positive future in the private space of your own journal, or you might brainstorm with a partner or trusted friend. Thinking of imagination as a *practice* is key: your vision will be iterative, evolving over time as you evolve and as the world around us shifts. Some questions to guide your visioning could include:

    • What do you hope your personal life looks like in ten to twenty years? In twenty to forty years? (For the purpose of this exercise, you can pick just one time point if that feels easier.)
    • What might an ideal day look like for you and your family in the future? How might your day-to-day lifestyle or relationships be different than they are now?

- What do you hope our collective life looks like in the coming decades? How do you hope current systems and ways of being have shifted?
- What role could you imagine yourself playing in the movement for climate action and climate justice in the coming years?

If you haven't already seen the film *2040*, I highly encourage you to check it out as an inspiration for your visioning practice. It's a "visual letter" from the filmmaker to his then-four-year-old daughter, offering a hopeful exploration of what the future could look like in 2040 if we embraced the best possible climate solutions we already have. Having a positive vision for the future in mind will help sustain you as you engage in climate action in the coming months and years.

3. **Take inventory.** For parents juggling the challenges of everyday life with small children, it's not always easy to carve out the space for deep reflection. But the challenges of the coming years demand that we meet them with clear eyes and clear hearts. See if you can find an hour of quiet time (or better yet, a quiet hour with a partner or trusted friend) to reflect on the following questions:

    - How are you spending your time, energy, and money? If you have the time, it can be helpful to sketch out a typical day, week, or month. You might also take a look at recent bank statements. What patterns do you notice?
    - What is your family's current carbon footprint? This is another way to look at how you're spending energy, in a very literal sense, and there are a number of carbon footprint calculators available online. I like the EPA's calculator, as it allows you to see in concrete terms how much you can save in terms of dollars and carbon emissions by making simple changes at home: https://www3.epa.gov/carbon-footprint-calculator/

- Is the way you're using your time, energy, and money right now in alignment with the future you want? What values are you honoring well right now? Where does your current life feel misaligned with those values?
- If nothing about the way you spend your time, energy, and money changed significantly in the next ten years, how would that impact the future?
- How do you want to act on your responses?

4. **Take action.** After reflecting on the questions above, choose a place to begin taking action in your own life. Sometimes, people will feel an intuitive nudge towards a particular next step: for you, maybe it makes the most sense to start at home, moving towards a plant-rich diet, reducing your overall carbon footprint, or reducing food waste. Maybe it's carving out an hour or two each week to devote to volunteering with a climate action group, getting involved in your local elections, or starting the process of figuring out how to divest your money from banks that invest in fossil fuels. Choose a starting place that feels challenging enough to inspire you, but not so challenging that it's unrealistic or overwhelming.

   If it's helpful to take to your journal or discuss this with a partner or friend, here are some questions and ideas that can support you in choosing an action you'll be successful with:

   - Where do you want to begin taking action? Is there a specific goal you'd like to set? When setting goals, it's often helpful to create a clear goal statement that's SMART: *specific, measurable, action-oriented, realistic,* and *time-bound.* In coaching, goals are often set with a three- to six-month time frame in mind, but for some climate-related goals, a shorter time frame may make more sense. Some example goal statements: (1) By the end of March, we will be eating a fully plant-based diet three days a week. (2) By the end of next month, we will reduce our household food waste by at least 25% through planning our meals. (3) By the end of this week, I will make an appointment with a climate-aware therapist. (4) By the end of this year, we will reduce our household carbon footprint by at least 25%.

- How does this goal or action align with your values and your hopes for the future?
- What personal strengths or past successes could help you with this goal or action?
- What barriers or obstacles could potentially arise? How might you overcome them?
- What "small wins" might support this goal or action? For example, if your goal is to move towards a plant-rich diet, small wins could look like buying a plant-based cookbook, trying a new meat or dairy substitute, experimenting with a new recipe, or dining at a plant-based restaurant.
- Who might offer support or accountability? (We're more likely to achieve our goals if we have others cheering us on!)

5. **Consider creating a family climate emergency plan—and start thinking about longer-term climate adaptations, as well.** One of the things that can cause the most anxiety when it comes to climate change is the fear of being in a natural disaster, such as a hurricane, flood, or wildfire. Knowing that you have a plan for dealing with climate threats, such as a go-bag for wildfires or an emergency kit for hurricanes, can go a long way towards easing that anxiety. If you haven't already spent time learning about how climate change is likely to affect your geographic region in the coming years, make this a priority. In the United States, the National Climate Assessment is a great place to start, as it breaks down climate impacts region by region. (Also, make it a priority to take care of yourself emotionally: this learning can be difficult to take in.) If you're in a geographic area that's under threat for specific natural disasters, identify

the concrete ways you could prepare ahead of time to make sure your family will be as safe as possible.

While a climate emergency plan can help you prepare for acute threats, climate adaptation invites us to think as well about how we might need to adapt the way we live on a day-to-day basis. The field of climate adaptation seeks to anticipate the adverse impacts of climate change and to proactively address them in order to minimize their potential damage. Around the world, climate adaptation efforts are already happening at the national, state, and local levels, but I think it's worthwhile for families to consider what adaptation could look like at the household level, as well. Some questions to consider:

- How is climate change likely to impact your job or career path? Are there changes you could make now to better prepare for these impacts?
- How is climate change likely to affect your local community and neighborhood? How might you help your community adapt to climate change? Your community may already have a climate adaptation plan—if so, it's worth taking the time to read it. If not, how could you advocate within your community for a climate adaptation plan to be created?
- How is climate change likely to affect your home or living space? Are there changes you could think about making that would help your home be more able to withstand climate threats?
- How might climate change affect your closest loved ones? How could you support them in thinking about how to prepare for climate change?

A note about emergency and adaptation planning: it can be easy to shift into a "prepper" mindset while thinking about these things, and I emphatically *don't* encourage that. The "prepper" movement, which encourages individuals to be prepared for apocalyptic climate disasters, tends to be highly individualistic, emphasizing personal survival over community resilience. In truth, your personal resilience in the context of climate change will be inseparable from the resilience of your community. It's possible to take personal preparation efforts seriously as a matter of responsibility while remembering that we also have a responsibility to support the well-being of our communities (and when we do, we'll all be better off for it).

Long-term commitments

6. **Commit to being a lifelong student of racial justice.** The issue of climate change is inseparable from racial justice: toxic, exploitative white supremacy is the root cause of both climate change and systemic racism. For far too long, white environmentalists have ignored or minimized the need to address racial justice in every aspect of climate solutions. The injuries of climate change already have and will continue to fall disproportionately on Black, Indigenous, Latinx, and Asian communities, and a just, equitable response to climate change must center these communities' needs, leadership, and voices. Many climate action groups are still disproportionately led and represented by white people, and there's much work to be done to dismantle white supremacy and white privilege within the environmental movement. As a white person, I know I will be doing this work for the rest of my life. Two great starting places for learning more about the connections between environmental justice and racism are the Intersectional Environmentalist website (www.intersectional environmentalist.com) and the Climate Justice Alliance (www.climatejusticealliance.org). Further reading suggestions can be found in Appendix E.

7. **Start thinking of yourself as a climate activist.** Most of our behaviors are driven by an internalized sense of identity. The way we live our lives on a day-to-day basis has a lot to

do with who we believe ourselves to be. Chapter 9 describes the idea of identity-based habits: if you want to set a goal to complete a marathon, it's going to be much easier to do if you think of yourself as a runner, and take small steps that reinforce this "runner" identity. Likewise, if you want to actively participate in climate solutions, you'll be much more effective in this endeavor if you think of yourself as a climate activist. (And if you don't like the word "activist," feel free to substitute another word that resonates more, like "advocate" or "change maker.") I've met many parents who shy away from the idea of activism because the identity of "parent" doesn't seem compatible with many of the stereotypes about activism, but I don't believe these two identities are mutually exclusive at all. Parents, fueled by a love for their children, are capable of a kind of fierce, determined, "failure is not an option" optimism that is powerful fuel for climate action. If you don't already, start thinking of yourself as a climate activist, and begin looking for the small wins that will help you reinforce this identity. (A small win I can't recommend highly enough: join a climate action group that meets regularly. Seeing other people who are committed to this new identity will go a long way towards helping you embrace it yourself.)

8. **Make your money count.** In order to transition to a just, sustainable world, we will need to divest our money from fossil fuels, both collectively and as individuals. Fossil Free (www.gofossilfree.org) is an organization supporting global fossil fuel divestment efforts, and offers a country-by-country guide to local divestment campaigns (as well as information about how to start one yourself!). Their website offers a comprehensive list of organizations and companies that have already made a commitment to divest from fossil fuels, from universities and faith-based organizations to companies and local towns. For individuals, two books that can help you learn how to shift your investments out of fossil

fuels are *The Do-Gooder's Guide to Investing*, by Adrian Reif, and *Investing to Save the Planet*, by Alice Ross.

If divesting your retirement investments from fossil fuels seems like a daunting place to start (I know it was for me—this is a step our family is still working on!), start smaller. Switch to an ethical bank for your everyday purchases and savings accounts. Switch to a socially and environmentally responsible credit card. One of my favorite resources in the United States for making your money count is Green America, which offers a user-friendly *Guide to Social Investing and Better Banking* to help people make the switch to greener banks and investments. You can find the guide online here: https://www.greenamerica.org/magazine/guide-socially-responsible-investing-and-better-banking

Other sustainable switches can help ensure that your money is contributing to a sustainable world. In some places, it's easy to switch to a renewable energy provider: SwitchIt, a U.K.-based global campaign to divert money from the fossil fuel industry, offers a simple tool to help consumers in the U.K. switch to renewable energy providers (they can also help with switching to ethical banking and investing; you can find them online here: www.switchit.money). Switching to a plant-rich diet is a way of making your money count. Choosing to buy everyday items like clothing, toys, and baby gear used instead of new is a way of making your money count. Choosing to avoid spending money on single-use plastics is a way of making your money count. Choosing not to buy things you don't really need—that plastic toy your child will forget in a week, that kitchen gadget you'll only use twice—that's a powerful way of making your money count, too.

Another powerful way to make your money count is to funnel any donations you make to environmental causes towards organizations working explicitly for environmental justice, like the Climate Justice Alliance (www.climatejustice alliance.org), which mobilizes communities on the front lines of climate impact to organize for a just transition.

These groups receive far less funding than mainstream climate organizations, thanks to systemic racism in the allocation of environmental funding, and are doing important work. Consider a monthly donation to a climate justice organization—even a small amount can make a difference.

Start where you are. While it can seem intimidating to think about all of the ways your money is connected with environmental harm, remember that every dollar you choose to redirect towards a sustainable future matters.

9. **Find support for your parenting.** Parenting is hard; parenting in a changing climate is harder. In the coming years and decades, climate change will present a multitude of stresses that will directly impact parents and families. When parents are under stress—as I'm sure you know well!—children struggle, too. And when our children struggle, our stress as parents increases even more.

Every parent deserves emotional and practical support in meeting the day-to-day challenges of parenting, though this support is often in short supply for a multitude of reasons. For me, the Hand in Hand Parenting approach has been invaluable in offering practical ideas for resilient, connected parenting. The Hand in Hand model focuses heavily on *parents'* need for support, encouraging practices like a *listening partnership*, in which two parents exchange intentional listening time with each other each week to offload the emotional challenges of parenting. Hand in Hand's model also includes practices like *staylistening* and *playlistening*, both of which help children process emotional difficulties with the support of an adult's attentive presence. While my own children are too young to have experienced climate anxiety directly yet, I can easily envision using Hand in Hand's approach to help them process climate distress as they get older, and I have used listening partnerships to help process my own climate distress. An easy introduction to this model is the book *Listen: Five Simple Tools to Meet Your Everyday Parenting Challenges*, by Patty Wipfler; the

Hand in Hand website (www.handinhandparenting.org) offers an extensive library of blog posts and classes for those looking to dive deeper.

Ideally, support for parents would extend far beyond the things we can do individually; sweeping systemic changes are needed to increase paid parental leave, ensure that every family has access to affordable childcare, and encourage employers to offer flexibility for working parents. Let's advocate for all of these changes, and in the meantime, find as much practical day-to-day parenting support as we can.

10. **Strengthen your local community and practice mutual aid.** While climate change is a global problem, it largely impacts us locally. The challenges faced in my home state of North Carolina will be distinctly different than those faced in California or Australia or the United Kingdom. And the challenges faced by wealthy white communities in any given geographic location will be distinctly different than those faced by communities of color, as was painfully illustrated by Hurricane Katrina in 2005. Our individual resilience in the face of future climate threats will be directly tied to our collective resilience, and to the quality of our relationships with others. In the future, we will need each other more than ever to stay safe and informed. If your town is hit by a heat wave or a storm-related power outage, for example, you can play a critical role in ensuring that vulnerable neighbors are safe. Knowing that there are people you can trust nearby in the event of a crisis can also go a long way towards supporting your mental health. It's your local friends and neighbors who will grieve with you if your town is hit by a devastating hurricane or wildfire, and your local community who can show up to share resources and keep spirits high.

If you don't already know your neighbors, it's time to meet them. Getting involved in local groups and projects— think community gardens, book clubs, neighborhood organizations, PTAs, kids' sports teams, or local events—can be a great way to build authentic, long-term relationships within your community. Another way to help strengthen your local community is to ensure that it has a climate resilience and adaptation plan. If such a plan exists, there's a good chance you can find it and read it online. If there isn't a climate resilience plan for your community yet, it's time to start advocating for one by contacting your city or town council.

Intentionally engaging in "mutual aid" is also a powerful way to cultivate climate resilience, actively dismantle systems of oppression, and to facilitate the transition to a more just, sustainable world. In systems of mutual aid, individuals work together to support the well-being of everyone in their community. "Mutual aid is a form of solidarity-based support," wrote journalist Amanda Arnold in a September 2020 article for *The Cut*, "in which communities unite against a common struggle, rather than leaving individuals to fend for themselves. While underserved and systemically oppressed communities have long organized mutual-aid networks, in the past year, the groups have proliferated across the country, and the concept has increasingly gained mainstream recognition." While charity often functions as a top-down handout that can reinforce power imbalances between "haves" and "have-nots," mutual aid embraces the idea that everyone in a community has something of value to contribute, and everyone in a community has needs.

While most of us understand the importance of self-care to resilience, far fewer of us—especially those of us who are white, straight, and cisgender—have lived experiences of offering or receiving community care, thanks to our capitalist, individualistic Western culture. In practice, engaging in mutual aid might look like building a network of fifteen to thirty community members with whom you are willing to commit to long-term relationship, and freely sharing skills and resources within your community "pod." You might offer to bring meals or pick up groceries for a community member who is ill, offer childcare support to a single parent who needs a break, or help translate for a neighbor who doesn't speak the dominant local language. In turn, you might gratefully receive extra tomato seedlings from a neighbor who loves to garden or a listening ear in a difficult moment. Emotional support is also a powerful part of mutual aid.

Mutual aid is not just for disaster situations, like COVID-19 or a hurricane, but much can be learned about the power of community networks in times of crisis. To learn more about the practice of mutual aid and community care:

- Mutual Aid Disaster Relief (a U.S.-based grassroots disaster relief network): www.mutualaiddisasterrelief.org
- Big Door Brigade (guide to mutual aid from organizer Dean Spade): www.bigdoorbrigade.com
- Milkwood Permaculture (Australian organization that offers courses on everyday permaculture, which prominently feature the concept of mutual aid and collective interdependence): www.milkwood.net
- Article: *COVID-19, the Climate Crisis, and Mutual Aid*: https://www.commondreams.org/views/2020/12/21/covid-19-climate-crisis-and-mutual-aid
- Article: *So You Want to Get Involved in Mutual Aid*: https://www.thecut.com/2020/09/what-exactly-is-mutual-aid-how-to-get-involved.html
- Book: *The Care Manifesto*, by The Care Collective

11. **Commit to long-term civic engagement.** Electing officials who care about the environment and will prioritize climate action at the levels of local, state, and federal government is critical to a successful collective response to climate change. Your vote matters more now than it ever has. Local elected officials will play a critical role in climate resilience and adaptation efforts in your own community. Look up the dates of your upcoming local elections for the year and put

them on your calendar. Commit to voting in every single local election from this point forward, not just presidential elections. Make sure you're registered to vote in your county, especially if you've recently moved, and make a point to research pro-environmental candidates before every election. If possible, donate your time and money to political candidates who are committed to addressing climate change and environmental justice. Encourage everyone you know to vote. One of my favorite ways to engage in get-out-the-vote efforts as a busy mother over the last few years has been writing postcards to voters (www.postcardstovoters. org). This is great to do while watching escapist television, in a group of friends, or with your kids (if they're anything like mine, they will love putting on the stamps!).

Troublingly, racist voter suppression efforts remain rampant in the United States, particularly in the South. You can support efforts to fight voter suppression by supporting Stacey Abram's organization Fair Fight Action (www. fairfight.com), which combats voter suppression in Georgia, and Black Voters Matter (www.blackvotersmatterfund. org), which works to increase voter engagement in Black communities. Another organization to consider getting involved with is the Environmental Voter Project (www. environmentalvoter.org), a nonpartisan get-out-the-vote group that encourages voters who care about environmental issues to make their voices heard at the polls.

12. **Spend time in nature with your kids—and cultivate wonder.** For both children and adults, being in intentional relationship with the natural world offers profound benefits in terms of mental, physical, and spiritual well-being. Children, especially young children, approach nature with an infectious sense of wonder that's both delightful and healing for adults to witness. In 2005, author Richard Louv coined the term "nature deficit disorder" to describe the human costs of alienation from the natural environment and to call attention to a disturbing trend: as more and more of our

lives have moved onto screens, we've spent less and less time outdoors. Recent research suggests that children spend an average of forty-four hours a week in front of screens and fewer than ten minutes a day playing outside, and access to green space is often limited by racial and socioeconomic disparities. The majority of adults report spending fewer than five hours a week outside as well. According to Louv, nature deficit disorder contributes to "diminished use of the senses, attention difficulties, higher rates of physical and emotional illnesses, a rising rate of myopia, child and adult obesity, Vitamin D deficiency, and other maladies." When we spend less time in nature, we are less resilient. We are also less connected to the planet we must act now to protect.

The wonder we experience in connection with the natural world, suggests ecologist H. Emerson Blake, is rarely given due attention in our hectic modern lives. "But maybe it's for just that reason—" he says, "how busy we are and distracted and disconnected we are—that wonder really is a survival skill. It might be the thing that reminds us of what really matters, and of the greater systems that our lives are completely dependent on. It might be the thing that helps us build an emotional connection—an intimacy—with our surroundings that, in turn, would make us want to do anything we can to protect them."

The simplest way to engage this step is to put away your screens, open your front door, and go outside. Another excellent resource for learning more about the importance of spending time in nature with children is the Children and Nature Network (www.childrenandnature.org), which supports leaders, educators, activists, and parents in moving towards a world where all children and families have safe, equitable access to nature.

13. **Practice grief.** We live in a culture that tends to disenfranchise and pathologize grief, and offers few practices for individual or collective healing. While grief isn't an "action step" that can be checked off a to-do list, it is a skill

that we can practice over time, and it's a necessary skill for living and parenting in a changing climate. We can practice grief by slowing down long enough to notice and acknowledge our own heartbreak. We can practice grief by writing about it in the pages of a journal, sharing it with a trusted confidante or group, or holding space for the heartbreak of another. We can practice grief by *allowing* our hearts to break at the systems of injustice and oppression that have caused so much harm to humans and the environment, rather than soldiering on as if everything is ok. As parents, we can practice grief by learning how to let our children grieve, rather than trying to fix their broken hearts with strategies designed to numb or distract them from their pain.

We experience grief to the extent that we have allowed ourselves to experience love; grief and love are inseparable twins. Many of the losses we will grieve with climate change will be surprisingly intimate, related to the loss of personally beloved people and places; other losses will feel broader in scope. Inevitably, these losses will continue throughout our lifetimes. Practicing grief now will help us to cultivate inner resilience and community resilience for decades to come.

My favorite grief resources include Being Here, Human, an organization that offers grief literacy classes for both individuals and professionals (www.beingherehuman.com); the work of my teacher Michelle C. Johnson, a social justice activist and yoga teacher whose latest book *Finding Refuge* explores practices for healing collective grief; and the Good Grief Network (www.goodgriefnetwork.org), which offers a unique ten-step support group to help individuals and communities cultivate resilience during these extraordinary times.

APPENDIX B:
CLIMATE CHANGE BASICS: TEN THINGS EVERY PARENT SHOULD KNOW

I'M GUESSING YOU ALREADY know a fair amount about climate change. Since you've picked up this book, you likely already understand that it's an issue that warrants concern and attention. But it's never a bad idea to review the basics, especially if you have children who are old enough to be asking questions: *Mom, I know the planet is getting warmer, but* WHY? Below are ten key ideas for parents to understand about climate change. (If you'd like to learn about climate science in more depth, I've included some of my favorite climate books in Appendix E.)

A fair warning: some of this may be difficult to read. While there *is* reason for hope (see #9 and #10 below), there is also ample reason for anxiety and grief. Know that whatever emotions arise for you as you read this part are normal, and take care of yourself accordingly.

I. **Climate change is real: the planet is getting warmer, and average warming trends are increasing over time.**
While there is still a vocal minority of climate deniers in

the United States, a striking 97% of climate scientists agree that climate change is real. Climate change is a fact, not an opinion. It's important to note that the *climate* is different from the *weather*. Climate describes long-term weather trends for a particular location, whereas weather describes the outdoor conditions on any given day. When scientists describe climate trends, they're looking at analyses of data that has been collected over a long period of time (generally, at least thirty years). On average, the planet is getting warmer every year, and these warming trends have increased sharply over the last twenty years. In 2020, the Earth's average global surface temperature was tied with 2016 as the hottest year on record, according to NASA.

The 2018 Intergovernmental Panel on Climate Change (IPCC) report found that if current warming trends continue, the earth is likely to reach an average of 1.5°C of warming between 2030 and 2052. While climate impacts and temperature changes won't be spread evenly around the globe, an average of 1.5°C of warming significantly raises the risk of adverse climate impacts, such as heat waves and extreme weather events. You can think of it like a fever: while an extra couple of degrees might not seem like a lot in terms of ambient outdoor temperature, a few additional degrees of body temperature when you're sick make a huge difference.

An excellent resource for learning more about the science behind climate change is climate scientist Katharine Hayhoe's series of videos about "global weirding." You can find them online at www.globalweirdingseries.com.

2. **Climate change is caused by human activities, especially the burning of fossil fuels.** The earth has experienced a range of climates in its long history, but the kind of climate change we're talking about here is indisputably human-caused. A key concept to understand when it comes to climate change is the *greenhouse effect*. Gases in the earth's atmosphere, such as carbon dioxide, trap the sun's heat

in much the same way that a glass roof traps heat in a greenhouse. We *need* greenhouse gases in the atmosphere in order to keep the earth at a livable temperature for human beings—the greenhouse effect isn't inherently bad! However, when we burn fossil fuels for energy, additional greenhouse gases are released into the atmosphere, and over time, they can end up trapping *too* much heat.

Human activities are impacting the climate in other ways, as well. Forests are an incredibly important *carbon sink* for the planet, absorbing carbon dioxide from the atmosphere as part of the process of photosynthesis. When forests are destroyed through intentional deforestation, we lose their capacity to absorb excess carbon from the atmosphere. The oceans are another critical carbon sink for the planet. In healthy ocean ecosystems, plants like seagrass and mangroves can absorb and hold carbon. The ocean also absorbs heat. But excess greenhouse gases in the atmosphere have exceeded the ocean's carrying capacity for carbon, leading to ocean acidification and the death of many ocean creatures, such as coral reefs.

3. **Climate change is making extreme weather events more common.** Scientists now know that increased global temperatures are making extreme weather events like wildfires, heat waves, droughts, and hurricanes more common. A recent analysis by Carbon Brief, a U.K.-based climate science website, found that of 405 extreme weather events documented in published, peer-reviewed scientific papers, 70% of them were found to have been made more likely or more intense by human-caused climate change.

When it comes to hurricanes, warmer ocean temperatures intensify the wind speeds of tropical storms, increasing the likelihood that they'll make landfall as stronger hurricanes, and warmer ocean temperatures have also been linked to hurricanes that produce more rain. The U.S. National Oceanic and Atmospheric Administration (NOAA) predicts that category four and five hurricanes may become more likely as the climate warms. (A science note: while *extreme* hurricanes are becoming more common, the science isn't yet clear on whether hurricanes themselves are becoming more frequent with climate change.) Climate change-related sea level rise means that coastal communities are more likely to be inundated with floodwaters when tropical storms and hurricanes hit, making these storms more damaging to infrastructure and dangerous for humans.

Climate change is directly related to an increase in extreme heat events. By mid-century, much of the world could see a dramatic rise in the number of days where the high temperature is above 90°F, leading to numerous risks to human health. Heat waves are the deadliest form of extreme weather in the United States, responsible for more deaths than hurricanes and floods combined. Extreme heat is associated with an increase in cardiovascular events, respiratory illness, and kidney disease, and is particularly harmful to outdoor workers, the elderly, low-income households, and children. Alarmingly, heat waves are also linked to poor pregnancy outcomes, such as an increased risk for preterm birth and stillbirth.

Increased temperatures are one way that climate change contributes to an increased risk for drought events, as warmer air increases evaporation from the soil. Hotter temperatures also increase evaporation from lakes, rivers, and other bodies of water. A 2015 Pew Research Center Survey found that of all the potential impacts of climate change, drought is the one that worries people the most. The risk of drought will not be evenly distributed around the world, however; in general, climate scientists expect the wetter parts of the world to get wetter in the coming decades, and the drier parts of the world to get drier. Drought can have a devastating impact on agriculture and the water supply, threatening food security and the livelihoods of farmers and agricultural communities. In communities living with food insecurity, households with children suffer the most.

Hot, dry conditions are also ideal for wildfires. Research shows the frequency of wildfires in the western United States has increased by 400% since 1970. Less predictable rainfall may make it more difficult to put these fires out once they've started, leading to significant damage to homes and infrastructure, and the devastating loss of life. In short, the extreme weather events that used to be considered "once in a lifetime" circumstances will become more and more commonplace, threatening existing infrastructure and testing our resilience.

4. **Extreme weather events and climate shifts contribute to "feedback loops" that worsen the problem.** One of the most troubling aspects of climate change—and there are many—is the existence of "feedback loops" in nature that are amplifying human's impact on the environment. An important example is melting glacial ice. Glacial ice acts as a cooling mechanism for the planet in several ways: not only does it cool the planet the way you'd cool your lunch with an ice pack, it also reflects sunlight because it's light-colored, limiting the amount of warming that sunlight can cause. Ice has a high *albedo,* meaning that it reflects most of the solar radiation that hits it back into the atmosphere. But as warming global temperatures cause ice to melt, darker-colored land and water is revealed below. Land and liquid water are low albedo surfaces, absorbing most of the sun's energy, and causing further warming. You can see how this is a vicious cycle: as warming temperatures cause ice to melt, the melting ice results in more of the sun's energy being absorbed by land and water, causing temperatures to rise even further and resulting in even more ice melting.

    Climate feedback loops are complex, and exist in many other systems—there are feedback loops in forests, soil, and permafrost, as well. An excellent resource for learning more about feedback loops is a five-part documentary series called *Climate Emergency: Feedback Loops.* The series is narrated by Richard Gere and available to watch online for free at https://feedbackloopsclimate.com/.

5. **Climate change is inextricably linked with other forms of environmental destruction, such as deforestation and biodiversity loss.** We won't be able to adequately address climate change without also addressing *all* forms of harm to the environment, from deforestation and biodiversity loss to land and air pollution. In part, this is practical: climate change and deforestation are dramatically increasing the rate of species loss, so fast that many scientists believe we are in the midst of a "sixth extinction." But stopping deforestation and protecting biodiversity are also climate solutions. Healthy, diverse ecosystems are better at sequestering carbon, and they strengthen the communities around them, increasing climate resilience.

    Aside from the practical reasons to address environmental destruction holistically, acknowledging that climate change isn't a standalone issue helps us to get closer to the root of the problem. *All* of the ways that we harm the planet are related to a fundamental disconnect from nature and a deeply internalized sense of entitlement to use and exploit the earth's resources. In his inspiring 2020 film *A Life on Our Planet*, celebrated naturalist David Attenborough explores the important connections between climate change and ecosystem loss, and powerfully advocates for "rewilding the earth." His eponymous memoir offers a clear call to action: "The next few decades represent a final opportunity to build a stable home for ourselves and restore the rich, healthy, and wonderful world that we inherited from our distant ancestors. Our future on the planet, the only place as far as we know where life of any kind exists, is at stake."

6. **The impacts of climate change will disproportionately harm vulnerable and oppressed populations around the world, including Black communities, Indigenous communities, and communities of color.** Just as the

COVID-19 pandemic has exacerbated already-existing social and health disparities, so will the climate crisis. Climate impacts will not be distributed equally or fairly, and globally, the communities that will feel the harshest impacts of climate change are those that have contributed least to the problem. Poor and marginalized communities have the fewest resources available to adapt to climate change, and often live in areas on the front lines of impact, such as flood-prone coastal neighborhoods or urban areas that are already suffering from air pollution. Waves of climate migration from drought-stricken Central America and North Africa have already begun, and are likely to dramatically increase in the coming decades as climate-related food insecurity worsens. Climate justice frames climate change as an ethical and political issue, and insists that climate solutions must be centered in justice and equity for all. Climate justice also acknowledges that the unjust political and economic systems that create social and racial inequities are the same systems that have created climate change, and tackling these systems must be part of addressing the root causes of climate change.

7. **The impacts of climate change will disproportionately harm children.** An obvious reason for climate change's disproportionate impact on children is that they will live longer than we will. Children born in the early part of the 21st century are likely to live past the mid-century time-point that scientists predict may herald a rapid increase in worsening extreme weather events. If we don't act now to mitigate climate change, our children will be left to deal with damage to the planet that may or may not be reversible decades into the future.

Climate change will also disproportionately harm children's health because of their smaller, still-developing bodies; this harm is already happening. Climate change is directly linked to poorer air quality. Rising temperatures and longer, more intense heat waves can increase ground level ozone, a pollutant that can cause asthma attacks in children. Warmer temperatures are contributing to longer, more intense pollen seasons that can trigger children's allergies. And poor air quality can have a devastating impact on children's health before they are even born. Globally, air pollution is linked to preterm birth, low birth weight, and 20% of newborn deaths. Hotter temperatures can make it dangerous for children to play outside due to an increased risk of heat-related illness, posing a barrier to children's need for exercise, sunshine, and fresh air.

Changing climatic patterns are also contributing to an increase in vector-borne diseases that threaten children, as the habitable range for vectors like the black-legged tick and the mosquitoes that carry dengue, malaria, and zika increases. These same changing patterns are linked to increased precipitation, stronger hurricanes, and larger wildfires. During and after severe rain events, flooding can promote the spread of diarrheal diseases that are especially dangerous for small children, and post-flood mold growth can threaten children's respiratory health. Agricultural systems are already being impacted by our changing climate, and households with children are at highest risk for food insecurity when food distribution pathways are disrupted. The trauma of living through major storms and other extreme weather events can have a harmful impact on children's long-term mental health, as can the prospect of worsening climate change itself. Children who live in vulnerable or marginalized communities, such as Black communities, Indigenous communities, and communities of color, are at increased risk for all climate impacts.

8. **We must act *now*. The next ten years are critical: what we do over the next decade will affect life on the planet for generations to come.** The IPCC's 2018 report described the impacts of different levels of global warming in stark detail. In no uncertain terms, the report made clear the importance of limiting global to 1.5°C, as higher levels of

warming—2°C or higher—would result in catastrophic extreme weather events and far greater levels of species extinction in the latter half of the 21st century. Meeting the 1.5°C warming target is critical, because at this level of warming, humans will have a far better shot at being able to adapt to a climate changed world. "Climate-related risks to health, livelihoods, food security, water supply, human security, and economic growth are projected to increase with global warming of 1.5°C and increase further with 2°C," the report states. "Poverty and disadvantage are expected to increase in some populations as global warming increases; limiting global warming to 1.5°C, compared with 2°C, could reduce the number of people both exposed to climate-related risks and susceptible to poverty by up to several hundred million by 2050."

Under the 2015 Paris Climate Accords, countries have promised to limit warming to well below 2°C, but this is already a lofty goal. Five years after the agreement, UN Climate Change reports that "current levels of climate ambition are not on track to meet our Paris Agreement goals." Urgent, justice-centered action is needed *now* to limit climate warming, and climate scientists agree that the next ten years are critical to protecting life on Earth for generations to come. If you're a parent of small children like I am, this may be especially difficult to take in: we can't postpone climate action until our children are older in the same way that we might be able to postpone other life goals or changes. We have to find ways to incorporate climate action into our lives and identities as parents *now*, because our children's futures depend on it.

9. **Climate solutions already exist!** Finally, some good news: the climate solutions we need to address global warming already exist. Project Drawdown's work shows that the world could reach drawdown—the future point in time when greenhouse gases in the atmosphere begin to decline—by mid-century, if we make the best use of the climate

solutions that are already available to us. We don't need to invent new technology to solve the climate crisis; we need to use the best technology and ideas we already have. As you've read in Chapter 8, some of the most important climate solutions are as simple as empowering women and girls, reducing food waste, and embracing plant-rich diets. The real work of addressing climate change is generating the political and social will needed to turn these ideas into our shared reality in the next decade.

10. **Public opinion is already on our side.** We are already well on our way to generating the social and political will we need. In the United States, data from the Yale Center for Climate Communication showed that in 2020, 63% of Americans were worried about global warming, and 71% were worried that global warming will harm future generations. Neither Americans nor Europeans believe their governments are doing enough to address climate change. While worry and dismay at the lack of government action doesn't necessarily translate into active civic engagement, it's fertile ground for a social movement. Political science researcher Erica Chenoweth has found that once 3.5% of a population is *actively* engaged in an issue through nonviolent means of civil resistance, positive change is all but inevitable. In other words, if those of us who say we care about climate change take bold, clear, consistent *action* on our values and bring others along with us, we have a pretty good chance of success.

APPENDIX C:
RESILIENCE-BUILDING EXPRESSIVE WRITING PROMPTS

E XPRESSIVE WRITING IS PROMPT-GUIDED writing about emotionally significant issues, written with therapeutic or healing intent. Often more structured than journaling, research has shown that expressive writing can offer powerful benefits to emotional and even physical well-being, including promoting resilience in trauma recovery. For many of us, climate change is or will be experienced as a trauma. And the stories we tell about trauma matter. As journalist Katie Orenstein says, "The story we tell becomes the world we live in." We need stories of resilience, resistance, and hope more than ever, and expressive writing is one way to cultivate these stories in our own lives.

Guidelines for writing

Expressive writing isn't meant to be shared with others. It's for your eyes only, unless you choose to share it, and there's no need to worry about spelling, structure, or grammar. Often, it's useful to use a timer to give yourself a "container" in which to respond to the prompt. Depending on the prompt, anywhere from two to twenty minutes may be an appropriate length of time. Try to keep writing in response to each prompt for the entire length of time, even if you find yourself repeating what you've already said—sometimes, new emotions or ideas will bubble to the surface unexpectedly. If you find yourself getting upset as you're writing and feel the need to take a break, please do so. Take a walk, stretch, get a glass of water, dance to a favorite song. And after writing, it's good practice to leave yourself as much space as possible for extra self-care. (Not always easy with little ones in the house, I know!)

The prompts below follow a loose progression. They're arranged in a specific order for a reason, but I also encourage people to use their intuition when engaging in expressive writing—if you feel particularly drawn to a prompt in the middle, start there, and see what comes up. You can tackle one prompt a day or even one prompt a week, or if you have a larger block of time, you can tackle several prompts at once. Take this at your own pace. You can't do this wrong.

After each writing prompt, whether you take them one at a time or choose to do several in one sitting, I strongly encourage a practice of reflecting on what you've written. Developed by writing researchers James Pennebaker and my mentor John Evans, the practice of writing post-writing reflections invites us to consider what the writing process was like for us. In each of the research and clinical settings that I've been a part of, I've heard writers express surprise at how many additional insights are gleaned from the post-writing reflections themselves. While it may seem like an unnecessary extra step, I encourage you to give it a try.

Post-writing reflection: Taking a mindful step back, write a few sentences about your experience of responding to the prompt: What did you notice? What surprised you? What felt difficult, and what flowed? How did your body feel as you wrote? *(Suggested time: two to five minutes, completed after each prompt)*

Prompts

Prompt 1: Write about a place you love. For the next several minutes, write about a place in nature that you deeply love. Consider all five senses in your writing: What are the sights, smells, sounds, tastes, and textures of this place? Who else in your life comes to mind when you think about this place? What meaningful memories does this location hold for you? What makes this place matter to you? *(Suggested time: five to ten minutes, followed by post-writing reflection)*

Prompt 2: Express difficult emotions. Write about your deepest thoughts and feelings about climate change. When did you first begin to understand the seriousness of climate change? What aspects of the climate crisis break your heart? What deeply-held values of yours are threatened? What do you fear or worry about the most, both for yourself and for others—for your children? How has climate change impacted your mental health, your relationships, and important life decisions? How is it related to other challenges you're aware of, personally or collectively? Try to use your writing time to explore the issues that are most personally significant for you at this time. *(Suggested time: fifteen to twenty minutes, followed by post-writing reflection)*

Prompt 3: Continue to express difficult emotions. After taking at least a brief pause after prompt 2 (a pause to complete the post-writing reflection is plenty), continue to write about what's hard or painful about climate change for you. Write about your climate-related anxieties, fears, regrets, shame, confusion, grief, trauma, or anything else that's present, even if you feel like you're repeating what you wrote in the first prompt. Keep going. *(Suggested time: fifteen to twenty minutes, followed by post-writing reflection)*

Prompt 4: Explore a new perspective. Now, write about your relationship to climate change from a different viewpoint. You might take the perspective of a future version of yourself, a wise friend or elder, a child, a divine ally, or anything else that comes to mind.

How could you see your own fears and worries differently? What unseen opportunities or gifts might be present in the challenges you and the world are facing? How could you view the climate crisis from a radically different perspective? *(Suggested time: fifteen to twenty minutes, followed by post-writing reflection)*

Prompt 5: Write a compassionate letter. Consider writing a letter of compassion to someone else, real or imagined, who might be struggling with the same challenges related to climate change that you are. Perhaps they're a busy parent who's doing the best they can to live up to their values around the environment, but also struggling to meet the demands of parenting day by day. Maybe they're someone who's struggling with the process of deciding whether or not to have an additional child. Or maybe they're someone who is feeling isolated or afraid. In your writing, empathize with the struggle your recipient is facing, acknowledging their challenges. You might also use the letter to name and encourage their strengths: their resourcefulness, resilience, integrity, their love for their children. Write as if the letter is for your eyes only, though you may choose to send it later if you wish. *(Suggested time: fifteen to twenty minutes, followed by post-writing reflection)*

Prompt 6: Read a poem, and respond. Read the following poems: "hieroglyphic stairway," by Drew Dellinger, and "Good Bones," by Maggie Smith (both are available to read online with a quick internet search). Both poems deal with themes of grief at the complicated reality of the world and how this influences our relationship with our children and grandchildren. In your writing, explore your emotional response to the poems. Which words or images stand out to you? Explore using the first line of each poem as a prompt. For example, "Life is short, though I keep this from my children…" might be a prompt for exploring what else you keep from your children; "it's 3:23 in the morning / and I'm awake" might be a prompt for exploring what keeps you awake in the darkest hours of the morning. You might even experiment with responding with a few lines of poetry of your own. *(Suggested time: fifteen to twenty minutes, followed by post-writing reflection)*

Prompt 7: Affirm strengths & resources. Each of us has a unique role to play in healing the climate crisis. We each bring an irreplaceable mix of personal experiences, strengths, talents, knowledge, connections, and other resources to the table. During the next few minutes, write about your own strengths and resources as they relate to climate change. See if you can write with the appreciation you would bestow upon a deeply respected friend. In what ways has life prepared you to play an active role in climate justice, healing, and resilience? How might your own strengths and gifts be of service to others—to your family, to your local community, and to the world? *(Suggested time: fifteen to twenty minutes, followed by post-writing reflection)*

Prompt 8: Personal vision for the future. When it comes to climate change, we often spend far more time focusing on our fears around the future than our hopes. In this writing exercise, see if you can explore a positive vision for your life in the context of climate change. What's a best-case scenario for you? How might you align your life with your most deeply-held values in a way that allows you and your family to thrive? What kind of person do you hope to become in the coming years? What kind of parent, activist, friend, partner, citizen? What might an ideal day look like for you, five or ten years into the future? What would help your children to thrive in a climate-changed world? Try to approach this writing exercise with an attitude of "stubborn optimism" or "active hope," acknowledging that while climate change *will* affect our future in profound ways, *how* it affects our future depends largely on our individual and collective action in the next several years. Use this prompt as a chance to practice using your hopeful, radical imagination. *(Suggested time: fifteen to twenty minutes, followed by post-writing reflection)*

Prompt 9: Write your own climate manifesto. A "manifesto" is a clear declaration of the intentions, motives, or views of its issuer, often written as an invitation to join the vision the writer wishes to make manifest. Considering your previous writing, write your own climate manifesto or mission statement. What is the story about your relationship to climate change that you want to carry into the future? What kind of world do you hope will be possible for your loved ones, community, and future generations? How will you contribute to creating this world with your unique gifts and resources? Try to tie together the threads of your writing from the previous assignments, and consider the prompts below as possible starting places.

I believe in a world where...
I believe in the value of...
I am creating a world where...
I will use my gifts to...
I will advocate for...
I will teach my children/future generations that...
I will leave behind...
I am committed to...

(Suggested time: fifteen to twenty minutes, followed by post-writing reflection)

Prompt 10: Mindful writing. The practice of mindfulness can help us to cultivate greater awareness in our lives. Mindful writing is an expression of compassionate, open-hearted, nonjudgmental awareness, often allowing us to witness our own inner experience with more clarity. This type of awareness is especially interested in how engaged we are in judging and categorizing our experiences and our patterns of reaction. In this writing of awareness, we are careful to simply notice judging as it comes up, not to judge the judging, simply to note its presence. Considering all that you've written about climate change so far, write in response to the prompt: "I am aware of / that..." You may wish to start each sentence of your writing with this prompt, or to respond in a less structured way. If you find yourself getting stuck, return again to the prompt and allow whatever arises to flow onto the page. *(Suggested time: ten minutes, followed by post-writing reflection)*

APPENDIX D:
FIVE MYTHS ABOUT PLANT-RICH DIETS (AND TIPS FOR MAKING THE SWITCH)

EMBRACING A PLANT-RICH DIET is one of the best things you can do for the planet—and it's also one of the best things you can do for your health. Plant-rich diets significantly reduce your carbon footprint, with Project Drawdown's findings suggesting that the traditional meat-rich Western diet is responsible for one-fifth of global carbon emissions. Research also shows that plant-based diets are linked to lower rates of chronic disease. While acceptance of plant-based eating has become far more widespread in recent years, many people are still hesitant to jump on board, thanks to a number of common misconceptions. Let's break them down.

Myth #1: It's expensive to eat a plant-rich diet.

Fact: For many people, eating a plant-rich diet is actually *less* expensive than eating a diet rich in animal protein. A recent survey of 1,072 Americans found that people eating plant-based diets spent an average of $23 less per week on grocery bills than people who eat meat. Plant-based proteins like beans, nuts, tofu, and tempeh tend to be less expensive than animal products, especially if you're cooking meals from scratch. While some people spend more on plant-based diets in the "learning curve" phase as they experiment with expensive animal protein substitutes, over time, it's a way of eating that can actually save money. It's also worth noting that in the United States, the government subsidizes the cost of meat to benefit the livestock industry, so the price that consumers pay for animal protein at the grocery store doesn't reflect its true cost.

Myth #2: Plant-rich diets are boring.

Fact: Plant-rich diets can be endlessly creative! Ditching or reducing animal products may inspire you to embrace a wider variety of produce and plant-based proteins as you experiment with new recipes and new ways of preparing old favorites. More and more restaurants are offering excellent plant-based fare, and there's no shortage of amazing plant-based cookbooks and mouthwatering food blogs. (You can find a list of the cookbooks we use the most at my house in Appendix E.) Mindfully embracing a plant-rich diet can also offer an opportunity to more intentionally honor the long chain of labor that went into getting food to our table, from the labor of migrant farmworkers to the work of the employees at your local grocery store. Eating with the well-being of the planet in mind can attune us to the well-being of others in multiple ways— and that's anything but boring.

Myth #3: It's impossible to get enough protein if you don't eat animal products.

Fact: According to the Physician's Committee for Responsible Medicine, most Americans consume *double* the amount of protein they actually need, often to the detriment of their health. Research has linked eating large amounts of animal protein with a significantly higher risk of death from diabetes and cancer than for those consuming less animal protein. While it does require some planning at first, it's absolutely possible for individuals of all ages and activity levels to meet their protein and other nutrient requirements on a plant-rich diet. (Some of the world's most elite athletes swear by plant-rich diets, like Ironman triathlete Brendan Brazier and ultrarunner Scott Jurek.) If you're concerned about making sure you or your children are getting your nutritional needs met on a plant-rich diet, don't hesitate to make an appointment with a dietitian or nutritionist who can help you create a meal plan that will work for your family.

For more inspiration about the health benefits of going plant-based, check out the 2011 documentary *Forks Over Knives*. The Forks Over Knives website is a fantastic resource for those who are new to plant-based eating: www.forksoverknives.com

Myth #4: It's not a meal if there's no meat.

Fact: Most of us were raised eating meat, and our food memories are often rich with emotion. If your mother or grandmother always insisted on "square meals" that included a serving of meat every time you sat down at the table, changing this habit may feel like rejecting a part of your family or cultural history. In truth, it's absolutely possible to eat a well-rounded diet that doesn't include animal products, and it's also possible to begin a transition to a plant-rich diet by starting out with meat substitutes like the Impossible Burger or any of Beyond Meat's delicious options. You may even find new ways to make your family's favorite recipes that taste just as good as the original version—with far less impact on the planet. When you find yourself resisting the idea of a meal without "real" meat, remind yourself that eating animal products is just a habit, and habits can be changed over time.

Myth #5: My kids/partner will never go plant-based, so this just won't work for our family.

Fact: While you can't force anyone else to embrace a plant-rich diet (trust me, I've tried), don't let your family's resistance stop you from making changes that will benefit your own health and the planet. If you make plant-rich eating look delicious, your family will eventually want to join in on the fun. And remember that for all of us, change takes time. Pediatric nutritionists tell us that young children often have to be exposed to new foods ten to twenty times before choosing to eat them. So if your kids have balked at tofu the first few times you've experimented with it, don't give up on them yet! Another way to encourage your children to try new foods is to get them involved in the cooking process. Kids love to cook, and they'll likely be eager to try a meal they've helped prepare. Try browsing through a family-oriented plant-based cookbook with your kids (like Dreena Burton's excellent *Plant-Powered Families*) and make plant-rich cooking a family affair.

Behavior change tips

The most important first step in making any behavior change is understanding your *why*. How does a plant-rich diet align with your values? How does it align with the future you want for yourself and the world? Once you have a clear understanding of what's inspiring you to reduce your consumption of animal products, starting with small, doable steps is key to long-term success. Here are some bite-sized ways to begin moving in the direction of a plant-rich diet:

- Check out a plant-based cookbook from the library.
- Explore plant-based food blogs.
- Make a list of recipes you'd like to try.
- Commit to trying one new recipe a week.
- Ask someone you care about to join you in reducing your consumption of animal products—making changes is always easier with a friend!
- If you're a research nerd like me, read the EAT-Lancet Commission summary report on Food, Planet, Health—I think you'll be as inspired as I was by the science behind why shifting towards a plant-rich diet is so important for the health of our planet: https://eatforum.org/eat-lancet-commission/

- Try one new plant-based meat or dairy substitute at the grocery store each week (a few of my personal favorites: anything by Beyond Meat, Follow Your Heart vegan cheese, and Ben & Jerry's non-dairy ice cream).
- Invite your friends over for a plant-based potluck.
- Join a local vegetarian group.
- If you're a fan of takeout, explore cuisine from another culture—Indian, Thai, Korean, and Ethiopian restaurants often have fantastic plant-based fare.
- Experiment with having one fully plant-based day each week, such as a "Meatless Monday."
- Try plant-based baking—I recommend banana bread and pumpkin bread as excellent starting places.
- If you're trying to get your kids to try new plant-based foods, experiment with food play, especially if they're younger or tend to be picky eaters. This was a technique taught to us by Milo's occupational therapist when he was going through an especially difficult picky eating phase, and it's backed by solid research. Food play is a form of "sensory-based food education," encouraging children to touch, smell, and taste a wide variety of foods. Researchers from Finland found that preschoolers who received sensory-based food education were more likely to choose fruits and vegetables from a buffet compared with children who didn't receive it. When you're trying to help your children expand their food repertoires, every interaction they have with a new food can be considered a small win—even if it takes time for them to fully embrace it.

APPENDIX E:
RECOMMENDED READING

Climate change

If you want to learn more about climate science and climate solutions, there's a wealth of fantastic books available. These are the ones I've found the most inspiring, motivating, and hopeful to read, and the ones I'd recommend without hesitation to parents. (Each of these would make a great read for a climate change book club!)

- *All We Can Save: Truth, Courage, and Solutions for the Climate Crisis*, edited by Ayana Elizabeth Johnson and Katharine K. Wilkinson

- *The Future We Choose: Surviving the Climate Crisis*, by Tom Rivett-Carnac and Christiana Figueres

- *The Parents' Guide to Climate Revolution: 100 Ways to Build a Fossil-Free Future, Raise Empowered Kids and Still Get a Good Night's Sleep*, by Mary DeMocker

- *Raising Elijah: Protecting Our Children in an Age of Environmental Crisis*, by Sandra Steingraber

- *A Field Guide to Climate Anxiety: How to Keep Your Cool on a Warming Planet*, by Sarah Jaquette Ray

- *How to Talk to Your Kids About Climate Change: Turning Angst into Action*, by Harriet Shugarman
- *Beyond Climate Grief: A Journey of Love, Snow, Fire, and an Enchanted Beer Can*, by Jonica Newby
- *The Future Earth: A Radical Vision for What's Possible in the Age of Warming*, by Eric Holthaus
- *From What is to What If: Unleashing the Power of Imagination to Create the Future We Want*, by Rob Hopkins
- *The Good Ancestor: A Radical Prescription for Long-Term Thinking*, by Roman Krznaric
- *Parents for a Future: How Loving Our Children Can Prevent Climate Collapse*, by Rupert Read
- *Drawdown: The Most Comprehensive Plan Ever Proposed to Reverse Global Warming*, edited by Paul Hawken
- *We Are the Weather: Saving the Planet Begins at Breakfast*, by Jonathan Safran Foer
- *Letters to the Earth: Writing to a Planet in Crisis*, multiple contributors
- *Our House is on Fire: Scenes of a Family and a Planet in Crisis*, by Greta Thunberg, Svante Thunberg, Malena Ernman, and Beata Ernman
- *On Fire: The Burning Case for a Green New Deal*, by Naomi Klein
- *Being the Change: Live Well and Spark a Climate Revolution*, Peter Kalmus

Racism, Indigenous voices, and environmental justice

Being an effective climate advocate requires becoming a lifelong student of racial and environmental justice. This is far from an exhaustive listing of the many excellent books about these topics, but a handful of the books that have had the biggest impact on me.

- *How to Be an Antiracist*, by Ibram X. Kendi

- *So You Want to Talk About Race*, Ijeoma Oluo

- *White Rage: The Unspoken Truth of Our Racial Divide*, by Carol Anderson

- *The Sum of Us: What Racism Costs Everyone and How We Can Prosper Together*, by Heather McGhee

- *Caste: The Origins of Our Discontents*, by Isabel Wilkerson

- *Raising White Kids: Bringing Up Children in a Racially Unjust America*, by Jennifer Harvey

- *This Book is Anti-Racist: 20 Lessons on How to Wake Up, Take Action, and Do the Work*, by Tiffany Jewell (aimed at youth ages 11 to 15, but also a helpful guide for parents)

- *Braiding Sweetgrass: Indigenous Wisdom, Scientific Knowledge, and the Teachings of Plants*, by Robin Wall Kimmerer

- *As Long as Grass Grows: The Indigenous Fight for Environmental Justice, from Colonization to Standing Rock*, by Dina Gilio-Whitaker

- *Climate Justice: Hope, Resilience, and the Fight for a Sustainable Future*, by Mary Robinson

Young children's books

There are far too many wonderful children's books about nature in general to list here, and as noted in Chapter 7, any books that encourage a sense of wonder and love for the natural world are excellent. The books below are a great starting place for introducing young children to the idea that we need to help protect the environment, and they can help gently initiate climate conversations.

- *We Are Water Protectors*, by Carole Lindstrom and Michaela Goade (ages 3-6)

- *Wangari's Trees of Peace: A True Story from Africa*, by Jeannette Winter (ages 3-7)

- *Our House is On Fire: Greta Thunberg's Call to Save the Planet,* by Jeannette Winter (ages 3-8)

- *Greta and the Giants*, by Zoe Tucker and Zoe Persico (ages 4-7)

- *Winston of Churchill: One Bear's Battle Against Global Warming,* by Jane Davis Okimoto and Jeremiah Trammell (ages 4-8)

- *The Boy Who Grew A Forest: The True Story of Jadav Payeng,* by Sophia Gholz and Kayla Harren (ages 5-8)

- *The Story of Climate Change: A First Book About How We Can Help Save Our Planet*, by Catherine Barr and Steve Williams (ages 5-8)

- *One Plastic Bag: Isatou Ceesay and the Recycling Women of the Gambia*, by Miranda Paul and Elizabeth Zunon (ages 5-9)

- *The Boy Who Harnessed the Wind* (picture book edition), by William Kamkwaba and Bryan Mealer (ages 6-8)

- *Our World Out of Balance: Understanding Climate Change and What We Can Do,* by Andrea Minoglio and Laura Fanelli (ages 8-12)

While not a book, *Bad Future, Better Future: A guide for kids, and everyone else, about climate change—and what we can do about it* deserves special mention. Written by science reporter Julia Rosen, this New York Times feature functions like an online book, and is beautifully illustrated by Yuliya Parshina-Kottas. You can find it online here: https://www.nytimes.com/interactive/2021/04/18/climate/climate-change-future-kids.html

Another great resource for parents who want to read to kids is Social Justice Books (www.socialjusticebooks.org), which has a number of carefully curated book lists for children, young adults, and educators.

Books to support resilient living, resilient communities, and resilient parenting

These books aren't necessarily about climate change, but they all speak to skills that will be much needed in the coming decades: navigating grief, strengthening community, parenting by connection, and loving the natural world bravely.

- *Finding Refuge: Heart Work for Healing Collective Grief,* by Michelle Johnson
- *Radical Joy for Hard Times: Finding Meaning and Making Beauty in Earth's Broken Places,* by Trebbe Johnson
- *Emergent Strategy: Shaping Change, Changing Worlds,* by adrienne maree brown
- *Active Hope: How to Face the Mess We're in Without Going Crazy,* by Joanna Macy and Chris Johnstone
- *Coming Back to Life: The Updated Guide to The Work That Reconnects,* by Joanna Macy and Molly Brown
- *The Community Resilience Reader: Essential Resources for an Era of Upheaval,* edited by Daniel Lerch
- *Hope in the Dark: Untold Histories, Wild Possibilities,* by Rebecca Solnit
- *Listen: Five Simple Tools for Meeting Your Everyday Parenting Challenges,* by Patty Wipfler

Plant-based cooking

There are *so* many excellent plant-based cookbooks available on the market these days, and once again, this list won't begin to do them justice. But these are the books we reach for most often at our own house—I have no doubt you'll find recipes you and your family will love in this collection.

- *Forks Over Knives: The Cookbook*, by Del Sroufe
- *Plant Powered Families: Over 100 Kid-Tested, Whole Foods Vegan Recipes*, by Dreena Burton
- *Minimalist Baker's Everyday Cooking*, by Dana Schultz
- *Clean Food; Clean Start;* and *Eat Clean, Live Well*, all by Terry Walters
- *The Oh She Glows Cookbook*, by Angela Liddon
- *The Joy of Vegan Baking*, by Colleen Patrick-Goudreau
- *Protest Kitchen*, by Carol Adams and Virginia Messina
- *The Homemade Vegan Pantry*, by Miyoko Schinner
- *Crazy Sexy Kitchen*, by Kris Carr and Chad Sarno
- *Eating Clean*, by Amie Valpone
- *Grub: Ideas for an Urban Organic Kitchen*, by Anna Lappe and Bryant Terry

APPENDIX F:
CLIMATE ACTION COMMUNITIES

I F YOU TAKE ANY single action after reading this book, I hope it's that you join a climate community. I recommend grabbing a favorite beverage and spending fifteen to twenty minutes browsing through the list below until you find at least one or two groups whose missions resonate with you. All are doing good work, but you may find that some approaches appeal to you more than others (and what matters most is that you find a climate community that encourages you to stay engaged in climate action for the long haul). Many of the groups below have local chapters around the world, and there's no better way to get involved in climate action than to connect with neighbors in local climate groups. If you're a member of a faith community, check to see if your denomination or place of worship has a group working on climate change or environmental issues—more and more, spiritual communities are connecting the dots between faith and our relationship with the natural world.

If you don't yet have the energetic bandwidth to join regular meetings, start by signing up for one or two email lists or following the groups that resonate with you on social media. And when you do attend your first climate community meeting, be sure to bring a friend.

Family-oriented climate and environmental groups

- 1000 Grandmothers: www.1000grandmothers.com
- Climate Action Families: www.climateactionfamilies.org
- Climate Dads: www.climatedads.org
- Climate Mama: www.climatemama.com
- Dear Tomorrow: www.deartomorrow.org
- EcoAction Families: www.ecoactionfamilies.life
- Elders Climate Action: www.eldersclimateaction.org
- Grandparents for Climate Action Now: www.grandparentscan.org
- Moms Clean Air Force: www.momscleanairforce.org
- Mothers' Climate Action Network: www.mothers-can.org
- Mothers Out Front: www.mothersoutfront.org
- Our Kids Climate: www.ourkidsclimate.org
- Parents for Future: www.parentsforfuture.org
- Science Moms: www.sciencemoms.com

General climate and environmental groups

- 350.org: www.350.org
- Citizen's Climate Lobby: www.citizensclimatelobby.org
- Climate Action Network International: www.climatenetwork.org
- Climate Coaching Alliance: www.climatecoachingalliance.org
- Climate Generation: www.climategen.org
- Climate Justice Alliance: www.climatejusticealliance.org
- Climate Reality Project: www.climaterealityproject.org
- EarthJustice: www.earthjustice.org
- Environmental Defense Fund: www.edf.org
- Extinction Rebellion: www.rebellion.global
- Fridays for Future: www.fridaysforfuture.org
- Friends of the Earth International: www.foei.org
- GenderCC – Women for Climate Justice: www.gendercc.net
- Good Grief Network: www.goodgriefnetwork.org
- GreenPeace: www.greenpeace.org
- Health and Environment Alliance: www.env-health.org

- Indigenous Environment Network: www.ienearth.org
- Julie's Bicycle: www.juliesbicycle.com
- Natural Resources Defense Council: www.nrdc.org
- Naturefriends International: www.nf-int.org
- Oceanic Global: www.oceanic.global
- Our Climate Voices: www.ourclimatevoices.org
- Pachamama Alliance: www.pachamama.org
- Project Drawdown: www.drawdown.org
- Rainforest Action Network: www.ran.org
- Sierra Club: www.sierraclub.org
- Stop Ecocide: www.stopecocide.earth
- Sunrise Movement: www.sunrisemovement.org
- World Wildlife Fund: www.worldwildlife.org

APPENDIX G:
LETTER TO A GENERATION OF GRANDPARENTS

Dear Grandparents,

I'll get right to the point: we need you in the climate movement.

When I first became pregnant, one of the moments I most looked forward to was the moment I would get to watch my own parents transform, crossing the threshold from *parent* to *grandparent*. I've heard many who have crossed this threshold say that being a grandparent is different. That as a grandparent, you love your grandchildren in a way that you didn't have the capacity to love before. That grandparent love is abundant, unfettered, full of delight.

I am profoundly lucky to have received this kind of love from my own grandparents, all of whom have now passed. And it has been an extraordinary gift to watch this new kind of love emerge in my parents. Some of the photos I treasure most from the early days after the twins' birth are the pictures of my parents holding them. Of my mother looking with awe and adoration at a tiny, swaddled bundle in the NICU; of my father, beaming and draped with two sleeping babies on our couch at home. I treasure the wobbly iPhone video we recorded of the first time my husband's parents saw the babies. Veteran grandparents, they were just as enchanted by the twins as if they hadn't already watched six grand-children grow up.

Grandparents, you are magic. As Alex Haley said, "Nobody can do what grandparents do. Grandparents sort of sprinkle stardust over the lives of little children."

(You also, as I have discovered, sprinkle toys. Most of them we have loved. Mom and Dad, I have still not completely forgiven you for the plastic, remote-controlled race cars whose off-tune electronic jingles sometimes start whining on their own from odd corners of the house, but that's a conversation for another day.)

Yet I'm increasingly worried that *I* won't get to experience being a grandparent. That I won't get to cross the same magical threshold in my later years. The threat of the climate crisis is, quite understandably, frightening more and more young people away from the idea of having children at all. If we cannot get the climate crisis under control while there is still time, the experience of loving grandchildren may become as rare and unique as I'm told the experience *feels*. I am heartbroken when I think about this possibility.

So grandparents, we need you in the climate movement.

We need your time, your energy, your resources. We need your wisdom, skills, and influence. We need you to join climate groups, to organize within your faith communities, to call your representatives and demand climate action. We need you to work alongside of us to reduce your carbon footprints, divest from fossil fuels, and mobilize your social groups to do the same. We need you to shout from the rooftops that all future generations—mine, my children's, and all those yet to come—deserve the chance to become grandparents, too.

And of course, we need your love. Our *children* need your love, that particular flavor of stardust that is uniquely yours. (But maybe, just maybe, fewer battery-operated plastic toys?)

Thank you for everything.

With love and deep respect,
Elizabeth

APPENDIX H:
BOOK CLUB DISCUSSION GUIDE

I T'S MY DEEPEST HOPE that *Parenting in a Changing Climate* is a book that will be read and discussed in community. I'm a believer in the power of conversations about climate change, as you've no doubt gathered through reading the book. Climate conversations can broaden our awareness, help shift social norms, invite creative thinking, promote individual and community resilience, and perhaps most importantly, help us feel less alone as we navigate this challenging territory.

One approach for a book club would be to read the book week by week, chapter by chapter, following each chapter's reflection prompts as a guide for group discussion. (If you're a busy parent, taking the book one chapter at a time may feel most doable!) Another approach would be to discuss the entire book at once in a longer session, if a weekly commitment is unrealistic. Below are sample structures for discussion:

Sample book club structure:
Eleven weeks, week-by-week format
Suggested time per session: Sixty to ninety minutes

- **Icebreaker & introductions:** Begin with icebreaker and introductions (spend more time on introductions in the first week; in subsequent weeks, use introduction time for name reminders as long as needed).

- **Group guidelines:** Set group guidelines, and ask for group feedback and agreement.
- **Discussion:** Depending on how much time you have, you can either move through discussion of each question from the week's chapter reflection section or pick a few that feel most relevant. The first week would include discussion of both the introduction and Chapter 1.
- **Closing:** Invite each participant to share one word, idea, perspective, or action step that they're taking away from the week's discussion, and remind participants of the following week's meeting time. If there's time, invite participants to share how they will be cultivating joy and/or resilience in the coming week.

Sample book club structure:
Discussion of entire book at once

Suggested time: Two to three hours

- **Icebreaker & introductions:** Begin with icebreaker and introductions.
- **Group guidelines:** Set group guidelines, and ask for group feedback and agreement.
- **Discussion:** I suggest dividing discussion into three segments, with one segment devoted to each section of the book (*Pain*, *Possibility*, and *Practice*). The book club organizer may wish to spend some time in advance selecting one or two questions from each chapter to guide discussion.
- **Take breaks:** In a longer discussion, breaks are essential. Encourage participants to take breaks as needed, but also invite a group break midway through the discussion.
- **Closing:** Invite each participant to share one word, idea, perspective, or action step that they're taking away from the discussion. If there's time, invite participants to share how they will be cultivating joy and/or resilience moving forward.

General book club tips

- **Ideal size:** In my experience, the ideal size for a book club is between two and ten people, as this allows space for everyone's voices to be heard in discussion.

- **Group guidelines:** Setting group guidelines or agreements in the first session (or at the beginning of a single-session discussion) can go a long way towards creating an environment of safety and trust. Some guidelines you may wish to name include honoring confidentiality within the group, requesting that participants not offer unsolicited advice to others, speaking from the heart, allowing equal time for everyone to speak, and in online settings, encouraging participants to remain on mute when not speaking to minimize background noise.

- **Welcome children:** Since this is a book aimed at parents, there's a good chance some participants will have to navigate childcare during discussion sessions. Naming up front that kid interruptions are expected and welcome (particularly in online settings, where participants may be coming to the discussion from their own homes) can help create an environment that is supportive of parents with young children.

- **Inclusive nametags:** Providing nametags that have a space for participants to indicate their correct pronouns (or putting your pronouns in your name on platforms like Zoom) is a step towards inclusivity.

- **Icebreakers:** Icebreakers are a wonderful chance to help a new group get to know each other. For this context, I love icebreaker questions that relate to the natural world, such as, "What are you noticing in nature this week?" or "When was the last time something in the natural world made you smile?" Icebreakers are also a great opportunity to introduce a note of humor and levity to a potentially heavy discussion. You might ask participants with young children, "What's the funniest thing your child did this week?" or, "If you had to parent as an animal, which animal would you want to be?"

- **Sensitive topics:** This book touches on difficult and sensitive topics, such as infertility, pregnancy loss, and reproductive choice. If you are leading a group, it may be helpful to know in advance if any of your participants are in the middle of actively navigating any of these things, and to ask them what you can do to ensure that they feel safe and supported during conversations that may touch on these subjects. It may also be helpful to consider in advance how you might handle discussions about family size (or, how you might choose in advance *not* to explicitly discuss this, if it is likely to feel like a charged topic within your particular group). I encourage adopting an attitude of unconditional support for the decisions (and decision-making processes) of everyone in the group.
- **Mental health support:** Please encourage all members of the group to seek out professional support if difficult or unmanageable emotions arise in discussions of climate change. Climate distress is a *normal* response to environmental destruction. While it's been my experience that open, supportive conversations about climate change are often helpful for mental health, as they provide space for processing difficult emotions in community, sometimes an additional layer of support is needed. Don't hesitate to check in privately with group members who may be struggling. Finding a climate-aware therapist (such as those listed in the Climate Psychology Alliance directory: https://www.climatepsychology.us/climate-therapists) can powerfully support this work.
- **Encourage joy and resilience practices:** Throughout the discussion of a book like this, it can be helpful to focus intentionally on cultivating personal resilience, recognizing that your individual resilience and well-being has a direct impact on your ability to contribute to the well-being of your family and community. If there is time at the end of a discussion, you might ask participants, "How will you practice joy this week?" or "How will you tend to your own resilience?"

- **Keep reading:** If reading *Parenting in a Changing Climate* is your first experience with a climate-related book club, don't let it be your last. There's a growing number of extraordinary books on climate change, many of which would make excellent book club books (such as *All We Can Save, A Field Guide to Climate Anxiety,* and *The Future We Choose,* just for starters). Keep reading and talking about climate change with others—these discussions matter.

If you do read *Parenting in a Changing Climate* with others, I'd be delighted to hear about your reading communities! Use the hashtag **#parentinginachangingclimate** on Instagram to share photos, or reach out to me via my website (www.elizabethbechard.com) to share more about your experience. I hope you'll enjoy reading this book as much as I have enjoyed writing it.

ACKNOWLEDGEMENTS

THIS MAY SEEM LIKE a strange place to begin an acknowledgements section, but stay with me: I am grateful, first and foremost, for the butterflies.

Less than a month after completing the manuscript for this book, we found ourselves in the midst of a harrowing health crisis with Milo that was eventually diagnosed as pediatric acute-onset neuropsychiatric syndrome, or PANS. I spent the evening of my sixth Mother's Day in a padded chamber of the local emergency room with Milo, panicked and undone by his sudden, shocking change in behavior. Later that week, just hours after bringing him home from the emergency room for the second time, I was sitting in our dining room—exhausted, heartbroken—when a small flutter of motion caught my eye. The fish tank-turned-terrarium that had housed Heimlich and his fellow caterpillars the previous summer had been sitting empty in our dining room for months, save a thin layer of dirt at the bottom. Or at least, we *thought* it had been empty. That afternoon, on one of the very worst days of my life, a butterfly that had been overwintering in the fish tank for nine months—entirely unbeknownst to us—crawled out of its chrysalis, wings crumpled but determined. The twins knew exactly what to do. We brought the tank outside, took the butterfly out, and Milo held it as it tried to fly, his hands gentle for the first time in weeks.

I have learned that in moments of crisis, sometimes things are not as they seem on the outside. That what looks like a thin, barren layer of dirt might just be incubating a tiny miracle. That sometimes, miracles overwinter. I have learned that we are connected with the natural world in ways that we cannot yet begin to fathom. I have learned to trust the butterflies and their strange, surprising journey of becoming. And I am so grateful for them.

The community that showed up for my family with such love and support during Milo's health crisis—sending meals, offering childcare and healing skills, listening to me as I wept with fear and grief—was the same community that showed up with so much love and support throughout the process of writing this book. I'm deeply grateful for my incredible community of friends and colleagues, many of whom were early readers for the manuscript. Words feel painfully inadequate to express this gratitude, but I'll try. I offer my sincere apologies in advance for anyone I may inadvertently leave out.

Alaya, our conversations about the environment and motherhood over the past few years were one of the biggest inspirations for writing this book. Thank you for countless Marco Polo exchanges that always make me feel seen, for introducing me to Hand in Hand Parenting, for being an early reader with such a keen eye, and for being such a beloved friend.

Stacey, there isn't a day that goes by that I am not grateful for your friendship. You've been one of the steadiest forces of love, compassion, and authenticity in my life for so long, and I can't imagine doing life without you. Thank you for being an early reader and giving such good feedback. And mostly, thank you for just being you.

Jessie, thank you for twenty years of friendship, long walks and runs, and deep conversations about pretty much everything. Thank you for being one of the bravest truth-tellers and paradigm-challengers I have ever met, and for knowing that after the spring from hell, an ant farm was just what our family needed.

Mark, thank you for teaching me so much about what it means to listen. You've been the one listening on the other end of the phone line during most of the best, worst, and weirdest moments of my life over the last several years, and you've cheered on even my craziest ideas (like writing a book in the middle of a pandemic!) as if they made all the sense in the world. I am so glad you are in my life.

Megan, your friendship has been such an anchor for me over the past decade, and it has been an absolute joy to experience motherhood with you. Thank you, soul sister, for your constant support, for being an early reader for the book and giving such incredible feedback, and for sending us pizza all the way from California when Milo was sick. You're the best.

Alix, our conversations about climate change and motherhood influenced so much of this book. Your vulnerability and heart and fierce love for the world make me so grateful to count you as a friend. Thank you for being you.

Gael, you have taught me more than anyone else about what it means to love children who are different, and to understand how perfect and divine these differences are. Our exchanges always anchor me in the magic of the world and I am so grateful for you.

Marla, fellow eco-warrior, you inspire me every day with your work in the world. Thank you for being with me on this path of transformation and for being such a steady friend for almost two decades. I can't wait to see what you do next.

Dana, you were the first mom friend I talked to about climate change in a way that made me feel seen and understood in my grief and alarm. Our first conversation about climate change—and a shared love for Sandra Steingraber's writing—gave me the courage to keep talking.

Erica, you have been on the path of fighting for the environment for so much longer than I have, and your fierce dedication to understanding and protecting the natural world has been an inspiration to me since high school. Our conversations about climate change changed everything for me. I'm so grateful for your friendship.

Ruth, fellow twin mama and dear friend, thank you for taking that picture of me holding your babies years ago. The rest is history.

To my little book club community—Shivani, Patty, Stacy, Melissa, and Jen—thank you for being a safe space to talk about hard things, from climate change to motherhood. You've convinced me that reading books and talking about them in community is exactly the medicine the world needs right now, and I can't wait to keep reading with you.

I'm deeply grateful to all of the friends who offered me feedback and cheered me on at various stages of this project, including Teresa, Marion, Katherine, Mary, Mara, Maureen, Megan, Liz, Rachel, Kristen, Whitney, Jody, Anna, Kim, Patty, Caroline, Abby, Jenny, Marie, Susan, Kat, Heather, and Sarah. Your words shaped and clarified my ideas, and your support inspired me to keep going even in the moments when writing felt impossible. Jonica, thank you for sending me photos of parrots, echidnas, and kangaroos all the way from Australia during the final stretch of this book marathon! I'm grateful to everyone I've met in the Hand in Hand Parenting community, especially Kelly, Shelley, Marcie, Kathy, and Marilupe: each of you has supported me the way every parent deserves to be supported, and I'm a better mother because of you.

I am grateful for my teachers, mentors, and guides. Sherrie Dillard, thank you for your clear vision and encouragement to keep going. Janet Raftis, thank you for your love and for reminding me that I've never been alone. Michelle Johnson, you are magic. Thank you for all of you have taught me about justice, liberation, and grief—I know I will keep learning from you for years to come, and your influence is throughout this book. My understanding of grief has been shaped, too, by the rich teachings of Rachelle Bensoussan and Michelle Williams of Being Here, Human and by the deep work of Amy Wright Glenn of The Institute for the Study of Birth, Breath, and Death.

John Evans, thank you for being a mentor and colleague for so many years, and for your rich body of work with expressive writing. You have taught me so much about legacy.

I am so grateful for my clients. You know who you are, and I love each one of you so much. It has been an honor to bear

witness to your hopes, your fears, your grief, and your love. Our
conversations have shaped me in so many ways, and this book
would never have happened without you.

I am so grateful to my incredible colleagues, especially my
friends in the climate change coaching community. To my CCC
friends—Charlotte, Katie, Peter, Anne-Marie, May, and Max—
thank you for holding space with me for so many months to talk
about what it means to be a coach and changemaker during these
extraordinary times. Thank you for unconditionally believing in
me in a way that made me think I could actually write a book.
Katie and Peter, thank you especially for being early readers of
the book and for such enthusiastic support. I'm beyond lucky to
know each one of you.

To Charly Cox and Sarah Flynn, thank you for your innovative work with the Climate Change Coaches, which was my first
introduction to the idea that coaches could be changemakers in the
climate movement. I'm deeply grateful to have been your student
at exactly the right time—you are powerful catalysts.

To my Game Changer Intensive colleagues, thank you for
sharing space for such important conversations over the past year
and for offering deep encouragement and support. I am especially
thankful for Eve Turner. Eve, your work with the Climate Coaching Alliance and the way you show up in the world inspires me
every day. I feel profoundly lucky to have met you.

To the Wayfinders—Megan, Ed, Becca, Marc, Anne Jo,
Theresa, Laura, Carol, Niko, and Julia—thank you for incredible conversations, for seeing me as the person I most wanted to
become, and for believing in me in moments when I found it hard
to believe in myself. You landed in my life at the perfect moment.

To the NBHWC DEI committee, I am so lucky to know each
one of you. Thank you for showing me what it feels like to dream
in community.

To everyone I have met through Citizen's Climate Lobby and
the Climate Reality Project, thank you for modeling what it looks
like for everyday citizens to show up for climate activism. I have
drawn inspiration and hope from each one of you. To my teachers and colleagues from the Yale Climate Change and Health

Certificate program, thank you for doing such important work in the world and for inspiring me to go back to graduate school to study public health.

I'm deeply grateful to the women who started writing and talking about climate change, environmental crisis, and environmental justice long before I did, because their voices made me believe that my voice might matter, too. I bow especially to the influences of Sandra Steingraber, Joanna Macy, adrienne maree brown, Sarah Jaquette Ray, Harriet Shugarman, Mary DeMocker, Ayana Elizabeth Johnson, Naomi Klein, Katharine Wilkinson, Leslie Davenport, Renee Lertzman, Britt Wray, and Katharine Hayhoe. I'm grateful for the influence of Elizabeth Cronise McLaughlin, who daily #ResistanceLive broadcasts and activist training helped me to see myself as an activist again for the first time in years. I am deeply grateful, too, for the extraordinary network of climate activists of all genders around the world whose work inspires me every day. Each one of you reminds me that I'm not alone and that together, we *will* make the world better for our children. Thank you for your work in speaking truth to power.

I'm beyond grateful to my little book team that has made my dream of being an author come true. Penelope Love, thank you for your friendship and the extraordinary love and support you put into your work at Citrine Publishing. I couldn't have asked for a better publishing partner than you; I'm so glad the stars aligned for us. And none of this would have happened without the support of Stacy Walsh, my editor and writing coach. Stacy, you were the first person I told when the surprise butterfly showed up. Thank you for understanding what I was trying to do with this book right from the beginning, and for encouraging me to throw out that first draft and write from my heart. I am so glad to know you.

Finally, thank you to my family. It is for you, most of all, that words feel inadequate. I am grateful for my incredible in-laws, who offered steady love and support from Vermont during a year that the COVID-19 pandemic kept us from visiting. I am grateful for my parents, who encouraged me in this project every step of the way, read early drafts, started composting, planted a garden, and wrote hundreds of postcards to voters with me. I am grateful to my loved ones who have passed, and especially to my grandmother, great aunt Anne, and Haven: your deaths broke me open, but I have felt your presence with me every single day. Carlton and Connie, you are like family to me too. Thank you for inviting me into your home on a February day that I'll remember forever.

To my husband, Bart: none of this would have happened without your unfailing love and support. Thank you for being my first reader for every chapter, for letting me tell a story that is really our story, for patiently making breakfast for the kids on so many early mornings while I sat on the couch typing away and trying to ignore the rest of the family. Thank you for buying me those noise-cancelling headphones. Thank you for loving me so well, every day. I love you.

Minnie and Milo, you are my life's very best teachers. Thank you so much for choosing me to be your mama. Minnie, as I'm writing this, we are sitting outside on the deck on a summer day and you are collecting basil and mint from our garden as if you were born knowing how to make magic with plants. Your deep love for the natural world and your innate ability to find and create beauty under any circumstances makes my world—our world—a better place every day. I love you.

And Milo, you are, as always, searching for small, crawling things. Your sensitivity, your intense curiosity, and your fierce devotion to anything that might catch your interest are superpowers I will do everything I can to protect. You remind me every day that people who experience the world differently than most are exactly the medicine the world most needs. I love you.

SELECTED REFERENCES

Introduction

1. "Australia Fires: Life during and after the Worst Bushfires in History." 2020. BBC. April 2020. https://www.bbc.co.uk/newsround/52410744.

2. "North Carolina Climate Blog." n.d. *North Carolina State Climate Office* (blog). Accessed April 21, 2021. https://climate.ncsu.edu/climateblog/.

3. "Overview of Durham History - Museum of Durham History." n.d. Museumofdurhamhistory.Org. Accessed July 14, 2021. https://www.museumofdurhamhistory.org/learn/overview-of-durham-history/.

4. Office of Legacy Management. n.d. "Environmental Justice History." Energy.Gov. Accessed April 15, 2021. https://www.energy.gov/lm/services/environmental-justice/environmental-justice-history.

5. Ray, Sarah Jaquette. 2021. "Climate Anxiety Is an Overwhelmingly White Phenomenon." *Scientific American*, March. https://www.scientificamerican.com/article/the-unbearable-whiteness-of-climate-anxiety/.

6. Holden, Emily. 2019. "'A Lot at Stake': Indigenous and Minorities Sidelined on Climate Change Fight." The

Guardian. October 3, 2019. https://www.theguardian.com/world/2019/mar/10/environment-climate-change-movement-indigenous-minorities-sidelined.

Chapter 1: Waking Up to Climate Change

7. Peach, Sara. 2020. "A Fertility Coach on Having Kids in a Time of Climate Change." Yale Climate Connections. June 26, 2020. https://www.yaleclimateconnections.org/2020/06/a-fertility-coach-on-having-kids-in-a-time-of-climate-change/.

8. Watts, Jonathan. 2018. "We Have 12 Years to Limit Climate Change Catastrophe, Warns UN." The Guardian. October 8, 2018. http://www.theguardian.com/environment/2018/oct/08/global-warming-must-not-exceed-15c-warns-landmark-un-report.

9. WWAY News. 2018. "Florence 'Has Forever Changed the Landscape' of Oakdale Cemetery." WWAY3. September 27, 2018. https://www.wwaytv3.com/2018/09/27/florence-has-forever-changed-the-landscape-of-oakdale-cemetery/.

10. Steingraber, Sandra. 2013. *Raising Elijah: Protecting Our Children in an Age of Environmental Crisis*. London, England: Da Capo Press.

11. Friedman, Thomas L. 2010. "Global Weirding Is Here." The New York Times. February 17, 2010. https://www.nytimes.com/2010/02/17/opinion/17friedman.html.

12. "Australia Fires: Life during and after the Worst Bushfires in History." 2020. BBC. April 2020. https://www.bbc.co.uk/newsround/52410744.

13. Duncan, C. 2019. "Researchers Say NC May Feel like Florida from Climate Change." The News & Observer. February

15, 2019. https://www.newsobserver.com/latest-news/article226204535.html.

Chapter 3: Risk Perception and our Children's Health

14. Eibach, Richard P., and Steven E. Mock. 2011. "The Vigilant Parent: Parental Role Salience Affects Parents' Risk Perceptions, Risk-Aversion, and Trust in Strangers." *Journal of Experimental Social Psychology* 47 (3): 694–97.

15. Marshall, George. 2015. *Don't Even Think about It: Why Our Brains Are Wired to Ignore Climate Change.* New York, NY: Bloomsbury.

16. Stoknes, Per Espen. 2015. *What We Think about When We Try Not to Think about Global Warming: Toward a New Psychology of Climate Action.* Chelsea Green Publishing Company.

17. Stoknes, Per Espen. 2017. *How to Transform Apocalypse Fatigue into Action on Global Warming.* USA: TED. https://www.ted.com/talks/per_espen_stoknes_how_to_transform_apocalypse_fatigue_into_action_on_global_warming.

18. Howe, Peter, Matto Mildenberger, Jennifer Marlon, and Anthony Leiserowitz. 2015. "Yale Climate Opinion Maps – U.S. 2014." Yale Program on Climate Change Communication. November 16, 2015. https://climatecommunication.yale.edu/visualizations-data/ycom/.

19. Leiserowitz, Anthony, Edward Maibach, Seth Rosenthal, John Kotcher, Parrish Bergquist, Matthew Ballew, Matthew Goldberg, Abel Gustafson and Xinran Wang. 2020. "Climate Change in the American Mind: April 2020." https://climatecommunication.yale.edu/publications/climate-change-in-the-american-mind-april-2020/5/.

20. Roser-Renouf, Connie, Edward Maibach, Anthony Leiserowitz, Geoff Feinberg, Seth Rosenthal and Jennifer
Kreslake. 2015. "Global Warming's Six Americas' Perceptions of the Health Risks." https://climatecommunication.
yale.edu/publications/global-warmings-six-americas-per-
ceptions-of-the-health-risks/.

21. American Public Health Association, and U.S. Department of Health and Human Services. n.d. "Climate Change
Decreases the Quality of the Air We Breathe." https://www.
cdc.gov/climateandhealth/pubs/air-quality-final_508.pdf.

22. American Public Health Association, and U.S. Department of Health and Human Services. n.d. "Climate Change
Decreases the Quality of the Air We Breathe." https://www.
cdc.gov/climateandhealth/pubs/air-quality-final_508.pdf.

23. Leiserowitz, Anthony, Edward Maibach, Seth Rosenthal,
John Kotcher, Parrish Bergquist, Matthew Ballew, Matthew
Goldberg, Abel Gustafson and Xinran Wang. 2020. "Climate Change in the American Mind: April 2020." https://
climatecommunication.yale.edu/publications/climate-
change-in-the-american-mind-april-2020/5/.

24. "Australia Fires: Life during and after the Worst Bushfires in
History." 2020. BBC. April 2020. https://www.bbc.co.uk/
newsround/52410744.

25. Bekkar, Bruce, Susan Pacheco, Rupa Basu, and Nathaniel
DeNicola. 2020. "Association of Air Pollution and Heat
Exposure with Preterm Birth, Low Birth Weight, and
Stillbirth in the US: A Systematic Review: A Systematic
Review." *JAMA Network Open* 3 (6): e208243.

26. Muglu, Javaid, Henna Rather, David Arroyo-Manzano,
Sohinee Bhattacharya, Imelda Balchin, Asma Khalil, Basky
Thilaganathan, Khalid S. Khan, Javier Zamora, and Shakila
Thangaratinam. 2019. "Risks of Stillbirth and Neonatal
Death with Advancing Gestation at Term: A Systematic

Review and Meta-Analysis of Cohort Studies of 15 Million Pregnancies." *PLoS Medicine* 16 (7): e1002838.

27. United States Environmental Protection Agency. n.d. "Children's Environmental Health Disparities: Black and African American Children and Asthma." https://www.epa.gov/ sites/production/files/2014-05/documents/hd_aa_asthma. pdf.

28. American Public Health Association, and U.S. Department of Health and Human Services. n.d. "Climate Change Decreases the Quality of the Air We Breathe." https://www. cdc.gov/climateandhealth/pubs/air-quality-final_508.pdf.

29. Leiserowitz, Anthony, Edward Maibach, Seth Rosenthal, John Kotcher, Parrish Bergquist, Matthew Ballew, Matthew Goldberg, Abel Gustafson and Xinran Wang. 2020. "Climate Change in the American Mind: April 2020." https:// climatecommunication.yale.edu/publications/climate-change-in-the-american-mind-april-2020/5/.

30. "Australia Fires: Life during and after the Worst Bushfires in History." 2020. BBC. April 2020. https://www.bbc.co.uk/ newsround/52410744.

31. Duncan, C. 2019. "Researchers Say NC May Feel like Florida from Climate Change." The News & Observer. February 15, 2019. https://www.newsobserver.com/latest-news/ article226204535.html.

32. Eibach, Richard P., and Steven E. Mock. 2011. "The Vigilant Parent: Parental Role Salience Affects Parents' Risk Perceptions, Risk-Aversion, and Trust in Strangers." *Journal of Experimental Social Psychology* 47 (3): 694–97.

33. Friedman, Thomas L. 2010. "Global Weirding Is Here." The New York Times. February 17, 2010. https://www.nytimes. com/2010/02/17/opinion/17friedman.html.

34. Guardian staff reporter. 2020. "Girl's Asthma Death a 'canary' Warning for London Pollution, Inquest Told." *The Guardian*, December 9, 2020. http://www.theguardian. com/environment/2020/dec/09/girls-asthma-death-canary-warning-london-pollution-inquest-ella-kissi-debrah.

35. Laville, Sandra. 2020. "Air Pollution a Cause in Girl's Death, Coroner Rules in Landmark Case." *The Guardian*, December 16, 2020. http://www.theguardian.com/ environment/2020/dec/16/girls-death-contributed-to-by-air-pollution-coroner-rules-in-landmark-case.

36. Katz, Cheryl. 2012. "People in Poor Neighborhoods Breathe More Hazardous Particles." *Scientific American*, November 1, 2012. https://www.scientificamerican.com/article/people-poor-neighborhoods-breate-more-hazardous-particles/.

37. "More than 90% of the World's Children Breathe Toxic Air Every Day." n.d. Who.Int. Accessed April 8, 2021. https://www.who.int/news/item/29-10-2018-more-than-90-of-the-worlds-children-breathe-toxic-air-every-day.

38. Bennett, William D., Kirby L. Zeman, and Annie M. Jarabek. 2008. "Nasal Contribution to Breathing and Fine Particle Deposition in Children versus Adults." *Journal of Toxicology and Environmental Health, Part A* 71 (3): 227–37.

39. Miller, Mark D., and Melanie A. Marty. 2010. "Impact of Environmental Chemicals on Lung Development." *Environmental Health Perspectives* 118 (8): 1155–64.

40. Brown, Matthew R. G., Vincent Agyapong, Andrew J. Greenshaw, Ivor Cribben, Pamela Brett-MacLean, Julie Drolet, Caroline McDonald-Harker, et al. 2019. "Significant PTSD and Other Mental Health Effects Present 18 Months after the Fort McMurray Wildfire: Findings from 3,070 Grades 7-12 Students." *Frontiers in Psychiatry* 10: 623.

41. "January 1992 nor'easter." 2021. Wikipedia. January 7, 2021. https://en.wikipedia.org/w/index.php?title=January_1992_nor%27easter&oldid=998869110.

42. United Nations. n.d. "United Nations Conference on Environment and Development, Rio de Janeiro, Brazil, 3-14 June 1992 | United Nations." Accessed July 8, 2021. https://www.un.org/en/conferences/environment/rio1992.

43. "Hurricane Andrew." 2021. Wikipedia. 2021. https://en.wikipedia.org/w/index.php?title=Hurricane_Andrew&oldid=1017520112.

44. Shaw, Jon A. 1993. "A Study of the Psychological Effects of Hurricane Andrew on an Elementary School Population." *FMHI Publications* 44. https://scholarcommons.usf.edu/fmhi_pub/44/.

45. "Disability-Adjusted Life Years (DALYs)." n.d. World Health Organization. Accessed April 15, 2021. https://www.who.int/data/gho/indicator-metadata-registry/imr-details/158.

46. Philipsborn, Rebecca Pass, and Kevin Chan. 2018. "Climate Change and Global Child Health." *Pediatrics* 141 (6): e20173774.

47. "Climate Change Poses Significant Risks to Children's Health and Well-Being." 2019. UNICEF. December 2019. https://data.unicef.org/topic/climate-change/overview/.

48. WWAY News. 2018. "Florence 'Has Forever Changed the Landscape' of Oakdale Cemetery." WWAY3. September 27, 2018. https://www.wwaytv3.com/2018/09/27/florence-has-forever-changed-the-landscape-of-oakdale-cemetery/.

49. Haelle, Tara. 2020. "Our Brains Struggle to Process This Much Stress." Elemental. August 17, 2020. https://elemental.medium.com/your-surge-capacity-is-depleted-it-s-why-you-feel-awful-de285d542f4c.

50. Prieto, Luis, and José A. Sacristán. 2003. "Problems and Solutions in Calculating Quality-Adjusted Life Years (QALYs)." *Health and Quality of Life Outcomes* 1 (1): 80.

51. Thunberg, Greta. 2019. "'Our House Is on Fire': Greta Thunberg, 16, Urges Leaders to Act on Climate." *The Guardian*, January 25, 2019. http://www.theguardian. com/environment/2019/jan/25/our-house-is-on-fire-greta-thunberg16-urges-leaders-to-act-on-climate.

Chapter 4: The Emotional Climate

52. "Explore Hazards." n.d. Climate.Gov. Accessed April 8, 2021. https://toolkit.climate.gov/steps-to-resilience/explore-hazards.

53. "Good Grief Network." 2020. Goodgriefnetwork.Org. November 25, 2020. https://www.goodgriefnetwork.org/.

54. "Helping the World Cope with Grief - A Grieving World." 2020. Drkkevorkian.Com. April 28, 2020. https://www. drkkevorkian.com/.

55. Albrecht, Glenn A. 2019. *Earth Emotions: New Words for a New World*. Ithaca, NY: Cornell University Press.

56. Duncan, C. 2019. "Researchers Say NC May Feel like Florida from Climate Change." *The News & Observer*. February 15, 2019. https://www.newsobserver.com/latest-news/article226204535.html.

57. Gleason. n.d. "National Climate Report - September 2015." Noaa.Gov. Accessed April 8, 2021. https://www.ncdc.noaa. gov/sotc/national/201509.

58. Buzzell, Linda, and Craig Chalquist, eds. 2010. *Ecotherapy: Healing with Nature in Mind*. Berkeley, CA: Counterpoint.

59. Macy, Joanna R. 2021. *World As Lover, World As Self (30th Anniversary Edition)*. Berkeley, CA: Parallax Press.

60. Haaland, Marie. 2020. "Majority of Young American Adults Say Climate Change Influences Their Decision to Have Children." SWNS Digital. April 20, 2020. https://www. swnsdigital.com/2020/04/majority-of-young-american-adults-say-climate-change-influences-their-decision-to-have-children/.

61. Newport, Frank and Joy Wilke. 2013. "Desire for Children Still Norm in U.S." Gallup. September 25, 2013. https://news.gallup.com/poll/164618/desire-children-norm.aspx.

Chapter 5: Stories for Resilience in a Long Emergency

62. Bechard, Elizabeth, John Evans, Eunji Cho, Yufen Lin, Arthi Kozhumam, Jill Jones, Sydney Grob, and Oliver Glass. 2021. "Feasibility, Acceptability, and Potential Effectiveness of an Online Expressive Writing Intervention for COVID-19 Resilience." *Complementary Therapies in Clinical Practice* 45 (101460): 101460.

63. "Expressive Writing for COVID-19 Resilience for Parents." n.d. Clinicaltrials.Gov. Accessed April 15, 2021. https://www. clinicaltrials.gov/ct2/show/NCT04589117.

64. Haelle, Tara. 2020. "Our Brains Struggle to Process This Much Stress." Elemental. August 17, 2020. https://elemental. medium.com/your-surge-capacity-is-depleted-it-s-why-you-feel-awful-de285d542f4c.

65. Rendon, Jim. 2016. *Upside: The New Science of Post-Traumatic Growth*. New York, NY: Simon & Schuster.

66. Pennebaker, James W., and John Evans. 2014. *Expressive Writing: Words That Heal*. Enumclaw, WA: Idyll Arbor.

67. Cook-Shonkoff, Ariella. 2019. "Parenting in the Age of 'Eco-Anxiety': Wildfire Fears, and a Deeper Dread," December 5, 2019. https://www.washingtonpost.com/lifestyle/2019/12/05/parenting-age-eco-anxiety-wildfire-fears-deeper-dread/.

68. "Maternal Stress from Superstorm Sandy Affected Babies." 2018. Cuny.Edu. October 19, 2018. https://sum.cuny.edu/maternal-stress-from-superstorm-sandy-affected-babies/.

69. "Resilience." 2015. Harvard.Edu. March 19, 2015. https://developingchild.harvard.edu/science/key-concepts/resilience/.

70. "Trauma and Adverse Childhood Experiences (ACEs)." 2020. Hhs.Gov. April 7, 2020. https://eclkc.ohs.acf.hhs.gov/publication/trauma-adverse-childhood-experiences-aces.

71. "Our Climate Voices." n.d. Ourclimatevoices.Org. Accessed April 7, 2021. https://www.ourclimatevoices.org/.

72. Rodriguez, Favianna. 2020. "Harnessing Cultural Power." In *All We Can Save*, edited by Ayana Elizabeth Johnson and Katharine K. Wilkinson, 121–27. New York: One World.

73. Macy, Joanna R., and Molly Young Brown. 2014. *Coming Back to Life: The Updated Guide to the Work That Reconnects*. Gabriola Island: New Society.

74. "Hand in Hand Parenting." 2020. Handinhandparenting. Org. September 3, 2020. https://handinhandparenting.org/.

Chapter 6: Imagining the Many Futures in Our Hands

75. Pierre-Louis, Kendra. 2020. "Wakanda Doesn't Have Suburbs." In *All We Can Save*, edited by Ayana Elizabeth Johnson and Katharine K. Wilkinson, 138–44. New York: One World.

76. Figueres, Christiana, and Tom Rivett-Carnac. 2021. *The Future We Choose: A Stubborn Optimist's Guide to the Climate Crisis*. New York: Vintage.

77. Holthaus, Eric. 2020. *The Future Earth: A Radical Vision for What's Possible in the Age of Warming*. New York, NY: HarperOne.

78. Ray, Sarah Jaquette. 2020. *A Field Guide to Climate Anxiety: How to Keep Your Cool on a Warming Planet*. Berkeley, CA: University of California Press.

79. brown, adrienne maree. 2017. *Emergent Strategy: Shaping Change, Changing Worlds*. Edinburgh, Scotland: AK Press.

Chapter 7: How to Talk About Climate Change (or, What Not to Say in a Moms' Group)

80. Leiserowitz, Anthony, Edward Maibach, Seth Rosenthal, John Kotcher, Parrish Bergquist, Matthew Ballew, Matthew Goldberg, Abel Gustafson and Xinran Wang. 2020. "Climate Change in the American Mind: April 2020." https://climatecommunication.yale.edu/publications/climate-change-in-the-american-mind-april-2020/5/.

81. Howe, Peter, Matto Mildenberger, Jennifer Marlon, and Anthony Leiserowitz. 2015. "Yale Climate Opinion Maps – U.S. 2014." Yale Program on Climate Change Communication. November 16, 2015. https://climatecommunication.yale.edu/visualizations-data/ycom/.

82. Leiserowitz, Anthony, Edward Maibach, Seth Rosenthal, John Kotcher Matthew Ballew, Matthew Goldberg, and Abel Gustafson. 2019. "Climate Change in the American Mind: December 2018." https://climatecommunication.yale.edu/wp-content/uploads/2019/01/Climate-Change-American-Mind-December-2018.pdf.

83. McKenzie-Mohr, Doug. 2011. *Fostering Sustainable Behavior: An Introduction to Community-Based Social Marketing.* 3rd ed. Gabriola Island: New Society.

84. Colgate, Orla, and Paul Ginns. 2016. "The Effects of Social Norms on Parents' Reading Behaviour at Home with Their Child." *Educational Psychology* 36 (5): 1009–23.

85. Hayhoe, Katharine. 2018. "Transcript of 'The Most Important Thing You Can Do to Fight Climate Change: Talk about It.'" Ted.Com. 2018. https://www.ted.com/talks/katharine_hayhoe_the_most_important_thing_you_can_do_to_fight_climate_change_talk_about_it/transcript?language=en.

86. Marshall, George. 2015. *Don't Even Think about It: Why Our Brains Are Wired to Ignore Climate Change.* New York, NY: Bloomsbury.

87. Stoknes, Per Espen. 2015. *What We Think about When We Try Not to Think about Global Warming: Toward a New Psychology of Climate Action.* Chelsea Green Publishing Company.

88. Alliance for Climate Education. 2017. "The Secret to Talking about Climate Change." YouTube. November 20, 2017. https://www.youtube.com/watch?v=RkklaXhbTuA.

89. Ballew, Matthew, Edward Maibach, John Kotcher, Parrish Bergquist, Seth Rosenthal, Jennifer Marlon and Anthony Leiserowitz. 2020. "Which Racial/Ethnic Groups Care Most about Climate Change?" Yale Program on Climate Change Communication. April 15, 2020. https://climatecommunication.yale.edu/publications/race-and-climate-change/.

90. Wally, Maxine. 2020. "Green Girl Leah on Why Environmentalists Must Speak up for Black Lives Matter." Wmagazine.Com. W Magazine. July 22, 2020. https://www.

wmagazine.com/story/green-girl-leah-thomas-intersectional-environmentalism-the-people-interview/.

91. "Intersectional Environmentalist." n.d. Intersectionalenvironmentalist.Com. Accessed April 8, 2021. https://www.intersectionalenvironmentalist.com/.

92. McAlees, Melissa. 2018. "Sweden's 'Skogsmulle' Teaches UK's Forest School Children Resilience." Daynurseries.Co.Uk. April 25, 2018. https://www.daynurseries.co.uk/news/article.cfm/id/1595071/Green-trolls-make-magical-appearance.

93. Power, Lucy. Email to Elizabeth Bechard. 2021, February 26, 2021.

94. Ray, Sarah Jaquette. 2020. *A Field Guide to Climate Anxiety: How to Keep Your Cool on a Warming Planet.* Berkeley, CA: University of California Press.

95. Thunberg, Greta, Svante Thunberg, Malena Ernman, and Beata Ernman. 2020. *Our House Is on Fire: Scenes of a Family and a Planet in Crisis.* Penguin Group.

96. Burke, Susie E. L., Ann V. Sanson, and Judith Van Hoorn. 2018. "The Psychological Effects of Climate Change on Children." *Current Psychiatry Reports* 20 (5): 35.

Chapter 8: Climate Solutions at Home

97. "Project Drawdown." 2021. 2021. https://drawdown.org/.

98. "Health and Education." 2020. Drawdown.Org. February 5, 2020. https://drawdown.org/sectors/health-and-education.

99. World Health Organization. 2014. "Gender, Climate Change and Health." https://www.who.int/globalchange/GenderClimateChangeHealthfinal.pdf.

100. Smith, Heather. 2017. "We're Teaching Kids the Wrong Ways to Fight Climate Change." *Sierra*, July 12, 2017. https://www.sierraclub.org/sierra/we-re-teaching-kids-wrong-ways-fight-climate-change.

101. "The Women's Leadership Gap." n.d. Americanprogress. Org. Accessed April 14, 2021. https://www.americanprogress.org/issues/women/reports/2018/11/20/461273/womens-leadership-gap-2/.

102. Ballew, Matthew, Edward Maibach, John Kotcher, Parrish Bergquist, Seth Rosenthal, Jennifer Marlon and Anthony Leiserowitz. 2020. "Which Racial/Ethnic Groups Care Most About Climate Change?" Yale Program on Climate Change Communication. April 15, 2020. https://climate communication.yale.edu/publications/race-and-climate-change/.

103. Harrington, Samantha. 2019. "Countries with More Female Politicians Pass More Ambitious Climate Policies, Study Suggests." Yale Climate Connections. September 12, 2019. https://yaleclimateconnections.org/2019/09/countries-with-more-female-politicians-pass-more-ambitious-climate-policies-study-suggests.

104. Haines, Andy. 2017. "Health Co-Benefits of Climate Action." *The Lancet Planetary Health* 1 (1): e4–5.

105. Battaglia Richi, Evelyne, Beatrice Baumer, Beatrice Conrad, Roger Darioli, Alexandra Schmid, and Ulrich Keller. 2015. "Health Risks Associated with Meat Consumption: A Review of Epidemiological Studies." *International Journal for Vitamin and Nutrition Research. Internationale Zeitschrift Fur Vitamin- Und Ernahrungsforschung. Journal International de Vitaminologie et de Nutrition* 85 (1–2): 70–78.

106. "Reduced Food Waste." 2020. Drawdown.Org. February 6, 2020. https://drawdown.org/solutions/reduced-food-waste.

107. Flagg, Kathryn. 2014. "Mandatory Composting: Coming Soon to a Trash Can near You." *Seven Days*, April 30, 2014. https://www.sevendaysvt.com/vermont/mandatory-composting-coming-soon-to-a-trash-can-near-you/Content?oid=2359984.

108. "Composting." n.d. Durhamnc.Gov. Accessed April 14, 2021. https://durhamnc.gov/935/Composting.

109. "CompostNow." n.d. Compostnow.Org. Accessed April 14, 2021. http://www.compostnow.org.

110. "Plant-Rich Diets." 2020. Drawdown.Org. February 6, 2020. https://drawdown.org/solutions/plant-rich-diets.

111. Ritchie, Hannah. 2019. "Which Countries Eat the Most Meat?" *BBC*, February 4, 2019. https://www.bbc.com/news/health-47057341.

112. Moore, Andrew. 2019. "Amazon Rainforest Fires: Everything You Need to Know." Ncsu.Edu. September 23, 2019. https://cnr.ncsu.edu/news/2019/09/amazon-rainforest-fires-everything-you-need-to-know/.

113. Brown, Natalie. 2020. "7 Reasons Why Meat Is Bad for the Environment." Greenpeace UK. August 3, 2020. https://www.greenpeace.org.uk/news/why-meat-is-bad-for-the-environment/.

114. "Indigenous Peoples' Forest Tenure @ProjectDrawdown #ClimateSolutions." 2020. Drawdown.Org. February 6, 2020. https://drawdown.org/solutions/indigenous-peoples-forest-tenure.

115. Neff, Roni A., Danielle Edwards, Anne Palmer, Rebecca Ramsing, Allison Righter, and Julia Wolfson. 2018. "Reducing Meat Consumption in the USA: A Nationally Representative Survey of Attitudes and Behaviours." *Public Health Nutrition* 21 (10): 1835–44.

116. Lee, Lucy, and Ian Simpson. 2016. "Are We Eating Less Meat? A British Social Attitudes Report." https://www. bl.uk/collection-items/are-we-eating-less-meat-a-british-social-attitudes-report.

117. EAT-Lancet Commission. 2019. "Food Planet Health: Healthy Diets from Sustainable Food Systems. Summary Report of the EAT-Lancet Commission." https://eatforum. org/content/uploads/2019/01/EAT-Lancet_Commission_ Summary_Report.pdf.

118. Riley, Tess. 2017. "Just 100 Companies Responsible for 71% of Global Emissions, Study Says." *The Guardian*, July 10, 2017. http://www.theguardian.com/sustainable-business/2017/jul/10/100-fossil-fuel-companies-investors-responsible-71-global-emissions-cdp-study-climate-change.

119. Mark, Jason. 2019. "Yes, Actually, Individual Responsibility Is Essential to Solving the Climate Crisis." Sierraclub.Org. November 25, 2019. https://www.sierraclub.org/sierra/yes-actually-individual-responsibility-essential-solving-climate-crisis.

120. McKenzie-Mohr, Doug. 2011. *Fostering Sustainable Behavior: An Introduction to Community-Based Social Marketing.* 3rd ed. Gabriola Island: New Society.

121. Loeffelholz, Tracy Matsue. 2020. "The 25% Tipping Point - YES! Magazine." Yesmagazine.Org. November 3, 2020. https://www.yesmagazine.org/issue/what-the-rest-of-the-world-knows/2020/11/03/how-social-change-happens.

122. DeMocker, Mary. 2018. *The Parents' Guide to Climate Revolution: 100 Ways to Build a Fossil-Free Future, Raised Empowered Kids, and Still Get a Good Night's Sleep.* Novato, CA: New World Library.

Chapter 9: Embracing Activism in Parenthood

123. Clear, James. 2018. *Atomic Habits: An Easy & Proven Way to Build Good Habits & Break Bad Ones.* Avery Publishing Group.

124. Clear, James. 2012. "Identity-Based Habits: How to Actually Stick to Your Goals This Year." Jamesclear.Com. December 31, 2012. https://jamesclear.com/identity-based-habits.

125. Herzog, Katie. 2016. "Surprise! A Third of Congress Members Are Climate Change Deniers." Grist.Org. March 8, 2016. https://grist.org/climate-energy/surprise-a-third-of-congress-members-are-climate-change-deniers/.

126. Leiserowitz, Anthony, Edward Maibach, Seth Rosenthal, John Kotcher, Jennifer Carman, Xinran Wang, Matthew Goldberg, Karine Lacroix and Jennifer Marlon. 2021. "Politics & Global Warming, December 2020." https://climatecommunication.yale.edu/publications/politics-global-warming-december-2020/5/.

127. Lopez, German. 2016. "Trump Was Elected by a Little More than a Quarter of Eligible Voters." Vox. November 10, 2016. https://www.vox.com/policy-and-politics/2016/11/10/13587462/trump-election-2016-voter-turnout.

128. Sabbagh, Dan. 2020. "Trump 2016 Campaign 'Targeted 3.5m Black Americans to Deter Them from Voting.'" *The Guardian*, September 28, 2020. http://www.theguardian.com/us-news/2020/sep/28/trump-2016-campaign-targeted-35m-black-americans-to-deter-them-from-voting.

129. Neumann, Sean. 2020. "Samuel L. Jackson Urges You to 'Vote Dammit! Vote!' in New Biden Ad on Voter Suppression." PEOPLE.Com. October 9, 2020. https://people.com/politics/samuel-l-jackson-urges-you-to-vote-dammit-vote-in-new-joe-biden-ad/.

130. Mahmood, Basit. 2020. "Why Is the Climate Change Movement So White?" Newsweek. September 10, 2020. https://www.newsweek.com/climate-change-race-inequality-xr-extinction-rebellion-1530892.

131. Valentine, Katie. 2013. "The Whitewashing of the Environmental Movement." Grist.Org. September 24, 2013. https://grist.org/climate-energy/the-whitewashing-of-the-environmental-movement/.

132. Jones, Rachel. 2020. "The Environmental Movement Is Very White. These Leaders Want to Change That." *National Geographic*, July 29, 2020. https://www.nationalgeographic.com/history/article/environmental-movement-very-white-these-leaders-want-change-that.

133. Riederer, Rachel. 2019. "The Other Kind of Climate Denialism." *New Yorker*, March 6, 2019. https://www.newyorker.com/science/elements/the-other-kind-of-climate-denialism.

Chapter 10: Grief and Love

134. Figueres, Christiana, and Tom Rivett-Carnac. 2021. *The Future We Choose: A Stubborn Optimist's Guide to the Climate Crisis.* New York: Vintage.

135. Johnson, Trebbe. 2018. *Radical Joy for Hard Times: Finding Meaning and Making Beauty in Earth's Broken Places.* Berkeley, CA: North Atlantic Books.

136. Scranton, Roy. 2021. "Opinion: I've Said Goodbye to 'Normal'. You Should, Too." *The New York Times*, January 25, 2021. https://www.nytimes.com/2021/01/25/opinion/new-normal-climate-catastrophes.html.

137. Jabr, Ferris. 2012. "How Does a Caterpillar Turn into a Butterfly?" *Scientific American*, August 10, 2012. https://www.scientificamerican.com/article/caterpillar-butterfly-metamorphosis-explainer/.

138. Villazon, Luis. n.d. "What Actually Happens When a Caterpillar Becomes a Butterfly? Is It a Pokémon Situation or More of a Cronenberg Thing?" Sciencefocus.Com. BBC Science Focus Magazine. Accessed April 9, 2021. https://www.sciencefocus.com/nature/what-actually-happens-when-a-caterpillar-becomes-a-butterfly-is-it-a-pokemon-situation-or-more-of-a-cronenberg-thing/.

139. "Johnnie Mercers Fishing Pier - WrightsvilleBeach.Com." n.d. Wrightsvillebeach.Com. Accessed April 9, 2021. https://www.wrightsvillebeach.com/johnnie-mercers-pier.html.

140. First Street Foundation. n.d. "North Carolina's Sea Level Is Rising." Sealevelrise.Org. Accessed April 16, 2021. https://sealevelrise.org/states/north-carolina/.

Epilogue

141. "Earth Overshoot Day - #MoveTheDate." 2021. Overshoot day.Org. April 23, 2021. https://www.overshootday.org/.

142. Dellinger, Drew. 2014. *Love Letter to the Milky Way: A Book of Poems*. Ashland, OR: White Cloud Press.

Appendix A: Thirteen Key Actions for Climate-Conscious Parents

143. "Children and Nature Network. Helping Children Thrive - Outside." 2020. Childrenandnature.Org. June 24, 2020. http://www.childrenandnature.org.

144. E360 Digest. 2017. "U.S. Study Shows Widening Disconnect with Nature, and Potential Solutions." Yale Environment 360. April 27, 2017. https://e360.yale.edu/digest/u-s-study-shows-widening-disconnect-with-nature-and-potential-solutions.

145. Suttie, Jill. 2016. "How to Protect Kids from Nature-Deficit Disorder." *Greater Good Magazine*, September 15, 2016. https://greatergood.berkeley.edu/article/item/how_to_protect_kids_from_nature_deficit_disorder.

146. Emerson Blake, H., ed. 2017. *Wonder and Other Survival Skills: A Selection of Essays from Orion Magazine*. Great Barrington, MA: Orion Magazine.

Appendix B: Climate Change Basics: Ten Things Every Parent Should Know

147. Cook, John, Naomi Oreskes, Peter T. Doran, William R. L. Anderegg, Bart Verheggen, Ed W. Maibach, J. Stuart Carlton, et al. 2016. "Consensus on Consensus: A Synthesis of Consensus Estimates on Human-Caused Global Warming." *Environmental Research Letters* 11 (4): 048002.

148. Brown, Katherine. 2021. "2020 Tied for Warmest Year on Record, NASA Analysis Shows." https://www.nasa.gov/press-release/2020-tied-for-warmest-year-on-record-nasa-analysis-shows.

149. Buis, Alan. 2019. "A Degree of Concern: Why Global Temperatures Matter." Climate Change: Vital Signs of the Planet. June 19, 2019. https://climate.nasa.gov/news/2878/a-degree-of-concern-why-global-temperatures-matter/.

150. "What Is the Greenhouse Effect?" n.d. Nasa.Gov. Accessed April 9, 2021. https://climatekids.nasa.gov/greenhouse-effect/.

151. "The Ocean, a Carbon Sink." 2016. Ocean-Climate.Org. December 3, 2016. https://ocean-climate.org/en/awareness/the-ocean-a-carbon-sink/.

152. "Ocean and Climate Change." 2010. The Ocean Foundation. August 7, 2010. https://oceanfdn.org/ocean-and-climate-change/.

153. "Mapped: How Climate Change Affects Extreme Weather around the World." 2021. Carbonbrief.Org. February 25, 2021. https://www.carbonbrief.org/mapped-how-climate-change-affects-extreme-weather-around-the-world.

154. Geophysical Fluid Dynamics Laboratory. 2021. "Global Warming and Hurricanes." Noaa.Gov. March 29, 2021. https://www.gfdl.noaa.gov/global-warming-and-hurricanes/.

155. National Weather Service. n.d. "Weather Related Fatality and Injury Statistics." Accessed April 9, 2021. https://www.weather.gov/hazstat/.

156. Bakalar, Nicholas. 2020. "Heat Waves May Be Bad for Your Pregnancy." *The New York Times*, November 16, 2020. https://www.nytimes.com/2020/11/16/well/family/heat-waves-hot-temperature-pregnancy-preterm-premature.html.

157. "The Facts about Climate Change and Drought." 2016. Climaterealityproject.Org. June 15, 2016. https://climaterealityproject.org/blog/facts-about-climate-change-and-drought.

158. Budiman, Abby. 2015. "Global Concern about Climate Change, Broad Support for Limiting Emissions." Pewresearch.Org. November 5, 2015. https://www.pewresearch.org/global/2015/11/05/global-concern-about-climate-change-broad-support-for-limiting-emissions/.

159. USDA Economic Research Service. n.d. "Key Statistics & Graphics." Usda.Gov. Accessed July 9, 2021. https://www.ers.usda.gov/topics/food-nutrition-assistance/food-security-in-the-us/key-statistics-graphics.aspx.

160. Earth.org. 2020. "Sixth Mass Extinction of Wildlife Accelerating- Study." Earth.Org. June 4, 2020. https://earth.org/sixth-mass-extinction-of-wildlife-accelerating/.

161. Attenborough, David. 2020. *A Life on Our Planet*. https://www.attenboroughfilm.com/.

162. Lustgarten, Abrahm. 2020. "The Great Climate Migration Has Begun." *The New York Times*, December 16, 2020. https://www.nytimes.com/interactive/2020/07/23/magazine/climate-migration.html.

163. American Lung Association. 2020. "Climate Change and Air Pollution." American Lung Association. March 14, 2020. https://www.lung.org/clean-air/climate-change/climate-change-air-pollution.

164. "Climate Change & Children's Health." 2019. Harvard.Edu. January 7, 2019. https://www.hsph.harvard.edu/c-change/subtopics/climate-change-and-childrens-health/.

165. Intergovernmental Panel on Climate Change. 2018. "Special Report: Global Warming of 1.5°C." https://ipcc.ch/sr15/.

166. UN Climate Change News. 2021. "'Climate Commitments Not On Track to Meet Paris Agreement Goals' as NDC Synthesis Report Is Published." United Nations Climate Change. February 26, 2021. https://unfccc.int/news/climate-commitments-not-on-track-to-meet-paris-agreement-goals-as-ndc-synthesis-report-is-published.

167. "Solutions." 2020. Drawdown.Org. February 10, 2020. https://www.drawdown.org/solutions.

168. Marlon, Jennifer, Peter Howe, Matto Mildenberger, Anthony Leiserowitz, and Xinran Wang. 2020. "Yale Climate Opinion Maps 2020." https://climatecommunication.yale.edu/visualizations-data/ycom-us/.

169. Mitchell, Travis. 2019. "U.S. Public Views on Climate and Energy." Pewresearch.Org. November 25, 2019. https://www.pewresearch.org/science/2019/11/25/u-s-public-views-on-climate-and-energy/.

170. Ash, Timothy Garton, Antonia Zimmermann, Dan Snow, and Eilidh Macfarlane. 2021. "What Europeans Say They Will Do to Combat Climate Change." Eupinions.Eu. April 19, 2021. https://eupinions.eu/de/text/what-europeans-say-they-will-do-to-combat-climate-change.

171. Robson, David. 2019. "The '3.5% Rule': How a Small Minority Can Change the World." *BBC*, May 13, 2019. https://www.bbc.com/future/article/20190513-it-only-takes-35-of-people-to-change-the-world.

Appendix D: Five Myths About Plant-Rich Diets (and Tips for Making the Switch)

172. "Plant-Rich Diets." 2020. Drawdown.Org. February 6, 2020. https://drawdown.org/solutions/plant-rich-diets.

173. Kim, Hyunju, Laura E. Caulfield, Vanessa Garcia-Larsen, Lyn M. Steffen, Josef Coresh, and Casey M. Rebholz. 2019. "Plant-Based Diets Are Associated with a Lower Risk of Incident Cardiovascular Disease, Cardiovascular Disease Mortality, and All-Cause Mortality in a General Population of Middle-Aged Adults." *Journal of the American Heart Association* 8 (16): e012865.

174. "Exploring Opinions on Plant-Based Eating - Sous Vide Guy." 2019. Sousvideguy.Com. December 4, 2019. https://sousvideguy.com/exploring-opinions-plant-based-eating/.

175. Physicians Committee for Responsible Medicine. 2021. "Protein." Pcrm.Org. 2021. https://www.pcrm.org/good-nutrition/nutrition-information/protein.

176. Kuzemchak, Sally. 2018. "Why You Should Let Kids Play with Their Food." Parents.Com. Parents. September 12, 2018. https://www.parents.com/recipes/scoop-on-food/why-you-should-let-kids-play-with-their-food/.

ABOUT THE AUTHOR

Elizabeth Bechard has been coaching professionally since 2011, and has taught in the health coaching certification program at Duke Integrative Medicine. For a decade, she worked for the research team at Duke Integrative Medicine, helping to coordinate, design, and implement studies exploring human resilience, wellness, and behavior change. She is a certified expressive writing facilitator and a graduate of Yale's Climate Change and Health Certificate program. Bechard is currently pursuing a master's of science in public health at the London School of Hygiene and Tropical Medicine, and serves on the Diversity, Equity, and Inclusion Committee for the National Board of Health and Wellness Coaching. Bechard lives with her husband and young twins in Durham, North Carolina. You can find her online on Instagram @elizabethbechard and at www.elizabethbechard.com.

PUBLISHER'S NOTE

Thank you for the opportunity to serve. If you would like to help share this message, here are some popular ways:

- **Reviews:** Write an online review; in social media posts, tag #parentinginachangingclimate and #elizabethbechard

- **Giving:** Gift this book to friends, family, and colleagues

- **Book Clubs:** Enjoy the *Book Club Discussion Guide* (Appendix H) and request an author appearance at your meeting: info@citrinepublishing.com

- **Speaking:** Invite Elizabeth Bechard to speak with your group or organization

- **Workshops:** Organize a *Parenting in a Changing Climate* workshop in your area: workshops@citrinepublishing.com

- **Bulk Orders:** Email sales@citrinepublishing.com

- **Contact Information:** +1-828-585-7030

We appreciate your book reviews, letters, and shares.

Made in the USA
Middletown, DE
13 October 2021